A Chanticleer Press Edition

Taylor's
Guide
to
Trees

Please return to B Puckey

Houghton Mifflin Company Boston

Based on Taylor's Encyclopedia of
Gardening, Fourth Edition, copyright © 1961
by Norman Taylor, revised and edited by
Gordon P. DeWolf, Jr.

Library of Congress
Cataloging-in-Publication Data
Taylor's guide to trees.
(Taylor's guides to gardening)
Based on: Taylor's encyclopedia of gardening.
4th edition. 1961.
Includes index.
1. Ornamental trees. 2. Ornamental
trees—Dictionaries. 3. Ornamental trees—
Pictorial works. I. Taylor's
encyclopedia of gardening. II. Title: Guide
to trees. III. Series.
SB435.T434 1987 635.9'77 87–26247
ISBN 0–395–46783–7 (pbk.)

Prepared and produced by Chanticleer Press,
Inc., New York
Cover photograph: Flowering Dogwood
by Charles Marden Fitch

Designed by Massimo Vignelli

Color reproductions made in Italy
Printed and bound in Japan

First Edition.

DNP   10 9 8 7 6 5 4 3 2 1

Contributors

Philip Chandler
Special consultant on Southern and West Coast tree species, Philip Chandler is a landscape designer, horticultural writer, and lecturer. He lives in Santa Monica, California.

Alan D. Cook
Author of the gardening essays and editor of the plant descriptions, Alan Cook is Director of Extended Services at the Dawes Arboretum in Newark, Ohio, with which he has been associated since 1970. He has written widely on gardening and horticulture, and served as guest editor of four Brooklyn Botanic Garden handbooks. He is Executive Director of the International Society of Arboriculture, and a member of the American Society of Consulting Arborists.

Gordon P. DeWolf, Jr., Ph.D.
Coordinator of the Horticultural Program at Massachusetts Bay Community College in Wellesley Hills, Massachusetts. Gordon P. DeWolf revised and edited the fifth edition of *Taylor's Encyclopedia of Gardening,* upon which this guide is based. Dr. DeWolf previously served as Horticulturist at the Arnold Arboretum of Harvard University.

Gordon E. Jones
General consultant for this book, Gordon Jones is Director of Planting Fields Arboretum in Oyster Bay, New York. He has written numerous articles on woody ornamental plants.

Katharine Widin
Author of the essay on pests and diseases, Katharine Widin holds an M.S. and a Ph.D. in plant pathology. She operates a private consulting firm, Plant Health Associates, in Stillwater, Minnesota.

Preface

Trees are the most valuable garden plants you can ever grow. A large specimen can be a major investment, but more importantly, trees offer both beauty and function on a scale and with a permanence unmatched by any other garden plants.

By their very nature, trees have an impact on our lives: Anyone who has gardened knows at least one tree as intimately as they do a family member, perhaps a gnarled old maple that hosts squirrels and woodpeckers and still manages to give shade and a blaze of fall color each year, or a gracefully branching dogwood that brightens the landscape each spring with its beautiful flowerlike bracts, just when azaleas bloom. Because of their beauty, utility, and longevity, trees can establish the tone and character of the landscape as potently as any architectural features, and can accommodate both the severely formal and the riotously informal. Trees grow in a bountiful variety of shapes and sizes, with all kinds of ornamental features—flowers, fruits or cones, bark, and colored leaves. They can be planted purely for their beauty, or to serve many other functions, from providing shade to screening.

This guide will show you how to properly select, plant, and maintain the right trees for your property, whether you live in Florida or Michigan, and whether you have never planted a tree before or you are an experienced gardener. Your efforts will be rewarded and enriched with the seasons and the years.

Contents

How to Use This

Trees—the largest and most permanent garden plants—play a great role in defining the nature and style of your landscape. Their varied shapes, sizes, and ornamental features offer a wealth of garden interest, from spring flowers to handsome foliage in summer, to fruits and cones in fall, to evergreen leaves or colorful bark in winter. Trees fulfill a range of landscape needs—they can act singly as focal points, be massed in groups for backgrounds or screens, or be used to provide shade.

Many homeowners are daunted by the prospect of choosing and caring for trees, but there is no secret for success, and in fact everything you need to know can be found in this book. You'll learn how to create a landscape that is the expression of your needs and tastes, and how to choose the right trees to enrich and beautify it. Even if you have a mature landscape, you will discover new species and new information on how to care for the trees you already grow. This book will also help you to identify those trees you admire in other gardens or nurseries.

How This Book Is Organized

The species presented in this guide were selected for their ornamental qualities and usefulness in landscape design. Trees notorious for their pest and disease susceptibility, rank growth, and maintenance problems have been omitted. The book contains three types of material: color plates, an encyclopedia of tree descriptions, and essays by experts to guide you through every aspect of gardening with trees.

The Color Plates

Nearly 200 of the most popular and attractive trees in cultivation today are illustrated in the color plates. Because the value of a tree is so intimately tied to its effective use, the color plates are arranged by the typical landscape functions of the three major tree groups: the deciduous trees, the broadleaf evergreens, and the needle-leaf evergreens. The first section, the deciduous trees, is divided into ornamental and shade trees. The second section, the broadleaf evergreens, is also divided into ornamental and shade trees, and includes the palms, tropical semi-woody plants. Finally, the needle-leaf evergreens are pictured in two sections, ornamentals and screens.

A view of the entire tree is shown first, together with a detail of its flowers, foliage, or fruit. Some photographs also present variations in color or seasonal changes. A few trees are represented with more than two photographs, or only by one. If you are a novice, browse through the color plates and familiarize yourself with the range of trees presented in each section. Even if you are unfamiliar with their common or scientific names, you will undoubtedly recognize many trees that you have seen before. To find out more about a particular tree, turn to the page noted in the caption.

Guide

Visual Key

The color section begins with the visual key, which adds another dimension to the plates. It illustrates the range of plants to be found within each major group and subgroup, and allows you to turn quickly to a photograph of the kind of tree you are interested in, and to compare that tree with others that are similar in form and use.

Captions

The captions that accompany the color plates provide essential information on each tree's physical characteristics and cultural requirements. To help you plan for a tree's long years to maturity, height is indicated at three stages: at 15 years, at 40 years, and at maturity. A bullet before the height indicates the approximate age and height of the tree pictured.

Also given here are the scientific and common names of the tree; the size and season of flowers, fruits, and cones; zone numbers that indicate the hardiness range of the tree; the tree's soil and climatic tolerances and preferences; and a mention of whether the tree is fragrant or has fall color. Finally, a page number reference directs you to a description in the Encyclopedia of Trees.

Encyclopedia of Trees

This section offers a full description of each tree shown in the color plates and specific information on how to grow it. The descriptions are based on the authoritative *Taylor's Encyclopedia of Gardening*, revised and updated for this guide. Entries are arranged alphabetically by genus and cross-referenced by page number to the color plates. (If you are unfamiliar with scientific names, you can easily find a tree by looking up its common name in the comprehensive index, which starts on page 471.) Each description begins with a heading indicating the genus name, followed by the common and scientific family names. Pronunciation of the scientific name precedes an overview of the genus.

Genus

This section describes the overall characteristics of the garden plants in the genus. It outlines broad growing requirements for the genus, including when and how to plant and prune.

Species, Hybrids, and Cultivars

After the genus description, you will find detailed information about each of the trees shown in the color plates and additional information about other popular cultivars. Each species description includes a tree's country of origin and the zones to which it is hardy. (You can find what zone you live in by referring to the map on page 16.) It also offers any growing tips that differ from the genus requirements, like the need for acid soil or a strong resistance

How to Use This Guide

to a particular disease common to the genus. A black-and-white illustration accompanies each species, and depicts a tree at both 15 years of age and at maturity. For deciduous trees, the branch structure reveals its winter silhouette.

Gardening Essays

These essays explain the complete process of choosing and caring for trees—from the basic principles of botany and landscape design to how and when to plant and transplant, how to prune and fertilize, and other important topics.

In the section on botany, beginners will learn how trees differ from other plants and the importance of scientific names. The illustrations of tree shapes show their different growth habits and how they work in the landscape. Essays on designing and planting offer sound advice on how to choose the right tree for any place in any landscape. The essay on record keeping tells how to remember what you plant and when and where you plant it. A gardening calendar provides a practical schedule for seasonal maintenance activities. Should a tree begin to falter, you can turn to the Pest and Disease Chart to identify your problem and cure it. The essentials of propagation are also explained, and a listing of trees to avoid will help you to judge often-planted trees of questionable merit. Common-sense advice on buying trees includes a list of nurseries and other sources. Finally, all the technical terms you may encounter are defined in the glossary.

Using the Tree Chart

The chart beginning on page 440 allows you to see at a glance which trees are best suited to your needs and the conditions in your garden. For example, suppose you live in Maryland (in zone 7) and want to plant a deciduous tree to shade your terrace from the summer sun. You need it to do so quickly, and you want the tree to give a display of fall color before it loses its leaves. Look in the chart in the section of Deciduous Shade Trees for trees with fall color that will grow rapidly. Then make sure these plants are hardy in your zone. Five trees may suit your needs: *Acer saccharinum,* *Fraxinus americana, Fraxinus pennsylvanica, Liriodendron tulipifera,* and *Quercus rubra.* Three, *Acer saccharinum* and the two *Fraxinus* species, will tolerate the city conditions of your urbanized neighborhood, so you can eliminate the other two. Turn to the color plates listed for these trees and read their descriptions and decide which appeals to you more.

Planning your landscape is both enjoyable and easy, and this guide will help you through every stage of growing trees for a lifetime of pleasure.

Basic Botany

Everyone knows what a tree is. But apparently it is difficult to define a tree precisely, since few authorities agree.

What Is a Tree?

Trees are one of three general types of woody perennial plants; the others are shrubs and vines. To be a tree, a plant must meet three criteria. First, a tree must have the potential to reach at least 20 feet or approximately six meters at maturity, in a temperate climate with reasonable rainfall or irrigation. Also, a tree has a single trunk, which may branch at an early stage into two or more ascending trunk-like branches of more or less equal importance. Finally, a tree is able to stand by itself. Shrubs are generally smaller than trees, and usually lack a central trunk. Vines, at least until very old, need supports upon which to twine or clasp.

How a Tree Grows

Trees grow taller and their branches spread outward only by the new growth produced each year from buds formed on the previous year's growth. Trunks and branches grow thicker—that is, expand in cross section—each year as the cambium layer beneath the bark forms a new ring of wood on the outside of the previous year's ring. A simple method to visualize the way a tree grows is to imagine a line of fence wire affixed to the trunk of a tree. The wire will not rise to higher levels as the tree grows, nor will it be pushed outward. However, in time the tree trunk will expand in circumference and engulf the wire.

Tree Roots

Roots of trees usually grow beneath the soil, and provide the above-ground tree with necessary water and minerals. Most tree roots grow in the upper two feet of soil, where aeration is best, and the roots of most trees extend well beyond the branch spread, often as much as three times beyond. On a hillside, other factors being equal, a tree's downhill roots are more numerous and grow farther than its uphill ones.

Deciduous or Evergreen?

A deciduous tree loses all or most of its leaves in the fall, remains bare for a time, then leafs out anew in spring. Most deciduous trees have broad, flat leaves. Some common examples are maples, birches, and ashes. In contrast, evergreen trees hold their leaves for at least a year, and are divided into two major groups. The broadleaf evergreen trees—hollies, certain magnolias, some oaks, acacias, and so on—bear leaves similar to those of deciduous trees, but hold them for at least a full year, so that the trees are never bare of foliage.

Needle-leaf evergreens also hold their foliage for a year or more, but their leaves usually are long and slender and resemble needles, such

Basic Botany

as the pines and spruces, or are somewhat flattened, such as the hemlocks and firs. A few have needles that are awl-shaped or scale-like, and sometimes both types of leaves appear on the same tree at the same time, as with the cedars and junipers. Needle-leaf evergreens are also called conifers because they bear cones. Some species produce berrylike fruits which are in fact modified cones. Classification systems usually have misfits. Larch, Bald Cypress, and Dawn Redwood trees bear cones and have needle-like foliage that drops in the fall, and so these trees are deciduous, even though they are conifers.

Palm Trees
Although evergreen, palms differ markedly from other trees. The palm family is botanically related to grasses and lilies, and its members don't form annual growth rings beneath their bark as do other trees, and are usually unbranched, with leaves alone forming their crowns. Palm leaves are usually large and compound, some structured palmately, as with the fan palms, others pinnately, as with the feather palms. For general purposes, they are considered broadleaf evergreens.

Scientific Names
Plants, as well as all other living things, are classified by family, genus, and species. Botanical classifications are made according to observable likenesses in plant characteristics, mainly concerning flowers and reproductive systems. A plant family may include one or many genera. Members of a genus have certain characteristics in common, but other characteristics are different enough to warrant further classification into species. Each genus in turn may include one or many species. Because of the reproductive similarities upon which classification is based, hybridization is most likely to occur among the species of a given genus.

Botanical Nomenclature
Plants are named in Latin, or in Latinized forms of other words, and are always printed in italics. A family name usually ends in "-aceae," pronounced "ay'see-ee." The beech family is *Fagaceae,* with six genera including beech and oak. Each plant, beyond the family level, has a two-word name, or binomial. The first word is the genus; the second, the species. Family and genus names are capitalized; species names are not. The generic name of oak is *Quercus,* a genus of about 450 species native to many temperate zone countries. Red Oak has the species name *rubra,* thus its binomial is *Quercus rubra.*
The common names of trees and other plants are often geographically limited, and the results can be confusing. For example, the names Black Tupelo, Black Gum, Upland Tupelo, Sour Gum, and Pepperidge all refer to one species—*Nyssa sylvatica.*

The name Red Maple causes frequent problems in nurseries. Is it a red-leaved form of Japanese Maple, *Acer palmatum;* a red-leaved form of Norway Maple, *A. platanoides;* or the "real" Red Maple, *A. rubrum*? Scientific names, though sometimes difficult to pronounce, serve an important function, and you will find it helpful to know the scientific name of any rare or unfamiliar tree that interests you.

Hybrids

Crosses between different species and sometimes between plants in different genera are known as hybrids, and rarely occur in nature. More commonly, hybrids are the result of controlled breeding by man. Crossing, selecting, backcrossing, and other manipulations can evolve progeny with the desirable characteristics of various ancestors, and without some of their drawbacks. Further, hybrids often produce progeny with qualities superior to those of their ancestors, a phenomenon called hybrid vigor. Hybrids are common among vegetables, garden flowers, and roses, but are relatively rare among trees, since evaluation and selection naturally take a great deal longer.

Hybrids are indicated by a multiplication symbol (×) preceding the appropriate generic or specific name. A generic hybrid is × *Cupressocyparis leylandii*, a cross between *Chamaecyparis nootkatensis* and *Cupressus macrocarpa*. The specific hybrid *Aesculus × carnea* comes from the cross-pollination of *Aesculus hippocastanum* and *A. pavia*.

Varieties, Cultivars, and Clones

A variety, botanically speaking, is a naturally occurring variant within a species, differing significantly in flower color, leaf characteristic, growth habit, or other traits. A variety usually can be propagated by seed.

"Variety" is often used interchangeably with the term cultivar. However, to be correct, a cultivar is also a variant within a species, but only if it is in cultivation. A cultivar may be the result of mutation, hybridization, or selective seedling breeding. Cultivars often are not capable of propagation by seed; asexual methods such as cuttings or grafting may be required to retain their desired characteristics.

Clones are groups of plants genetically identical to each other and to the parent plants. Cloned plants cannot be reproduced by seed or by grafting—layering, division, or cuttings, including tissue culture, are necessarily used to propagate them.

Getting Started

A large tree to shade the west bedroom window, a smaller ornamental tree to brighten the landscape near the patio, a tall evergreen to screen an unsightly view—the right tree in the right place increases the value of your property and improves your enjoyment of your home, and might even improve your health and well-being.

Selecting the right trees is among the most important landscaping decisions you will make, and the variety of ornamental trees available can be overwhelming. If you approach the task practically, understanding your needs and the assets and liabilities of the trees you are considering, then you can narrow the field to trees that are appropriate for specific locations on your property.

Winter Hardiness, Summer Heat Tolerance

The single most important factor that affects your choice of trees is the climate in your area. You may have been particularly taken with a glorious flowering tree you saw on a trip to the South, or a towering evergreen you saw in the mountains. But the former probably cannot withstand your sub-zero winters, and the latter may languish in your summer heat waves.

The ability of a tree to withstand winter cold is called its hardiness; its summer heat tolerance is self-explanatory. A tree will succeed if it is grown in a climate that exceeds neither of these two temperature extremes. Soil factors such as pH, moisture, drainage, and aeration also greatly influence what species will thrive in a particular area. Susceptibility to local problems—perhaps fireblight, or polluted air, or gypsy moths—is another important consideration when choosing a tree, but the proper hardiness zone is the overriding factor that determines whether you will be able to grow a given tree successfully.

Using the Zone Map

The United States Department of Agriculture Minimum Temperature Map on page 16 indicates the ten hardiness zones across the United States and Canada. The zones are numbered from north to south and are used in this book and in other planting guides to indicate the best areas in which to grow certain plants. The encyclopedic descriptions and photographic captions offer specific zone tolerances; use them both to help ensure success for every species pictured.

If, for example, your hometown is in zone 6 and the tree you like is described as suitable for zones 5 to 8, it should have little or no problem adapting to your climate. But if you live in zone 4, the tree probably will suffer cold damage during an average or worse winter. And in zone 9, the same tree probably will languish because it is genetically unsuited to a climate with very little cold and very hot summers. If a tree is described as semihardy in your zone, it means that many individuals are grown in the milder parts of your zone, but that the species is not reliably hardy there. You should plant the tree in a protected area and not stint on its care. Even so, it may suffer damage from severe winters or summers.

Local Variations and Microclimates

The hardiness map is a general guideline and cannot be exact—many variables in any locality affect plant adaptability. Valleys within a zone, though often sizable, are too small to include on the hardiness map. A nicely protected valley may be a full zone warmer than the surrounding area—zone 4 instead of 3, or 8 instead of 7. Conversely, a plateau may be a zone colder than surrounding lands only a few miles away.

A suburban lot, measured in feet and not miles, may have a microclimate big enough for one tree to thrive where it would die mere yards away. For example, the east side of a two-story house may protect a Southern Magnolia that couldn't survive a winter elsewhere on the lot.

Carefully observe which trees thrive in your locale, as well as which trees grow poorly or are absent. Such a survey will tell you quite a bit. Local experts—Cooperative Extension agents, qualified nursery personnel, horticulture instructors at colleges and technical schools, and long-time gardener residents—are excellent to talk to when you are unsure about how a tree will fare in your area.

Judging Your Site

A tree needs space. Not just for the day it is planted, but for its lifetime. Examine the proposed site of a tree carefully, and be sure that no potential hazards lie above, below, and to the sides before planting.

Height Restrictions

Look above the site. Wires, the canopies of other trees, roof overhangs, and other obstructions will undoubtedly cause damage to the tree or be damaged by the tree at a later date, and should be avoided. If you are planting a street tree, avoid severe pruning by line clearance crews by planting trees away from utility lines. Planting between the house and the sidewalk, and not in the so-called planting strip next to the curb, is often all that is needed. Don't plant a young tree too near an established one—neither will benefit from the competition. Heights at three stages of growth—at 15 years, at 40 years, and at maturity—are given in the caption information for each tree pictured. Use them to evaluate trees for restricted sites.

Underground Hazards

Know what lies below ground as well. Avoid a site with underground drain tiles, leach beds, or water, gas, or other utility lines. Any of these underground structures may require future

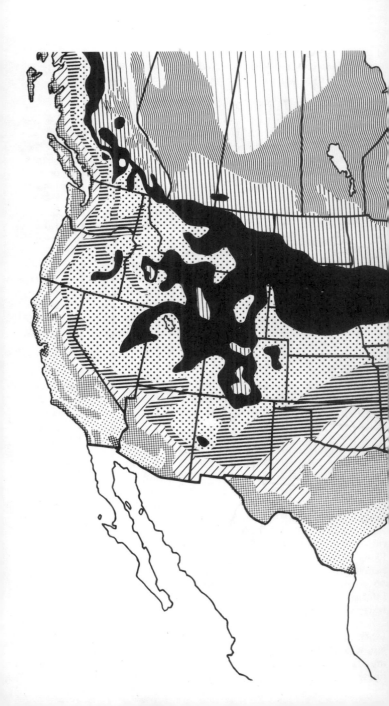

This map was compiled by the United States Department of Agriculture as a broad guideline to temperature extremes in your area.

The key below gives you the average minimum temperatures of the ten zones.

Determine if your area corresponds to its zone allocation by comparing your coldest temperatures with those given in the key.

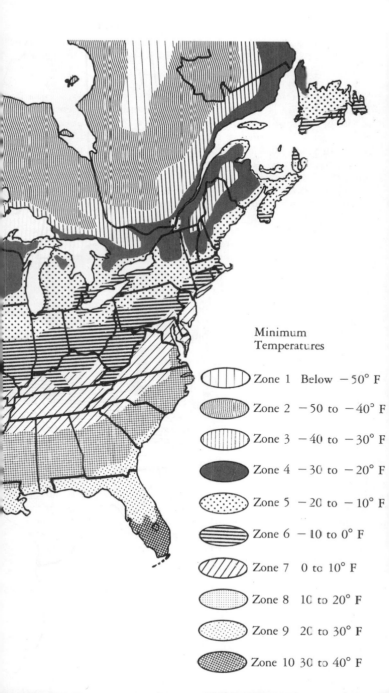

Minimum Temperatures

Zone 1 Below −50° F

Zone 2 −50 to −40° F

Zone 3 −40 to −30° F

Zone 4 −30 to −20° F

Zone 5 −20 to −10° F

Zone 6 −10 to 0° F

Zone 7 0 to 10° F

Zone 8 10 to 20° F

Zone 9 20 to 30° F

Zone 10 30 to 40° F

repair or replacement. A large tree will probably be killed by major excavations, and its roots may have caused the damage in the first place.

Width Restrictions
Be sure your site is wide enough to accommodate the eventual spread of a mature tree. If a description of a tree indicates a 40 foot mature height and equal or greater spread, plant the tree at least 25 feet from your house or your neighbor's property line. Storms can cause severe damage to trees and drop a branch through a roof or window, so be sure you plant sturdy species near the house and the street, and at a proper distance. Again, beware of possible interference with utility lines, street lamps, and traffic signs, especially when planting street trees. Unless you are purposely planting trees for a screen or to achieve a grove effect, space them so that they don't soon grow together and deform each other by competing for light and space. Trees for small spaces are indicated in the Tree Chart in the appendix.

Sun and Shade
Most trees give shade, but do not tolerate it. Flowering trees especially will wane if they don't receive plenty of light. If your yard has sun "most of the morning," or only "when the sun is just right," this is not adequate light. If a tree requires full sun, then it should remain unshaded throughout the day. So if your flowering cherry blooms only a bit and the crabapple hardly at all, shade may be the problem. Fall color, too, is diminished by shade.
However, a few trees will tolerate some shade, notably hemlocks, serviceberries, Flowering Dogwood, American Holly, and Redbud. If you need to place a tree in a shady area, read the encyclopedic descriptions or the Tree Chart to see whether your choice will grow in partial shade.

Wind
Severe winds will desiccate some trees. Cold winter winds are harmful to many evergreens, especially the hemlocks and some of the broadleaf evergreens. Hot summer winds can badly damage the same evergreens and also deciduous plants with vulnerable summer foliage. If you must expose trees to lots of wind, again check the encyclopedic descriptions to see whether a tree tolerates wind or will make an effective screen.

Soil
All soils are composed of three basic kinds of particles—very small particles of rock called clay; larger gritty particles of gravel and sand; and medium-sized silt particles. Loam is a balanced combination of all three components mixed with organic matter. These particles constitute about half of the volume of an ideal soil.

The remaining volume is made up of spaces or pores which trap water and air. Some of these pores are large enough to allow water to drain away and bring air into the soil. The balance are small enough to hold water against the pull of gravity, storing it and making it available to trees on rainless days.

Soil Problems

Unhappily, not all soils boast this ideal balance. Soil with a superabundance of tiny clay particles is usually soggy for a while after a rain, holding water but not air, then dries to the semblance of a good tennis court, holding not much of either water or air. Sandy soil will retain air while draining water, and will support only drought-tolerant plants unless water is regularly added by rain or irrigation.

So, if your soil has a good combination of clay, silt, and sand particles, you are well on your way to gardening success. But there is one more problem, called compaction. The process of compaction is easily demonstrated by squeezing a slice of fresh bread, which is full of pores, into a fraction of its former size. Construction equipment, for example, does to soil what squeezing does to bread. So can feet: those of children using a swing set, or those of chained dogs. So can wheels: those of family cars driven to shady spots for a wash, and those of lawn mowers and tractors. Compacted soils have little space for either water or air, and thus can support only the toughest, most tolerant of trees.

Soil Tests

Two simple, practical soil tests can help you to determine your soil's composition. Firmly (but not viciously) squeeze a handful of moist but not muddy soil to form a ball. Drop the ball from waist height onto a flat rock or other firm outdoor surface. If the ball deforms but does not crumble, the soil is mostly clay. If it crumbles in a discrete manner, the soil is mostly silt. If it scatters all over, or won't form a ball in the first place, the soil is mostly sand. If it breaks into particles pea-sized and smaller, the soil is a balanced loam.

The other soil test is one often used by building inspectors to see whether a septic system is allowable for a rural homesite. Dig a hole a foot deep and fill it with water. The next day, fill the hole to the top again and note the time. If all the water has not drained away within 12 hours, a soil-type or soil compaction problem is present. If the water drains very quickly, you have a very porous, sandy soil.

No easy, effective means exist to alter poor soils on the large scale trees require, and your only option is to select trees that will tolerate your soil conditions. The encyclopedic accounts and the captions that accompany the tree photographs offer specific information on each tree's soil tolerances and preferences.

Getting Started

Soil pH

The acidity or alkalinity of soils is indicated by pH ratings on a scale from 1 to 14, with 7 being neutral—the pH of pure water. If the pH is below 7, the soil is acid; values above 7 indicate alkaline soils. Interestingly, pH is expressed as a logarithmic function. This sounds daunting, but simply means that pH 4.0 is ten times more acid than pH 5.0, 100 times more than pH 6.0, and so on. Thus it is much more difficult to adjust the lower levels of soil pH, which indicate high acidity, than it is to change the pH of less acid soils.

Soils in the East and in the Pacific Northwest are largely acid. In much of the Midwest and West, soils are alkaline. Generally, soils are acid in areas of high annual rainfall and alkaline in drier regions, but local soils can vary considerably. Unfortunately, nothing as simple as squeezing will indicate the acidity or alkalinity of a soil. To judge the pH level of your soil, see your local Cooperative Extension office about having a soil sample analyzed, or purchase a home soil test kit from a garden center or mail-order house.

Since pH helps determine the availability of nutrients in the soil, it is relatively important to some tree species, radically important to others. Most trees tolerate both acid and alkaline soils. Hollies, Sour Gum, Sourwood, and Scarlet and Pin Oaks are among the trees that require a clearly acid soil—one with a pH below 6.0. Soil can be made more alkaline by adding lime, and more acid by adding sulfur. Soil test reports will indicate the proper amounts to add. Since trees require considerable soil areas, it is almost always better to choose a tree suitable to your existing soil pH than to try to change the soil to suit a given species.

Site Alterations

Altering a site prior to planting trees must be done on a rather grand scale to be effective. After all, we know that the roots of trees may extend three times farther than their branches. The roots of a mature shade tree can easily inhabit a 150-foot circle, two-fifths of an acre. In most cases, then, significant alterations can only be carried out in areas devoid of existing trees and shrubs, or with expendable trees and shrubs. The new homesite is often just such a place.

Landscape Changes

A variety of options can markedly alter the appearance of a landscape. Soil mounding is a popular device of some designers, and often helpful in reducing noise problems, in screening winds or unsightly views, and in relieving monotonously flat areas. Mounds and raised beds will also allow you to grow smaller trees and shrubs in areas with poor or wet soils, and are often quite effective in smaller urban lots. Terracing can provide usable flat areas on a hillside. Artificial ponds are feasible in areas with clay soil, and provide picturesque habitats for trees such as willows and bald cypresses. Grading changes, in conjunction with terracing and the use of retaining walls, can dramatically reshape a landscape, but alterations may adversely affect water drainage and runoff if carried out improperly.

Improving Drainage

Poorly drained sites cannot support moisture-sensitive trees such as Red Oak, Sugar Maple, and other species. To cope with excess ground water, you will need to build some form of drainage system. Changing the grade of a site to allow surface water to run off into storm drains or streams instead of pooling and stagnating is one alternative. Diversion terracing—forming a wide, shallow waterway or ditch that is usually planted with grass—will collect and divert water before it reaches the site, and is effective on hills and sloping areas. Drainage tiles laid in gravel will collect and carry ground water to lower areas. Check with your local USDA Soil Conservation office or an engineer with appropriate expertise before carrying out any large grading or drainage changes.

Soil Preparation

Since tree roots must cope with ambient soil sooner or later, the latest recommendations suggest little or no soil preparation when planting, not even amendments in backfill soil. If the tree you want is not tolerant of the general area, it is usually advisable to select one that is. But if you want to treat a large area, and are willing to accept the time and expense, there are ways to improve your soil. Soil pH can be altered by adding lime to increase alkalinity or sulfur to increase acidity. Avoid aluminum sulfate; it may harm plants. The amounts to add to soil depend upon the current pH, the soil type, its organic content, and the pH desired.
The soil structure can be improved by incorporating decayed organic matter deeply into the soil, and by adding gypsum. But soil changes take time and effort and expense, and they wear off, necessitating repeated treatments. If you decide to undertake large-scale site alterations, have your soil tested, obtain the advice of experts, and make the additions well in advance of planting the site—a year if possible, a month at the very least.

Obtaining Trees

Trees, as other plants, can be obtained by propagating them at home, by collecting them from the wild, or by purchasing them. Propagation methods are discussed in the Propagation essay later in this book.
Collecting trees from the wild is hard work, and it must be done early in spring before growth starts. Please remember that unless you own the land, you must obtain permission before you attempt

to transplant a wild tree. No matter how wild it may seem, all property has an owner. Watch for scheduled construction on woodsy sites; it should be easy to get permission to save a few small trees from the bulldozer. Wild trees have sparse roots and often are adapted to shady areas, and you may find it difficult to move them successfully, especially older trees.

The great majority of new trees are purchased from a nursery grower or dealer, either local or mail-order. The prices of trees should be compared, of course. But also consider guarantees, relative size, and the added value of seeing a tree's condition.

Local Suppliers

At a local source, you can inspect trees prior to purchase. First— and too few buyers do this—try to determine trueness to name. Check what you see against illustrations and descriptions, as in this book. Nurserymen are not infallible, especially with rare species and cultivars.

How to Judge a Tree

Look for sturdiness in a tree rather than choosing the tallest one. Check branching: buggy whips and fishing poles make poor trees. You want well-spaced branches—not sparse, and not crowded. The angle that branches make with the trunk is best if about 45 degrees, unless you are buying a narrowly upright cultivar.

Inspect the trunk. Reject trees with scars from careless handling, ragged pruning scars, brown cankerous spots, little borer holes, splits in the bark, and suckers from the base, especially if they look different from the upper twigs.

Inspect the foliage, unless the tree is deciduous and dormant. Spots, holes, poor color, or undersized, wilting, or dropping foliage are good reasons to reject a tree.

If you buy a bare-root tree (though not many are sold anymore), look for a full, fibrous, and symmetrical root system that is moist and flexible, and have it wrapped in something damp immediately after digging or removal from a bin.

Most trees are sold balled and burlapped or in containers. Is the root ball firm? Is the tree settled snugly in the can? Reject trees that seem to have roots loosely surrounded by floor sweepings, and those with dry or cracked root balls, girdling roots, or wobbly trunks.

Judging Nurseries

Good garden center sales people know plants. Ask about the advisability of various trees for the locations at your site. If every cultivar on the lot is "perfect for that spot," be wary and pay particularly close attention to any prospective purchases.

On the other hand, if you know what you want and can judge quality, don't be afraid to buy from a discount nursery. Often the stock there is shipped in from the same wholesale nursery that supplies high-priced sales centers.

Use good sense when bringing a tree home. Never allow fresh, unprotected foliage to be desiccated and injured by the winds created by a long drive from nursery to home. Have the seller wet the foliage and wrap the branches in damp burlap for a long trip, and be sure to wrap trunks to prevent injury.

Mail-order Suppliers

Because of limited demand, many local nurseries and garden centers and most discounters don't stock species and cultivars that are new, rare, or expensive. Your only source may be specialty mail-order dealers. Study catalogues and know the firms' policies or terms of sale, shipping dates, plant sizes, and guarantees. Order early for best selection, specify a shipping date when you know you will be able to plant, and specify a parcel service, which may cost more but is usually worth the expense in time saved.

Unpack the parcels immediately after receipt and inspect them for damage. Plant the trees as soon as possible. Read the "heeling in" instructions that should be in the parcel if you must delay planting. If there is any hint of dryness, soak the roots in a tub of water for three to four hours before planting.

If trees are broken, rotted, dried out, diseased, or in some other unacceptable condition, notify the supplier immediately, specifying whether you want a replacement or a refund.

See the section Nurseries for a list of reliable tree sources around the country. Whether you buy from a local garden center or a mail-order nursery, beware of extravagant claims for plant performance.

Designing with

Trees, as the largest and most permanent plants you can grow, play an essential role in determining the success of a landscape, whether you are starting from scratch or making changes in an existing design. Nothing else you can plant will have the presence and character of a tree. Its shape, height, color, and texture are attractive in themselves, and also give scale and architectural massing to your landscape; work to define garden rooms; frame a handsome view; screen bothersome noise, wind, or unpleasant views; and provide cooling summer shade. These dual needs of beauty and function are the keys to success in designing a landscape and selecting trees.

Some homeowners, faced with empty lots or daunted by the prospect of handling the design process themselves, hire a professional designer. (See the section Expert Help for guidelines to aid your search.) The decision is certainly wise in some cases, but you can find great satisfaction in creating your own design and watching it mature with the seasons and the years.

The Design Process
Because trees are expensive and difficult to move once planted, you must have a landscape plan. Working with such a plan will allow you to correct your mistakes before they become costly and unsightly problems. The plan is the culmination of the design process, which involves learning—about your site, about your wants and needs, about good design, and about the trees you may want to grow—as much as it involves planning and drawing. Creating the plan requires four essential steps—mapping your existing site; defining the public, private, and service areas of your property; understanding the basic elements of good landscape design; and using those elements to site the type of trees that will work in harmony to enrich your landscape. Once the mapping process is finished, you can then select the species and cultivars best suited to your climate, your needs, and your personal taste, aided by several features of this book.

Mapping Your Site
The first and most important step in designing is to record your property's features on paper at a convenient scale. Graph paper is easy to work with and is available in large sheets. Scales of one inch = eight feet and one inch = ten feet are most workable. For larger properties, one inch = 20 feet may be a better choice. Boundary dimensions and angles appear on your deed survey and are registered with your town or county clerk, or you can measure them yourself. After the property boundaries, sketch the house, any additional buildings, drives, walks, terraces, pools, existing trees and other vegetation, and all other physical features. Be as accurate as possible when recording their positions and sizes.

Don't forget to indicate overhead wires, underground pipes, leach

Trees

beds, high and low spots, wet and dry areas, and even trash cans. Note windy, sunny, and shady places. Indicate unsightly views and attractive ones, and sources of noise. Is your property encumbered by an easement or right of way? When detailing your plan, don't forget to include important house features such as windows, doors, and important views from windows and patios. When finished, have six or more copies made. File the original plan and use the copies as worksheets. This site map will be the basis of your planting plan, and it is nearly impossible to develop a workable design without one.

Public, Private, and Service Areas
Before choosing the site of even one tree, ponder the strengths and weaknesses of your property, and the general improvements you hope to make. Lists and brainstorming, and a good deal of reading on landscape design, will help immensely to clarify your thoughts and suggest what elements you should include in your design. You will find that all your wants and needs fall into three categories—public, private, and service. Translating these functions into actual areas creates the backbone of a landscape design.

On the first worksheet, use freehand ovals to make these areas. It may help you to use the analogy of these three areas as rooms, with discrete functions taking place in each landscape room. The public area, seen and used by visitors, is probably all or part of the front yard. Private areas are for play, relaxation, and entertaining. Service areas are for essential but obtrusive items and activities—trash containers, the compost bin, the dog kennel, a storage building, a vegetable garden. The site plan on page 26 represents the typical homesite at this stage of mapping.

The Principles of Landscape Design
Once you've mapped your site and laid out the public, private, and service areas, you are well on your way to beginning the process of landscape design. However, before you do so, you must have a working knowledge of the landscaping principles that underlie all successful designs. The following sections highlight the elements of formal and informal landscape design, and explain the principles that will allow you to use them in planning your own landscape.

Formal Designs
Landscape designs can be as varied as the tastes of their creators, but they are often described as being either formal or informal in style. Formal designs are symmetrical and controlled, with geometrically shaped beds, clipped shrubs, and terracing; they usually have paths, stairs, pools, and other architectural—rather than horticultural—features. Symmetry and balance, straight lines and right angles, with circular paths or beds for contrast, are the prized elements of formal design.

The Landscape Plan *Below is a plan of a new homesite, ready for the positioning and selection of trees.*

The house and other structures are drawn to scale, and future elements such as a swimming pool are sketched in. Natural features such as winds, views, sun, and shade are also indicated.

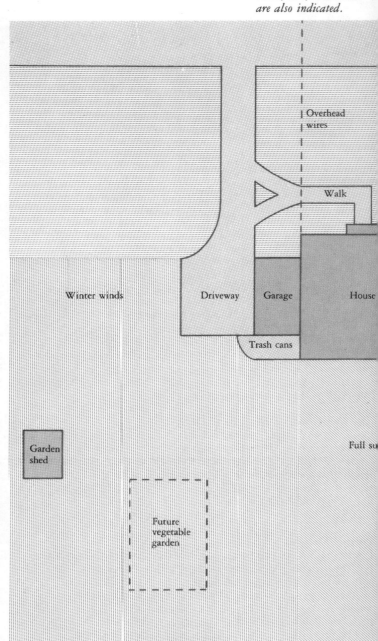

Overhead wires

Walk

Winter winds

Driveway

Garage

House

Trash cans

Garden shed

Full su

Future vegetable garden

Choosing trees according to each area's specific needs will improve the property's beauty and efficiency.

The 3 shaded blocks show the 3 functional areas of the landscape: public at top, service to the left, and private to the right.

Key
▤ Public
▥ Service
▨ Private

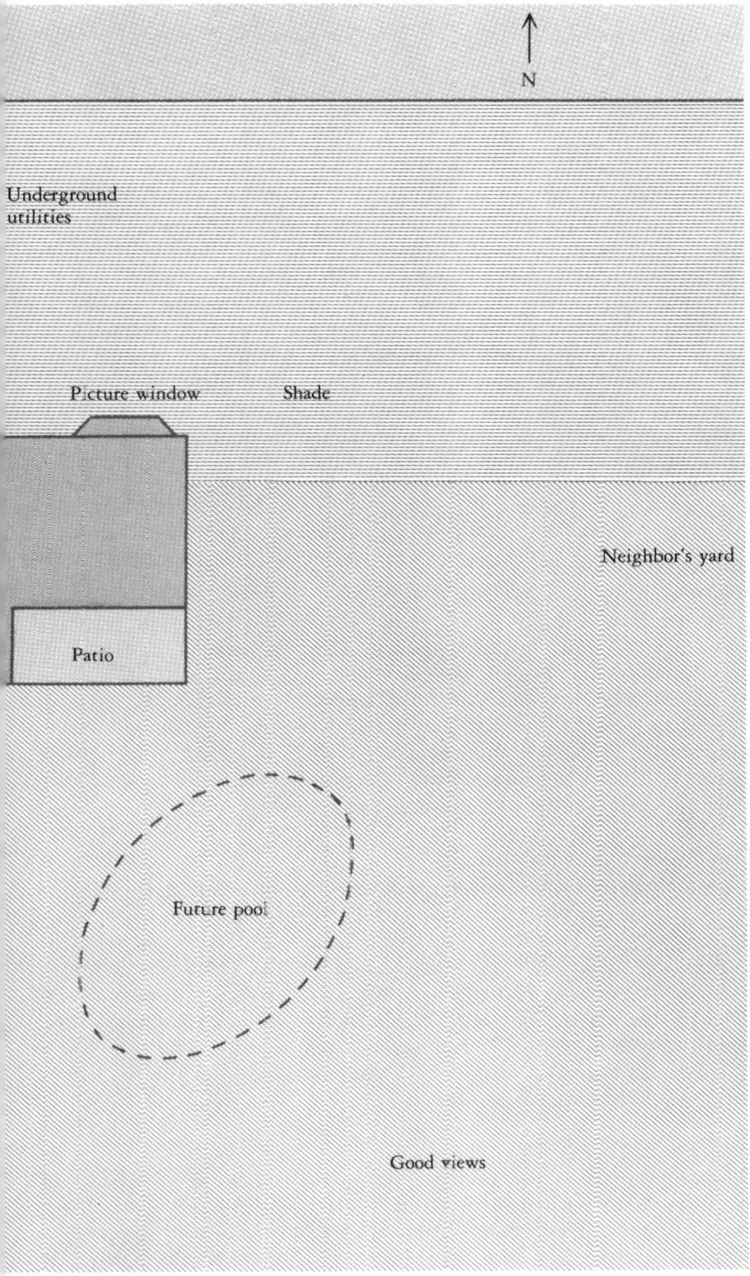

↑
N

Underground utilities

Picture window　　Shade

Neighbor's yard

Patio

Future pool

Good views

Designing with Trees

It takes time and effort to care for a formal garden. Frequent pruning, weeding, and general grooming are imperative to maintain the controlled look. But a simple formal design can be easier for an amateur to create than an informal one, precisely because there are strict rules and clearly evident patterns involved.

Intrusive Formal Elements

Formal designs are rare in residential America today, but unfortunately some residual formalities have been continued by unthinking homeowners. An example is the planting of paired trees on either side of a walk or driveway. Shrubs can be trimmed to be identical, but trees will be unavoidably different and so compete for attention. The straight-line screen planting is another awkward formal device that adds little aesthetically to the landscape and is nearly impossible to grow correctly. If one plant dies, its absence ruins the whole line, and a replacement, never matching, is like a patch on a Sunday suit. Sometimes we see foundation plantings in artificial geometrics; their smoothly sheared foliage is rigid and inappropriate. Avoid all such throwbacks to formal principles unless your landscape will be entirely formal.

Informal Designs

The rectangles, circles, and straight lines of formal designs give way in informal designs to irregular curves that take their cue from nature, yet artfully improve upon it. Features such as lawns, meadows, copses, groves, hedgerows, ponds, and glades are accentuated or introduced into the landscape, and though they appear to be wild features, they are in fact carefully planned and constructed. Note, though, that haphazard, cluttered collections of plants and garden structures are not informal designs, because they have no design principles guiding them.

Asymmetry and Balance

Informal designs allow plants to assume natural shapes, though their sizes may need control by artful pruning. Balance is not ignored; it is achieved asymmetrically. Instead of a pair of trees bracketing the entrance to a drive, imagine one large tree to one side of the entrance and three smaller trees or shrubs opposite it. Or imagine placing one large tree near the drive, balanced on the opposite side by a smaller tree some distance away. The principle is the same as that of a see-saw—a small mass far from the fulcrum will balance a large mass near it.

Specimen Trees

A specimen tree is one planted prominently alone. It may be in an open space, or backed by a screen or grouping of other trees. If too bold or gaudy, a specimen may detract from the rest of the landscape, especially on a small property. Blue Colorado Spruce, for example, is often prominently displayed in a modest front yard, shamelessly upstaging everything, including the house. The same tree would be appropriate in a group planting with other spruces, both blue and green, at the rear or side of a larger property. A less flamboyant tree with appealing traits—a magnolia or a crabapple, for example—is more safely used as a specimen. True, each tree has seasonal brilliance, but each has a better chance of harmonizing with the landscape by offering subtle, year-round interest after its brief display is over.

Group Plantings

If a property is large enough, grouping three or more trees of the same or similar species can be a valuable design feature. The group planting should harmonize, appearing as a unit rather than an assortment. Four or five pine trees; a group of three flowering trees of similar shape and foliage, even though different in their bloom times; and a small grove of shade trees are excellent examples of group plantings. Likewise, a screen planting, if space permits, is far more attractive if planted in a series of small groups rather than in a straight line. The effect can be enhanced by subtly varying the placement of the groups and the types of trees that compose them.

Scale, Size, and Shape

Trees should be scaled in relation to the lot, the house, and other plants. A massive Red Oak is majestic in a park or on an estate. On a 100-foot lot, it is overbearing, especially if growing in the front yard. It would be better planted behind the house, where it becomes a background, making the house seem comfortable rather than insignificant. Conversely, a tiny Sargent Crabapple set alone in the sizable front yard of an imposing three-story house shows the same inattention to proper scale. Choose a tree carefully, keeping in mind its mature height and its foliage mass.

Trees with common shapes are far easier to work with than those with weeping or very narrow outlines. Unusual trees should be treated as such; in a small landscape or in a given unit of a larger one, choose unusual shapes sparingly, as accents. A good guideline is to use no more than two different tree shapes in the same area. Planting variations of the same general shape—horizontal oval, mound, and round, for example—is even more effective.

To help you evaluate the form of a tree, the twelve basic tree shapes are illustrated on the following pages—umbrella, horizontal oval, round, mound, vase, broad triangle, upright oval, narrow triangle, narrow upright, weeping, columnar, and palm. The first four shapes are predominately horizontal and mix successfully. The second set of four shapes are vertical, and also complement each other. The last four shapes are unusual ones, and are best used as accents. Familiarizing yourself with these basic shapes will help you to visualize landscaping possibilities as you design.

Umbrella

Vase

This chart illustrates the 12 basic tree shapes. Use it to plan the types of trees for your landscape and to guide your pruning.

Horizontal Oval

Round

Mound

Upright Oval

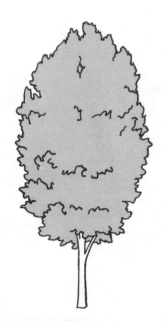

Trees with closely related shapes complement each other. Repeat 2 or 3 similar shapes in a given area of your landscape—in groves, as specimen trees, and in screens.

Broad Triangle

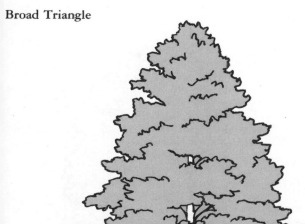

Narrow Triangle

Narrow Upright

Columnar

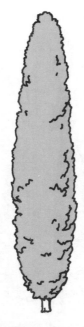

*Use unusual shapes—
narrow upright,
columnar, palm, and
weeping—sparingly, as
accents.*

Weeping

Palm

Designing with Trees

Color and Texture

Trees with year-round or seasonal color are like jewelry; they are tasteful in moderation. If an exception to this rule exists, it would be those deciduous trees with fall color. Instead of choosing only spring-flowering trees, balance your landscape with ornamental tree that offer a variety of attractions appearing at different times—flowers, foliage, fruit, or bark. Such a subtly changing landscape picture is always worth a second look.

Texture should be used with much the same restraint. The lacy foliage of Floss Silk Tree and the bold leaves of Southern Magnolia make a disturbing contrast. A Honey Locust, with its delicate foliage, would blend better with a Floss Silk Tree. Whenever possible, plan subtle modulations of foliage texture and·color. The restraint is soothing, and adds to the power of a deliberate contrast Texture can also be used to fool the eye, making a long, narrow lot appear wider and shorter, or a shallow lot appear deeper. Bold textures seem closer than they are, while fine textures recede. Remember, though, that deciduous trees usually have different textures after leaf drop. One can use similar design principles with color. Light colors jump out, dark colors seem shy. Thus, a screen of dark, finely textured hemlocks will seem farther away than one o bold, coarsely textured Colorado Spruces.

Near Entryways, Patios, and Decks

You may want to shade or frame an entryway with trees. A pleasing imbalance is often achieved by a tree planted on one side only, chosen for its scale, lack of messy or dangerous litter, and interesting features. Terraces and decks benefit from trees that provide shade, wind protection, screening, seasonal beauty, or fragrance. Trees soften the harsh borders of such architectural appendages and help them to blend with the landscape.

When choosing trees to overhang walks, drives, and outdoor living areas, know their litter propensities and pest and disease susceptibility, and choose accordingly. Some trees are mannered and tidy; others are boorish, discarding used parts—leaves, twigs, bark, petals, and fruits—with abandon. Their leaves, petals, and fruits can be hazardously slippery and may stain concrete and wood. Other trees are inherently subject to insect infestations, which induce trees to drip a sticky substance called honeydew.

Near Pools, Ponds, and Streams

Leaves, twigs, and other tree debris are abominable in a swimming pool, and so trees near pools should be limited to tidy upright types, preferably evergreens, planted at least 12 feet from the water. To shade a pool apron, use umbrellas or a slatted roof, not tree.

Ornamental ponds, streams, and small lakes usually don't suffer from fallen leaves as do swimming pools. Weeping trees are never so beautiful as when overhanging water, and reflecting water doubles the beauty of all trees, especially when in flower or in fall color. Painting the interior black gives a garden pool its best reflection.

Trees and streams are good companions. Planted on stream banks, trees reduce soil erosion. One precaution, however; the dikes of man-made ponds should be planted sparingly and only with shrubs or small trees. Tall trees, with root systems restricted by dike configurations, may topple in storms and breach the dike.

Mixed Plantings

Grass and trees coexist poorly. Grass, even those varieties touted as shade-tolerant, suffers from shade, but exacts revenge on trees through allelopathy, the excretion of toxins by one plant to the detriment of another. Trees grow best with nothing beneath them except organic mulch. But some smaller plants—ground covers, bulbs, perennials, and prostrate shrubs—interact well with trees. Check with local experts, look at other landscapes, or experiment on your own to find good combinations.

Large shrubs and other woody plants should not be planted beneath trees. They are best displayed in front of low-branching trees such as the evergreens, beeches, willows, and others. They are also effective simply planted nearby, in foundation plantings, beds, and borders.

Trees that Modify the Environment

Shade trees can moderate the temperature of roofs and walls, thus saving energy, possibly as much as one-quarter of annual heating and cooling bills. Trees shading a roof or an air conditioner are obvious energy-savers in summer. If those trees are evergreen, however, they can block solar energy in winter and negate summer savings. Near a house, especially on southern and western exposures, plant deciduous trees for summer shade and winter sun. Densely branching trees, though leafless, can still usurp a good deal of winter sunlight. In northern latitudes, experts can advise you where to position and how to limb-up trees to block the high-angled summer sun, yet allow low-angled winter sun to pass beneath branches and warm the house, especially through windows. Windbreaks made of trees are also valuable if properly designed. A badly positioned windbreak could possibly create turbulence above your dwelling and do more harm than good. Check with your local county Cooperative Extension agents or other experts for advice on windbreaks. While you have their attention, ask them how to use trees to make snowdrifts pile up out in the yard instead of in the driveway.

The noise reducing properties of trees and other plants are usually over-stated. Meeting the minimum specifications of such sound

Designing with Trees

barriers is of great importance if they are to be effective. A vegetative sound barrier should be at least 60 feet thick and planted as close as possible to the noise source. Low shrubs and trees are closest to the noise, then medium-sized trees, and finally tall trees. All the plants should have finely textured twigs and leaves, and there must be at least 60 feet between the barrier and the "hearer." By all means, consult a landscape designer of proven expertise before trying to muffle noises with trees.

Improving the Existing Landscape

Now that you are familiar with landscape design principles, you are ready to evaluate your existing landscape and plan an improved one. The temptation when designing is to be heavily influenced by your existing habits and landscape features. Let your imagination run freely. Forget existing trees, walks, drives, and flower beds for a time, even if you like them. Remember the rooms and windows in the house. What goes on in the rooms; what is seen from the windows? Drive up and down the road or street, looking, as if for the first time, at your property as you approach it. Does the house need trees for framing or for softening the roof line, or do trees need to be removed?

Use site photographs as drawing-board references. Within each area, work out the most efficient, pleasing arrangement of natural and constructed landscape elements. Pay careful attention to circulation. Does the path go where it's needed? Is the patio too close to the neighbor's house, and will shading it require planting a tree where the water line runs? Don't forget to account for future improvements, like a grassy lawn that may one day become a pool or tennis court. A word about bad views: it is not always possible or necessary to completely hide an eyesore. Indeed, partial screening may draw attention to it. Often it is enough to give the viewer something pretty to look at instead.

Siting Trees

Now you are ready to go back to your original map of the property showing good views, bad views, wind, wet spots, as well as private, public, and service areas. Start drawing circles to indicate the places you want to put trees. Do not scale the little circles to the size of a tree at planting time, but to the mature size you envision. Use the chart of tree shapes to help you choose the overall shapes of the trees, and sketch them in using generalized forms. Select narrow evergreens for screens, large, spreading trees for shade, and flowering trees for accents. Don't worry about identifying the tree species or cultivars just yet—choose trees to fit your needs, rather than adapting your plans to accommodate specific trees.

To help you complete your own site map, the plan on the following pages shows the original site map from page 26 after trees have

been positioned. The public, private, and service areas are clearly
defined by the placement of the trees, a simple solution that avoids
the use of expensive or high-maintenance features such as walls,
fences, or hedges. Evergreens of varying sizes are positioned at the
sides of the property in pleasingly irregular screens that offer
protection from winds, create privacy, and mask unsightly views.
Ornamental trees and small evergreens are used alone as specimens
and as highlights against the screens, or are grouped in groves that
work to define the functional areas of the landscape. Had the
property been larger, shade trees also could have been used in
groves, but here they are positioned to shade the patio, parking
court, and south side of the house from summer sun.
If your home is located in a cold climate, vertical tree shapes offer
the greatest selection of species. In warmer climates, horizontal
shapes might predominate. For example, spruces and firs could
compose the screens in cold climates, broadleaf evergreens in
warm ones. Upright shade trees would echo the triangular shapes
of the conifers, or any of several species of spreading oaks
would complement the rounded shapes of broadleaf evergreens.
Put your worksheet aside and wait a few days. Read the preceding
topics in this section again. Also read the chapters Getting Started
and Planting.
Then take another worksheet copy and deliberately draw something
entirely different. Think about the direct effects and side effects of
your choices. Have you eliminated something desirable? Will there
be too much shade for the rose bed? Will there be a way to get a
truck into the back yard if need be? Combine your first and second
plans, using the best features of both. Until you are satisfied,
continue to revise your plan. If you are unsure of the quality of
your final plan, seek a critique from an informed gardening friend
or make arrangements with a professional for a consultation; a fresh
perspective often sparks improvements.

Selecting Species and Cultivars
The last step is choosing the species and cultivars for the circles.
Each tree must be selected with care, with consideration of its
environmental adaptability and physical features. To help you
choose trees wisely, the color plates in this guide are organized by
the landscape functions of trees; use them in conjunction with the
caption information to identify the proper tree for each site. The
captions supply important facts about each tree's physical
characteristics and cultural requirements, including a tree's height
at two stages of growth, as well as at maturity. Next check the
Tree Chart, where you can easily compare the qualities of different
trees at a glance. And, of course, study the detailed descriptions in
the Encyclopedia of Trees before making any final choices. You will
discover that not only is landscaping with trees a worthy challenge,
but also fun.

Positioning Trees

The new homesite mapped earlier now has trees positioned on it. Selecting the proper species and cultivars will be the final step.

The evergreen screen to the west breaks winter winds, and a similar screen to the east provides privacy and blocks a poor view. An arc of ornamental trees and small evergreens accents the house.

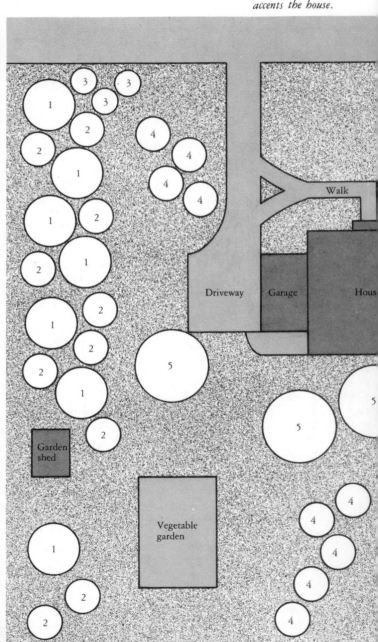

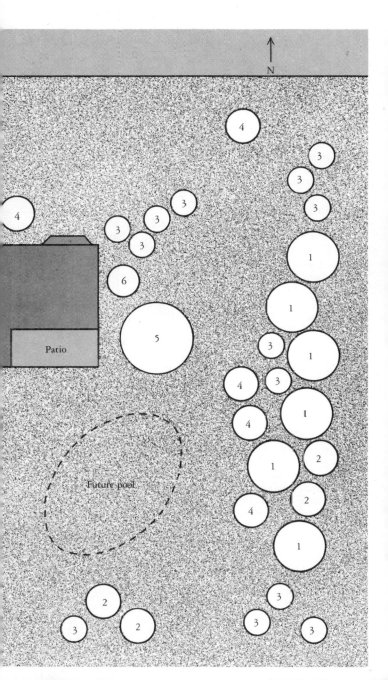

Large trees shade the driveway, patio, and south side of the house, and screen the service area. A semihardy tree grows in a sheltered east site.

Key
1 Large Evergreens
2 Medium Evergreens
3 Small Evergreens
4 Ornamental Trees
5 Shade Trees
6 Semihardy Trees

Planting

Often the most daunting question when considering a tree for planting is its size. This need not be so. Smaller container-grown, balled and burlapped, or bare-root trees are no more difficult to plant than many other garden plants. However, planting larger trees is among the most strenuous and dangerous of garden tasks. Judge your limitations realistically, and always buy a tree in a size you can safely handle. You are far better off planting or transplanting a smaller tree and waiting a few years for it to grow to size than risking possible injury by wrestling with a tree that should have been planted professionally. If you must have a large tree, employ professional tree movers; they have the equipment and expertise to plant landscape-sized trees safely and efficiently.

When to Plant

Most trees are best planted when dormant, in late winter or early spring, before new growth starts. Weather is relatively cool then, but soils are warming, and rain is likely during the following weeks in most climate zones. Roots may begin growth in their new environment before burgeoning new foliage requires large quantities of water.

Evergreens become dormant by late summer, and can be planted then. Fall planting is also fine for evergreens and most other species. Trees are dormant or soon will be, and the soil is warm enough for root growth before winter. Root growth continues until the soil temperature falls to 40 degrees Farenheit at a depth of eight inches. You should plant at least four weeks before the soil in your locality cools to that temperature. In zone 5, for example, most soils cool to 40 degrees by late November. Heavily mulching the planting site in late summer will delay soil cooling. Check with local authorities to find soil temperature data for your zone.

The cautions above are particularly important if trees are moved bare root, a procedure employed effectively with easily transplanted species when individual trees have trunks no more than two inches in diameter at the base. Roots must never be allowed to dry out. Trees sent by mail or other carrier should be planted as soon as possible after arrival. However, if the roots are dry, they should be soaked in water for three to four hours and planted immediately afterward.

Planting Sensitive Species

Some species, particularly evergreens, are best dug with a ball of soil about the roots, known as "balled and burlapped" or just "balled." Others are so sensitive to root disturbance that container growing is preferable to balling, and if balling is employed, it should be done before spring growth. Some of these trees are: all hornbeam, magnolia, hawthorn, and pear species, Sour Gum, White Oak, Madrone, Kentucky Coffee Tree, Sweet Gum, and Crape Myrtle.

Place a balled and burlapped tree in the hole with the burlap still attached. Cut ropes and check that the trunk-root juncture is at ground level, slightly higher in heavy soils.

Adjust depth, if necessary, and carefully cut away excess burlap. Remove wrappings, especially those that are not biodegradable.

Planting

Open containers with cutters. Do not pull trees loose. Check for girdling roots and cut them off near the trunk.

Pry encircling roots from the root ball and direct them into the new soil.

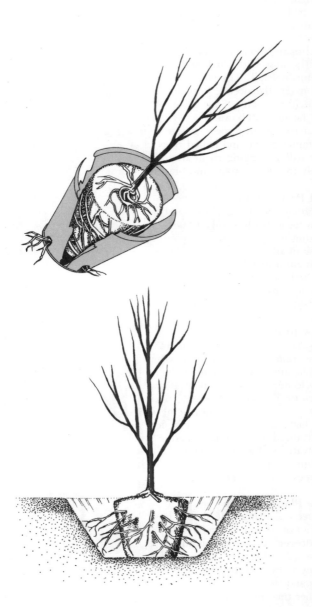

Most container-grown trees and those dug with a ball while dormant and properly stored in a nursery bed—the root ball plunged in wood chips and regularly watered—can be successfully planted all summer in cold climates and year-round in mild ones.

In climates where the soil freezes deeply in winter, a few species—mostly those with thick and fleshy roots—should be planted in spring, not fall. The most common of these trees are: all hornbeam and magnolia species, Weeping Nootka False Cypress, Tulip Tree, Golden-Rain Tree, Sour Gum, White Oak, Red Oak, English Oak, and Japanese Zelkova.

Treat trees with respect, before and after planting. Handle container-grown and balled trees carefully, by their containers or root balls; dragging them around by their branches or trunks is likely to damage roots and branches.

Soil Preparation

Improving your soil is easy and worthwhile for a bed of annuals, or even for a sturdy shrub. Often it is not practicable, however, when dealing with a tree whose roots at maturity may spread 50 feet or more in all directions from the trunk. Since a tree's roots must cope with ambient soil sooner or later, the latest planting procedures call for little soil preparation—not even amendments in backfill soil. If the intended tree is not tolerant of the soil texture, pH, or drainage of the site, you will be much better off choosing a tree that is.

How to Plant

Always choose your planting site in advance. Sod and other vegetation may be sprayed a week prior to planting with glyphosate, a non-specific herbicide sold commercially as Roundup or Kleenup. This treatment allows you to turn the dead grass under when excavating; otherwise, you must remove the sod the hard way—by digging it and placing it aside. (Don't worry about residuals harming the roots of newly planted trees; glyphosate is neutralized within minutes after contact with soil particles.) Put the excavated soil at the edge of the hole. Use a tarp, or place all the soil in one pile for easy retrieval; it's amazing how much soil escapes into the grass.

The Planting Hole

A tree's planting hole should be at least three times wider than the spread of its roots, whether they are bare roots or a root ball, but no deeper. The roots should rest upon undisturbed soil, because loosened soil settles, bringing the tree too deeply into the hole. Many trees are killed by deep planting, especially in heavy soils. In clay and silt-loam soils, keep the trunk-root juncture several inches higher than grade, sloping backfill soil just to cover the roots. In sandy soils, plant at soil level, but no deeper.

Planting

If you find you have dug your planting hole too deeply, place a flat rock or a couple of bricks under the tree's roots. Lacking rocks and bricks, simply shovel backfill soil in the bottom of the hole and pack it hard so it won't settle later. This is the only time compacted soil is tolerated.

Once you've reached the right width and depth, lightly loosen the soil on the sides of the hole. A shiny soil face discourages penetration by new roots, even several years after planting. Holes dug with the augers and tree spades used by commercial nurseries are especially apt to have glazed surfaces, and you should watch commercial planters to make sure that they prepare the sides properly.

Preparing the Roots

All pots, cans, and other containers must be removed, even the pressed fiber pots that are supposed to decay and add humus to the soil. They will, but too late to help a choked tree. Container-grown trees may be root-bound. If so, carefully tug and pull at roots to loosen and spread them. In extreme situations, cut tightly wound roots, especially those near the trunk-root juncture. Such roots frequently become girdling roots, causing serious trouble even many years later as they grow and strangle the tree.

Planting Depth

Balled trees also may have some problems. After placing the tree in the hole at the proper level, remove the twine from the top of the root ball, and especially from around the trunk. Peel the burlap back and look for the first roots. Some nursery-grown balled trees have cultivation soil, mulch, or debris piled on the upper portion of the root ball, causing unsuspecting gardeners to plant these trees too deeply. Remove any excess duff and adjust the tree's depth, then cut away as much burlap as possible without undue disturbance of the soil ball. Always discard synthetic burlaps. If the root ball is encased in wire mesh, use wire cutters to remove as much as you can. Wire persists in the soil for several years and may interfere with root growth. Spread the roots of bare-root trees radially and prune away broken roots.

Filling the Planting Hole

For generations, homeowners and nurserymen alike have religiously mixed organic matter and other soil amendments with the backfill soil. Recent tests indicate little if any benefits result, especially with trees. In fact, raw humus in backfill may foster detrimental anaerobic conditions, and should be avoided.

Merely replacing the soil and tamping it gently will do the job. If soil test results indicate a need for fertilizer, mix the suggested amount—more is not better—into the backfill before filling the hole.

Handle bare-root trees with care, keep them moist, and plant them quickly upon receipt. Spread the roots radially and prune away broken ones.

Plant with the trunk-root juncture at ground level, slightly higher in heavy soils, and stake to prevent toppling by winds.

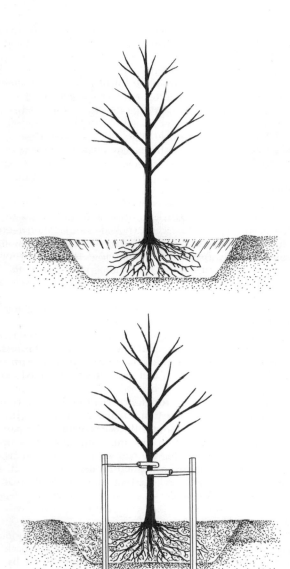

Mulching

Providing a circular dam, or a semicircular one on a slope, to hold water is fine, but mulching is better. Cover the disturbed soil to three times the root area with composted shredded bark, wood chips, leaf mold, mushroom compost, pine needles, and the like. In some areas, organic waste materials are available—peanut shells, cacao or buckwheat hulls, tobacco stems, or spent hops. These mulches may seem a bargain, but take care to inquire about unpleasant side effects such as odors.

Avoid mulching with fresh material at all costs. New grass clippings ferment and heat; fresh sawdust steals nitrogen from the upper soil; and so on. Inorganic mulches such as stones or marble chips are usually visually inappropriate for a home landscape, frequently alter soil pH, and become dangerous missiles when hit by the lawn mower.

Your mulch should be at least two inches deep, but no more than four inches deep. Leave a six-inch bare circle around the tree's trunk to deter fungus diseases and rodents. Water slowly and thoroughly immediately after planting, either before or after mulching, or both. If the mulch washes away, the water is running too fast.

Pruning and Wrapping

The ritual of pruning the tops of trees at planting time is not necessarily beneficial to the tree. The old rule about cutting off one-third of the top, according to recent studies, in fact may retard root growth. However, broken twigs and branches must be pruned, as should competing leaders—one central stem is enough. Also remove those branches growing inward, and those that mar the natural shape of the tree.

Wrapping the trunks of new trees seems not to prevent sunscald and other winter injury, contrary to popular gardening legend, although insect attacks are reduced. A coat of white latex paint or a covering of reflective material on the trunk and major branches will reduce sunscald, but seldom harmonizes with a home landscape. Rabbits inhabit many suburban neighborhoods and often eat the tender bark of ornamental trees, girdling trunks so badly that young trees may die. A cylinder of one-inch mesh chicken fencing, tall enough to stay well above your expected snow cover, will protect a tree's bark from their sharp incisors.

Staking

If a new tree requires staking to prevent leaning, as many bare-root trees do, use two sturdy stakes at least six feet long, pounded into the undisturbed soil at the bottom of the hole, far enough from the trunk to avoid damaging the roots. Secure the tree to stakes with heavy wire, with sleeves made of old garden hose to protect the bark from the wire. The wires must be loose enough to allow some movement of the trunk in the wind, or trunk strength will be sacrificed. Rigidly tied trunks, like arms in slings, become weak. Tree wraps and wires do nasty things as trees grow, so check periodically and loosen them as needed through the first growing season, and remove them altogether the following spring.

Transplanting

Sometimes a tree must be moved from one spot on a property to another. Occasionally a neighbor will offer a tree that is just right for your landscape plan, or a tree growing wild fits the plan. Remember that wild trees usually have wild, sparse roots and a meager tolerance to transplanting, so treat them with prudence and care.

Before starting, measure the diameter of the trunk of the tree six inches above the ground. The root mass for an easily moved species should be at least one foot in diameter for every inch of trunk diameter. Professionals can move trees of sizes up to 12 inches in trunk diameter at almost any time of year. Most gardeners should leave it to such experts to move sizable trees, and should observe some important timing guidelines for smaller trees.

When to Transplant

Transplant deciduous trees only when they are leafless. In cold zones 1 to 4, early spring is best, before new growth begins. In milder zones 5 to 8, fall is also fine for most deciduous trees, and in zones 8 and 9, you can transplant from fall to early spring. Follow this general timetable when transplanting evergreens, but keep in mind that evergreens in all areas also can be transplanted in late summer after their active growth is completed.

Transplanting Methods

You can use the bare-root method to transplant deciduous trees, except those with "tough to move" reputations. Move them in spring before growth starts so that they have a full year's growth before dormancy. Be aware that a tree with a three-inch trunk diameter is probably 15 feet tall, and even without soil it may weigh 150 pounds. Putting such a tree upright into a new hole is a great opportunity for frustration or calamity, and it may be better to obtain a smaller tree or hire a professional mover.

Evergreens and sensitive deciduous trees are best moved with a ball of soil. A tree with a two-inch trunk diameter may be as much as the collective family muscle can handle—with the two-foot ball it will weigh about 300 pounds. Trees this large or larger are best transplanted by professionals. The cost is little compared to the dangers you will avoid.

If the proposed move will put a shaded tree in full sun, exposure problems may result. You can risk damage or find another tree to move that has been growing in a similar location. Likewise, a tree with its front side sunny and its back side shady will adapt well to

Planting

Dig a trench around the tree, 1 ft. away from the trunk for each inch of its diameter. Dig down until you encounter no more roots, then undercut the root ball.

With help from another person, lift the tree and wrap the ball in burlap for transport, or gently dislodge soil from the roots if you are transplanting by the bare-root method.

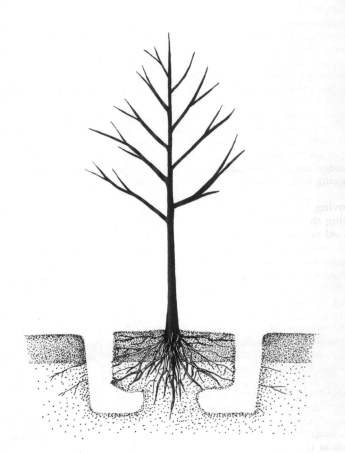

a site with a similar situation. To ensure proper orientation, mark one side before digging and align the tree in the same direction when replanting.

Trenching

Whether you plan to transplant a tree bare root or with a root ball, begin by digging a trench in a circle around the tree, leaving the appropriate root zone diameter—one foot for each inch of trunk diameter. Use a garden spade to cleanly cut the sides of the trench and roots encountered; use a long-handled shovel to remove loose soil from the bottom of the trench.

When the spading process hits no more roots, begin to slope the trench inward, toward the tree, and cut beneath the ball until it is free. Do so carefully, without prying with the spade, and leave the soil firmly intact about the remaining roots. This sounds simple; it is not always so. Wrenching and prying the root ball will only damage the tree; you should have patience and instead continue digging and trenching.

Moving the Tree

Using the spade beneath the ball, and perhaps a helper with the shovel or another spade beneath the ball, lift the tree from the hole and place it on a piece of burlap or an old tablecloth. This, too, sounds simple, but requires strength and agility.

The fabric should be ample enough to cover the root ball in roughly the manner of an old-fashioned diaper. If the new site is close by, two people may be able to grasp the fabric corners and carry the tree, or put it in a wheelbarrow. For farther transportation, tie the opposing corners snugly and web some stout twine around the ball to secure the fabric about the soil. Lift the ball carefully into a truck or trunk of a car. Once at the hole, proceed with planting as previously outlined.

Bare-Root Transplanting

To transplant a tree bare root, choose a cloudy windless day—a slight drizzle is good for the tree. Dig the new hole just slightly less deep than you anticipate the tree will need, and three times as wide as the depth.

Follow the transplanting procedure until your spade hits no more roots. Continue by cutting back the soil beneath the roots, but this time, pry and jiggle. Keep cutting and prying and jiggling until all the roots are free and bare.

If the new hole is close by, carry the tree to the site. The new hole by some chance may be just right. If so, plant. If not, mist the bare roots with water, adjust the depth of the hole, and plant.

If the new site is far away, or you forgot to dig the hole, remove the tree from its hole and place its roots on a large piece of sturdy plastic—at least enough to cover all the roots. Sprinkle the roots with water, and throw some dampened straw or sawdust or such around them. Bring the corners of the fabric together and tie. Do not let direct sunlight strike the plastic. After transporting the tree, proceed with planting as previously outlined.

Tubs, Boxes, and Planters

The roots of most plants can be killed by cold temperatures that are significantly higher than the temperatures lethal to dormant trunks and branches. For example, a researcher at the University of Massachusetts reported the death of roots of Saucer Magnolias at 23 degrees Farenheit. At Cornell University, the roots of Flowering Dogwoods died at 10 degrees. Yet the trunks and branches of both species are hardy to −20 degrees. Also, moisture in soil expands upon freezing and can easily damage containers. For both reasons, it is usually impractical to plant trees in above-ground containers in zones 1 to 7, unless you provide winter protection.

An ample soil volume is important for container-grown trees. A depth of three feet is minimal for smaller trees; five feet is better. The width, or diameter, of a tree planter should always be greater than its depth.

Drainage is paramount in successful container culture. Use a potting mixture with little or no soil for good drainage and for weight reduction. Commercial mixes are easy to use and are readily available. But remember, trees grown in containers require regular watering and scheduled fertilization.

Pruning

Exciting discoveries in recent years about how trees grow have reshaped our thinking about how to prune, and many time-honored practices, brought to scrutiny as never before, are no longer considered valid by the majority of professional arborists.

Why Prune Trees?

Trees should be pruned for purposes that will benefit the tree. Prune to remove dead and diseased wood, and to maintain or increase structural strength. Prune also to maintain or improve a tree's natural beauty, and to ensure good flowering or fruiting. Always remove water sprouts—those vigorous shoots arising from trunks and branches—and suckers—similar shoots arising from the bases of trees, often from the understocks of grafted or budded trees. You may need to prune a tree for safety reasons, such as keeping traffic views open or maintaining clearance for walks or drives. And, unfortunately, sometimes pruning is necessary to restrict a tree's size, usually because the tree was planted in a site too small for it.

Most lists of the reasons to prune trees include cutting back the branch structure when planting or transplanting to reduce shock and to keep the ratio of branches to roots in balance. Much research of late indicates that such cutting back does no good, and usually stunts a tree, and so should be avoided.

Use judgment before doing your own pruning. Sawing heavy limbs or working high in trees, near wires, or above buildings or traffic are jobs best left to qualified arborists.

When to Prune

If you want your trees to have their most vigorous response after pruning, then the best time to prune is in late winter or early spring, before new growth begins. If you are pruning for the greatest reduction of overall size, which is the most common reason for pruning, late spring or early summer is the best time. Remove water sprouts and suckers in summer. However, drastic summer pruning may weaken a tree, so save major pruning for a tree's dormancy. Also, if you are pruning deciduous trees, there will be no leaves to compound the mess.

Pruning Tools

A quality pruning tool given regular care will perform better and far longer than a bargain counterpart. Keep metal parts lightly coated with lubricating oil and keep wood parts painted or rub them monthly with linseed oil. Use bright colors when painting small tools, so they can't hide in the grass.

Hand-held pruning shears are of two general types: snap cut, with an anvil action, where a sharp blade impinges on a broad blade; and draw cut, with a scissors action. The latter makes a cleaner cut and is preferred. Hand pruners are good for cutting one-half-inch

Pruning

To remove a leader, cut
parallel to the bark
ridge.

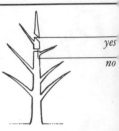

diameter branches, and three-quarter-inch branches if you are strong
enough.
Loppers are long-handled shears, operated with both hands. The
best models can slice through two-inch branches, but often tear
some bark when strained. You are better off using a small saw for
cuts that you can't handle with hand pruners.
Pruning saws have varying numbers of teeth per inch, called points.
An 8-point saw makes a fine cut; a 4½-point blade is coarse and
should only be used for removal work. A 7-point and a 5½-point
saw are fine for most weekend pruning. Purchase saws with
comfortable "D" or pistol-style handles, rather than the slightly
curved handles found on most folding saws.
Chain saws by their very nature are dangerous and difficult to use,
and are best left to professionals, or to skilled amateurs who use
them regularly.
Whatever pruning equipment you are using—shears, loppers, saws,
or chain saws—always wear heavy gloves and protective goggles to
avoid injury.

Making Cuts
When removing a side branch, cut the limb back to the trunk or a
larger branch. Never leave a stub. If you can hang your hat, you
have made a bad cut. On the other hand, a flush cut should also be
avoided. To make a proper cut, look for the branch collar—the
slight swelling at the base of the branch—and the branch bark
ridge—a roughened line of bark left on the trunk as the branch and
trunk grow longer. The cut should be at an angle equal to and
opposite the bark ridge, just leaving the branch collar. Refer to the
sketches on page 55, and make your cuts accordingly. To remove
part of a central trunk or of a main branch, choose a major side
branch and cut just above and parallel to the branch bark ridge.
The side branch chosen should be no less than half the diameter of
the removed trunk. The cuts will close quickly, and the chance of
decay will be minimized.
Most people cannot cut cleanly with pruners or a saw in one hand
while holding the branch in the other, and should use the three-cut
method. The first cut is made from below, a few inches from the
trunk and only about halfway through the branch. The second cut
is made about an inch farther along the branch. The final cut
removes the stub to the branch collar. To remove only part of a
main limb, cut back to a side branch with a good angle that is not
markedly smaller than the limb. Cut parallel to the branch bark
ridge.

Wound Treatments
Trees don't heal. A wound exists for the life of the tree; it is simply
covered by new annual growth. A time-honored wound treatment
recently has been found wanting: messy black tree paint is

Use the 3-cut method to remove large limbs. Undercut the branch about halfway through, then cut from above, slightly beyond the first cut, to remove the branch.

The third cut is made from above, parallel to the branch collar.

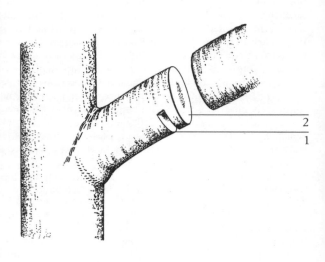

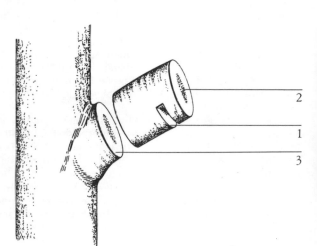

Pruning

ineffectual and often detrimental. Tree wounds cover over just as quickly without it, and the chance of decay is sometimes lessened. Make a clean, proper cut and leave the tree to do the rest. An exception is a sprout-inhibiting compound laced with napthalene acetic acid, applied after removing water sprouts and suckers.

If the bark of a tree trunk is accidentally gouged, do not cut the wound into the familiar ellipse shape, as this only hurts the tree further. Simply clean away torn and loose bark with a sharp knife, leaving as much bark intact as possible. Again, avoid tree wound dressing. Instead, wrap the trunk with black polyethylene film to completely cover the wound immediately after it has been cleaned. If the film is thin enough to let sunlight through, use several layers. Secure the plastic with black plastic electrician's tape, and leave it for one year. This method reduces decay and accelerates wound closure.

Cavities and Bleeding

Tree cavities were once vigorously scraped of decay and filled. Now we know that filling a cavity does not accomplish much, and that scraping is likely to spread decay into healthy tissue that may have walled off the infected area by a natural process called compartmentalization. Your best defense against the onset of decay is careful pruning, but if a tree becomes severely affected, it is best to remove it.

When pruned in spring, many trees respond with a copious sap flow called bleeding. Bleeding is unsightly, but it causes very little damage to a tree. There are vigorous Sugar Maples in New England that have gallons of sap removed each spring.

Topping and Thinning Out

Trees should never be pruned by topping, a method that indiscriminately removes or "tops" the upper branches of deciduous trees. A given tree in a given site has a largely predetermined height. After reaching that height, the tree, even a columnar cultivar, begins to spread, growing little if any higher. Topping simply seems to make a tree all the more determined to reach that height, but forces it to do so with many upright shoots rather than a natural pattern of trunk and branches. Topping destroys the natural beauty of a tree, causes wounds that can never heal, and results in broomlike clusters of epicormic shoots with weak attachment. In a few species, topping may actually increase wind resistance, and thus the likelihood of storm damage. Finally, topping reduces both a tree's value and its life expectancy.

The alternative to topping is thinning out by cutting back limbs to side branches without leaving stubs or right-angled truncations. Such thinning retains a tree's natural structure and shape, while reducing branch density and thus wind resistance. Some professionals call this method of pruning "drop crotching." Few amateurs should attempt this type of pruning, and instead should contact a professional pruner.

Training Young Trees

To prune a tree best, start early. However, pruning at transplanting may hinder or reduce growth, since it is now known that chemicals produced in leaf buds promote root growth, and cutting back at planting removes many of those buds. Instead, prune the second season after planting a tree, but avoid two common mistakes when pruning young trees. Don't neglect a young tree for several years, because forming a good branch structure will be all the more difficult. And do not begin limbing up young trees too soon. True, the limbs of a sizable tree should be high enough to allow head or vehicular clearance, but they needn't be that high immediately after planting. If side branches remain untrimmed, a tree will be stockier and shorter than its ideal. But if a tree's lower branches are completely removed very early, the trunk becomes spindly and weak.

To bring a young tree nearer to the ideal, cut back the lowest side branches by about one-third to smaller side branches. Remove those pruned branches entirely the next year, and head back the higher branches. Continue this process for several years until the lowest branches are at the desired height. All the while, see that the tree has one main vertical trunk. If secondary leaders develop, remove them immediately. The narrow crotches of multiple trunks are highly vulnerable to splitting.

When a tree becomes tall enough that its lower branches are to be permanent—four to six feet for a small flowering tree, eight or ten feet for a shade tree—begin forming a framework of strong, well-spaced branches. Branches should form a spoke pattern on the trunk, with about five branches to each wheel or tier of branches. Branches should form 45 degree angles with the trunk. For a large-growing shade or ornamental tree, the tiers of branches should be spaced so that one branch is at least three feet above the one directly below it. For a guide to ideal shapes, see the illustrations of tree shapes in the essay Designing with Trees.

Unfortunately, the branches of a live tree never grow like the ideal. If there is a missing spoke, perhaps a branch can be bent sideways by tying or bracing for a couple of months. Branch angles may be made larger by employing spacers or weights, smaller by using props underneath branches. Beware of using such corrective hardware without regular inspection; if branches begin to distort, adjust the ties and sticks. Paying attention to branch angles and spacing may add tremendously to the beauty and longevity of a tree.

Training a New Leader

If a young tree loses its leader or main upright stem, a new one

Pruning

Below is a tree about 4 years after planting, showing temporary training measures.

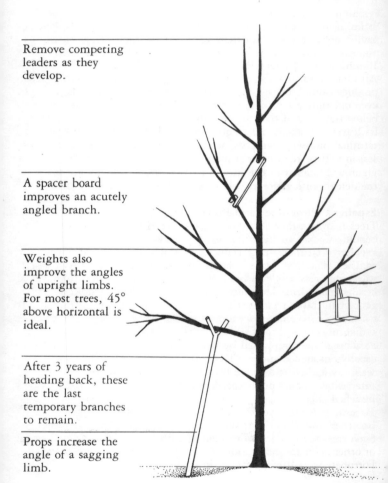

Remove competing leaders as they develop.

A spacer board improves an acutely angled branch.

Weights also improve the angles of upright limbs. For most trees, 45° above horizontal is ideal.

After 3 years of heading back, these are the last temporary branches to remain.

Props increase the angle of a sagging limb.

Early training and proper pruning will add greatly to a tree's beauty and longevity. Upon planting, remove only broken, crossing, or competing branches.

Year by year, head back the lowest branches and remove weak and poorly placed ones to form a spirally tiered pattern.

may be trained. Make the wound as clean as possible with pruners or a small saw. Select a side branch just below the wound and train it into a vertical position. Tie a stout stake half its length onto the remaining trunk and tie the new leader onto the upper part of the stake, using soft tying material. If a tree develops more than one leader, select the best and remove the others as soon as possible.

Pinching Needle-leaf Evergreens

All pines, and to a lesser extent spruces and a few other evergreens, produce candles of new growth in spring. If a dormant pine branch, even one only a year old, is cut in the middle, there are no buds below the cut and the stub will die. But if a tender candle—with its leaves still small and tightly appressed—is pinched back, a new terminal bud will form, and the growth for that shoot for that season will be reduced by half. Use this method to keep overly vigorous branches in check, and to slow the growth and increase the density of leggy evergreens.

Espaliers, Pleaching, and Pollarding

Trees may be pruned to a variety of distortions, artistic to some beholders, machinistic to others.

Espaliered trees are those trained more or less two-dimensionally on trellises, fences, or walls. Choose species that are dense and reach a small mature size—*Pyrus* and *Malus* are often employed. Traditional espaliers are formal, symmetrical, and sometimes elaborately geometric. More recent styles are free-form, and easier to begin and maintain. Espaliers require expert pruning knowledge, patience, and time.

Pleaching is accomplished by weaving tree branches to form, usually, an arched tunnel. Trees are planted on both sides of a walkway and their tops are bent inward and their branches intertwined. Some public gardens and a few private estates feature pleached allees.

Pollarding is the severe annual heading back of tree trunks or major branches, inducing dense short shoots from the truncated areas. Such trees are rendered into globes, cylinders, multiple pom-poms, or other artificial shapes. Like topping, the practice weakens trees. Fortunately, pollarding is rare in America.

Trees to Avoid

It has been said, "There are no bad trees, just trees in bad places." Indeed, a few trees that are maligned or even outlawed in some parts of the country are included in this book because they are valuable for use in specific, usually adverse, conditions. But some trees tend to be such nuisances that they are considered trees to avoid.

Common Tree Problems
Vigor—hardiness and adaptability to local conditions—and freedom from pests and diseases are not the only considerations when choosing a tree. A number of trees cause problems that overshadow their attributes.

Certain trees have invasive roots that can lift pavements, choke gardens, and clog drainage systems. Some trees drop large quantities of debris during a given season—petals, leaves, fruits—while others seem to litter constantly, shedding bark, twigs, and branches as well. A tree of this sort planted beside a patio may be a nuisance, but another tree of the same species growing in an open field may be a valued specimen.

You should also avoid trees with unusual foliage characteristics, or at least use them quite sparingly. For example, variegated leaves tend to scorch in hot, dry weather; yellow leaves often appear sickly; and large leaves shred and tear easily in the wind.

Trees with Severe Drawbacks
The 15 species and genera of trees that follow have severe drawbacks that limit their use only to the most extreme conditions, or that make them unworthy of planting at all. Commonly, they are rank and weedy, with invasive roots or suckers, they are susceptible to disfiguring or even fatal pest and disease infestations, they have weak wood and break easily in storms, or their physical attributes make their use in the landscape difficult. Remember that such evaluations are in measure subjective, and that a few trees on this list have been widely planted. Always investigate a tree's performance in your area and evaluate your landscaping needs before making a selection, wherever the tree is to be planted.

Using the Chart
On the chart you will find trees with questionable landscape merit in most areas. The description section explains why each species should be avoided. Despite the drawbacks given, if the tree is valuable for exceptional conditions, such as in polluted urban areas or in regions with dry, cold winters, this information is indicated under comment.

Name	Description	Comment
Acer negundo Box Elder	A weedy, fast-growing deciduous tree with brittle wood and no ornamental seasons. Attacked by Box Elder bugs.	Used in the Great Plains for temporary screening in cold, dry areas where few other trees will survive.
Aesculus hippocastanum Horsechestnut	A deciduous shade tree with a coarse appearance, nuisance fruits, and weak wood. Subject to disfiguring foliar diseases.	
Ailanthus altissima Tree-of-Heaven	A short-lived, weedy, and invasive deciduous tree with weak wood. Foliage and male flowers have a foul odor.	Endures the worst city conditions.
Aralia elata Japanese Angelica	An exotic-looking deciduous tree that is difficult to use in the landscape. Has dangerous thorns and invasive root suckers.	*Aralia spinosa*, a similar species, also should be avoided.
Betula populifolia Gray Birch	A short-lived, weak-wooded deciduous tree, often lasting only 20 years. Disfigured by leafminers.	

Trees to Avoid

Name	Description	Comment
Carya species Hickories	Deciduous shade trees, coarse in appearance, that drop litter, especially nuts. All are very difficult to transplant.	Sturdy and tolerant, but far more decorative species are available.
Elaeagnus angustifolia Russian Olive	A medium-sized ornamental deciduous tree subject to a variety of diseases, including Verticillium wilt, that weaken and disfigure it.	Silvery-gray foliage, most pronounced in youth, is not as decorative in maturity. Color can overpower other trees in the landscape.
Juglans nigra Black Walnut	The leaves, bark, and nuts of this fast-growing deciduous tree are messy and will stain most surfaces.	Nearby plants are killed by a toxic secretion of its roots.
Maclura pomifera Osage Orange	A deciduous tree with dangerous thorns and invasive roots. Female trees drop softball-sized fruits.	Thornless male cultivars exist, but are extremely rare.
Magnolia tripetala Umbrella Magnolia	The bold foliage can dominate the landscape, and the large leaves tear in the wind. Flowers have an unpleasant odor.	Other large-leaved magnolias have similar problems. Choose smaller-leaved species.

Name	Description	Comment
Platanus species Sycamores	Deciduous shade trees that litter heavily, dropping leaves, twigs, fruits, and bark. Subject to cankers and twig and leaf blights that weaken and disfigure trees.	Trees tolerate city conditions, but grow far too large to be effective in most urban areas.
Populus species Poplars	Fast-growing deciduous trees with brittle wood and invasive roots. Trees litter heavily and are susceptible to many pests and diseases.	Hybrids have been developed that tolerate the worst soils and conditions.
Prunus serotina Wild Black Cherry	A deciduous flowering tree with messy fruit. Subject to storm damage and tent caterpillar infestations.	
Robinia pseudoacacia Black Locust	A deciduous shade tree that ages poorly, often dying back from the branch tips. Host to numerous insect pests, especially borers and leaf miners.	
Ulmus americana American Elm	A deciduous shade tree subject to several pests and diseases, including Dutch elm disease and phloem necrosis, both fatal.	Efforts to breed resistant cultivars of this once-magnificent species so far have failed.

Trees, more than any other garden plants, make important and lasting contributions to the landscape. Because the value of a tree is so intimately tied to its effective use, the color plates are arranged by the typical landscape functions of the three major tree groups: the deciduous trees, the broadleaf evergreens, and the needle-leaf evergreens. The deciduous trees begin the color section, and are divided into ornamentals and shade trees. The broadleaf evergreens, also organized into ornamentals and shade trees, are next. This group includes the palms, which unlike the others are tropical semi-woody plants. Finally, the needle-leaf evergreens are pictured in two sections, ornamentals and screens.

Almost every tree is shown in at least two photographs. A view of the entire tree appears on the left-hand page, and a detail of its flowers, foliage, or fruit appears beside it on the right-hand page. A few trees are represented with more than two photographs, or only by one. Some photographs illustrate notable varieties of a species. The captions present important information on each tree's physical characteristics and cultural requirements. To help you plan for a tree's long years to maturity, height is indicated at three stages: at 15 years, at 40 years, and at maturity. A bullet before the height indicates the approximate height and age of the tree pictured.

Visual Key

The Visual Key shows the range of trees within each major group and subgroup. Using it allows you to quickly find a photograph of the kind of tree you are interested in, and to compare a tree with others that are similar in form and use.

Visual Key

The Deciduous Trees

Deciduous trees drop their leaves each fall; new foliage appears in spring. The 108 species shown are divided into ornamentals and shade trees.

Deciduous Ornamentals

Many of these trees provide spectacular spring flower displays. The smaller, compact trees are used as garden accents. If you want to add seasonal or year-round interest to your landscape, you can also choose from a number of trees with especially decorative bark, foliage, fruits, or branches.

Deciduous Shade Trees

You can plant these trees to provide a canopy of cooling summer shade. Nearly all are spreading and massive at maturity, but remember, decades may pass before some shade trees become truly effective. Several species turn a brilliant fall color before dropping their leaves.

To help you select the
right tree for your
needs, the color
plates are arranged in
three major groups:
deciduous trees,
broadleaf evergreens,
and needle-leaf

evergreens. Each group
has two sections that
reflect a tree's typical
landscape use.

Pages 72–185

Pages 72–139

Pages 140–185

Visual Key

The Broadleaf Evergreens	Broadleaf evergreens have broad, flat leaves that remain green year-round. The 50 species shown are grouped into ornamentals and shade trees.	
Broadleaf Ornamentals	If you want year-round greenery and showy flowers or fruits, consider the trees in this group. Most are native to warmer climates, notably the highly decorative but quite frost-sensitive palms.	 
Broadleaf Shade Trees	The species pictured here are evergreen counterparts to the deciduous shade trees, and many have handsome, waxy leaves. Most reach a great size, making them invaluable for constant shade in semi-arid, tropical, or coastal regions.	 

Pages 186–239

Pages 186–217

Pages 218–239

Visual Key

The Needle-leaf Evergreens	These evergreens, also called conifers, have needle-like or scale-like foliage. The 43 species shown are divided into ornamentals and screens.	
Needle-leaf Ornamentals	Use the distinctive forms and foliage textures of these evergreens to create year-round landscape accents. Choices range from the narrowly columnar cypresses to the gracefully tiered Norfolk Island Pine.	 
Needle-leaf Screens	The conifers in this group are particularly well-suited for screen and background plantings. The pines, spruces, firs, cedars, and hemlocks vary in shape from tapering spires to picturesque masses, while their foliage ranges in color and texture from subtle and delicate to vibrant and rugged.	 

Pages 240–287

Pages 240–257

Pages 258–287

The Deciduous

Trees

Many of these trees provide brief but spectacular spring flower displays. The smaller, compact trees are used as garden accents. If you want to add seasonal or year-round interest to your landscape, you can also choose from a number of trees with especially decorative bark, foliage, fruits, or branches.

Aesculus × *carnea* 'Briottii'

Ruby Red Horsechestnut
•Height at 15 years: 15 ft.
At 40 years: 35 ft.
At maturity: 50 ft.
Zones 5–9

Blooms in spring
Fruit summer to fall
Requires moist, acid soil
Tolerates light shade

Lagerstroemia indica

Crape Myrtle
Height at 15 years: 12 ft.
•At 40 years: 20 ft.
At maturity: 30 ft.
Zones 7–9

Blooms summer to fall

| *Aesculus* × *carnea* 'Briottii' | Ruby Red Horsechestnut
Flowers: ¾ in. long
Clusters: to 10 in. long | p. 297 |

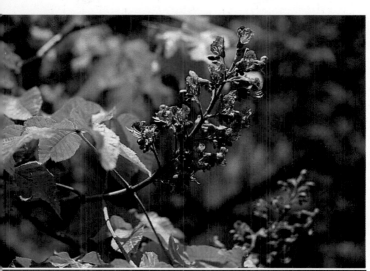

| *Lagerstroemia indica* | Crape Myrtle
Flowers: 1¼ in. wide
Clusters: 6–8 in. long | Fall color
p. 350 |

Chorisia speciosa   *Floss Silk Tree*   *Blooms in fall*
                          Height at 15 years:
                          30 ft.
                          •At 40 years: 50 ft.
                          At maturity: 60 ft.
                          Zones 9–10

Bauhinia blakeana   *Hong Kong Orchid*   *Blooms in winter*
                         Tree
                         •Height at 15 years:
                         10 ft.
                         At 40 years: 20 ft.
                         At maturity: 25 ft.
                         Zone 10

Chorisia speciosa   Floss Silk Tree   p. 319
                         Flowers: 3 in. wide

Bauhinia blakeana   Hong Kong Orchid   p. 305
                         Tree
                         Flowers: 6 in. wide
                         Fragrant

Delonix regia

Royal Poinciana
Height at 15 years:
20 ft.
•At 40 years: 40 ft.
At maturity: 50 ft.
Zone 10

Blooms in summer
Fruit fall to spring

Albizia julibrissin
'Rosea'

Hardy Silk Tree
•Height at 15 years:
15 ft.
At 40 years: 20 ft.
At maturity: 30 ft.
Zones 6–9

Blooms spring to
summer
Fruit in fall
Requires sun
Tolerates drought and
salt

Delonix regia   *Royal Poinciana*   *p. 328*
                         Flowers: 3–4 in. wide
                         Fruits: 2 in. wide, to
                         2 ft. long

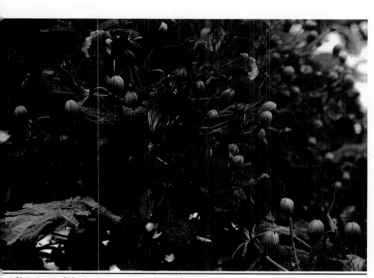

Albizia julibrissin   *Hardy Silk Tree*   *p. 298*
'Rosea'   *Flowers: 1 in. long*
                          Clusters: 3 in. wide
                          Fruits: 5–7 in. long

***Magnolia* ×
*soulangiana***

*Saucer Magnolia
Height at 15 years:
12 ft.
At 40 years: 25 ft.*
•*At maturity: 30 ft.
Zones 5–10*

*Blooms in spring
Requires moist, acid
soil*

***Prunus serrulata*
'Kwanzan'**

*Kwanzan Oriental
Cherry
Height at 15 years:
15 ft.*
•*At 40 years: 25 ft.
At maturity: 30 ft.
Zones 5–8*

Blooms in spring

Magnolia × *soulangiana*

Saucer Magnolia
Flowers: 6 in. wide

p. 355

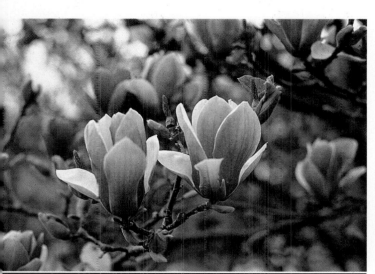

Prunus serrulata '**Kwanzan**'

Kwanzan Oriental
Cherry
Flowers: 2½ in. wide

Fall color
p. 383

Paulownia tomentosa

Empress Tree
Height at 15 years:
25 ft.
At 40 years: 40 ft.
•At maturity: 50 ft.
Zones 6–9

Blooms in spring

Jacaranda mimosifolia

Jacaranda
Height at 15 years:
20 ft.
At 40 years: 40 ft.
•At maturity: 40 ft.
Zones 10;
semihardy 9

Blooms in spring
Fruit in fall
Tolerates drought

Paulownia   *Empress Tree*   *p. 369*
tomentosa   *Flowers: 2 in. long*
                       Clusters: 8–10 in.
                       long
                       Fragrant

Jacaranda   *Jacaranda*   *p. 346*
mimosifolia   *Flowers: 2 in. long*
                       Clusters: 8 in. long
                       Fruits: 1¼ in. wide

Prunus subhirtella
'Pendula'

Weeping Higan Cherry
Height at 15 years:
12 ft.
•At 40 years: 25 ft.
At maturity: 30 ft.
Zones 6–8; semihardy
5

Blooms in spring

Cercis canadensis

Eastern Redbud
Height at 15 years:
10 ft.
•At 40 years: 22 ft.
At maturity: 35 ft.
Zones 5–8; semihardy
4

Blooms in spring
Fruit in fall
Tolerates shade, acid,
alkaline soil

Prunus subhirtella   Weeping Higan Cherry   p. 383
'Pendula'   Flowers: 1 in. wide
                         Clusters: 2–5 flowers

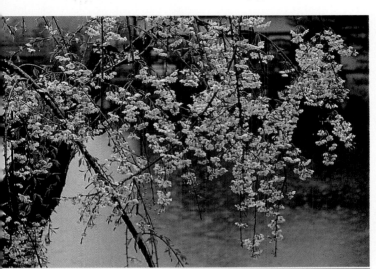

Cercis canadensis   Eastern Redbud   p. 317
                        Flowers: ½ in. long
                        Clusters: 1–2 in. wide
                        Fruits: 3 in. long

Prunus yedoensis *Yoshino Cherry* *Blooms in spring*
Height at 15 years:
12 ft.
•At 40 years: 25 ft.
At maturity: 40 ft.
Zones 6–8

Halesia carolina *Silver-Bell Tree* *Blooms in spring*
•Height at 15 years: *Fruit in fall*
12 ft. *Requires moist, acid*
At 40 years: 30 ft. *soil*
At maturity: 50 ft. *Tolerates shade*
Zones 5–8

Prunus yedoensis   *Yoshino Cherry*   *p. 384*
Flowers: ½ *in. wide*
Clusters: 5–6 *flowers*
Fragrant

Halesia carolina   *Silver-Bell Tree*   *Fall color*
Flowers: ½–¾ *in.*   *p. 344*
long
Clusters: 2–5 *pendant*
flowers
Fruits: 1½ *in. long*

| *Catalpa speciosa* | Northern Catalpa
Height at 15 years:
20 ft.
At 40 years: 50 ft.
•At maturity: 60 ft.
Zones 4–8 | Blooms in spring
Fruit in fall
Tolerates drought, wet |

| *Catalpa bignonioides* 'Aurea' | Southern Catalpa
•Height at 15 years:
18 ft.
At 40 years: 35 ft.
At maturity: 40 ft.
Zones 5–9 | Blooms in spring
Fruit in fall
Tolerates drought, wet |

Catalpa speciosa Northern Catalpa p. 312
Flowers: 2 in. wide
Clusters: 7 in. long
Fruits: 10–16 in.
long

Catalpa Southern Catalpa p. 312
bignonioides *Flowers: 1½ in. long*
Clusters: 7–10 in.
long
Fruits: 9–14 in. long

Pyrus calleryana
'Chanticleer'

Chanticleer Pear
Height at 15 years:
20 ft.
•At 40 years: 30 ft.
At maturity: unknown
Zones 5–9

Blooms in spring

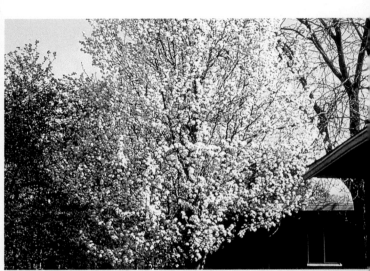

Prunus padus

European Bird Cherry
Height at 15 years:
15 ft.
At 40 years: 30 ft.
•At maturity: 40 ft.
Zones 4–7

Blooms in spring
Fruit in summer

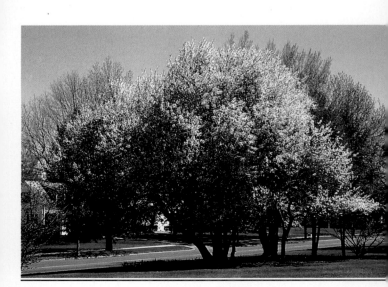

Pyrus calleryana   *Chanticleer Pear*   Fall color
'Chanticleer'   *Flowers: 1/3 in. wide*   p. 387
                Clusters: 3 in. wide

Prunus padus   *European Bird Cherry*   p. 383
                Flowers: 1/2 in. wide
                Clusters: 3–6 in. long
                Fruits: 1/2 in. wide
                Fragrant

Cladrastis lutea American Yellowwood *Blooms in spring*
 Height at 15 years: *Fruit summer to fall*
 15 ft.
 •At 40 years: 40 ft.
 At maturity: 50 ft.
 Zones 4–8

Koelreuteria Golden-Rain Tree *Blooms in summer*
paniculata •Height at 15 years: *Fruit fall to winter*
 15 ft. *Tolerates drought*
 At 40 years: 28 ft.
 At maturity: 40 ft.
 Zones 5–8

Cladrastis lutea
American Yellowwood   *p. 320*
Flowers: 1 in. long
Clusters: 10–15 in.
long, drooping
Fruits: 4–5 in. long

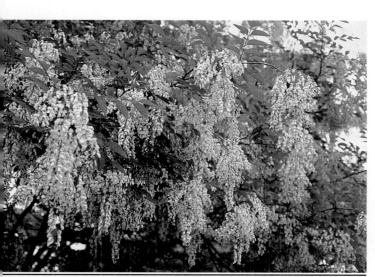

Koelreuteria
paniculata
Golden-Rain Tree   *p. 349*
Flowers: ½ in. wide
Clusters: 12–15 in.
long
Fruits: 2 in. long

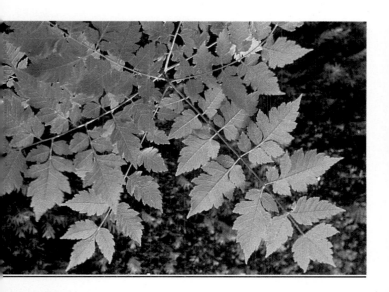

Sophora japonica   Pagoda Tree   Blooms in summer
    •Height at 15 years: Fruit fall to winter
    15 ft.
    At 40 years: 35 ft.
    At maturity: 70 ft.
    Zones 5–8

Koelreuteria   Chinese Flame Tree   Blooms in summer
bipinnata   Height at 15 years: Fruit in fall
    15 ft.   Tolerates drought
    •At 40 years: 30 ft.
    At maturity: 60 ft.
    Zones 8–10;
    semihardy 7

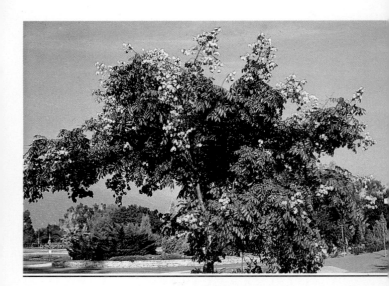

Sophora japonica *Pagoda Tree* p. 356
Flowers: ½ in. long
Clusters: 12–15 in.
long
Fruits: 2–4 in. long

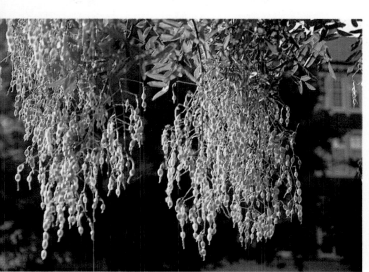

Koelreuteria *Chinese Flame Tree* p. 349
bipinnata *Clusters: 15 in. long*
Fruits: 2 in. long

| *Crataegus crus-galli* | Cockspur Hawthorn
Height at 15 years:
15 ft.
At 40 years: 20 ft.
•At maturity: 30 ft.
Zones 5–9 | Blooms in spring
Fruit fall to winter
Tolerates drought |

| *Crataegus ×*
lavallei | Lavalle Hawthorn
Height at 15 years:
10 ft.
•At 40 years: 18 ft.
At maturity: 25 ft.
Zones 5–9 | Blooms in spring
Fruit fall to winter
Tolerates drought |

Crataegus crus-galli *Cockspur Hawthorn*   *p. 323*
Flowers: ½ in. wide
Clusters: 2–3 in. wide
Fruits: ½ in. wide

***Crataegus* ×**   *Lavalle Hawthorn*   *Fall color*
lavallei   *Flowers: ¾ in. wide*   *p. 323*
Clusters: 3 in. wide
Fruits: ½ in. long

Crataegus phaenopyrum

Washington Hawthorn
Height at 15 years:
10 ft.
•At 40 years: 25 ft.
At maturity: 30 ft.
Zones 5–9

Blooms in spring
Fruit fall to winter

***Crataegus viridis* 'Winter King'**

Winter King
Hawthorn
•Height at 15 years:
15 ft.
At 40 years: 25 ft.
At maturity: unknown
Zones 5–7

Blooms in spring
Fruit fall to winter
Tolerates drought

| *Crataegus phaenopyrum* | Washington Hawthorn
Flowers: ½ in. wide
Clusters: 2–3 in. wide
Fruits: ¼ in. wide | Fall color
p. 324 |

| *Crataegus viridis*
'Winter King' | Winter King
Hawthorn
Flowers: ¾ in. wide
Clusters: 2 in. wide
Fruits: ⅜ in. wide | Fall color
p. 324 |

Malus
'Candied Apple'

*Weeping Candied
Apple Crabapple*
•*Height at 15 years:
12 ft.
At 40 years: 15 ft.
At maturity: 20 ft.
Zones 4–8*

*Blooms in spring
Fruit in fall*

Malus
'Dolgo'

*Dolgo Crabapple
Height at 15 years:
18 ft.
At 40 years: 35 ft.
•At maturity: 40 ft.
Zones 4–8*

*Blooms in spring
Flowers: 1³⁄₄ in. wide
Fruit summer to fall
Fruits: 1¹⁄₂ in. wide
p. 358*

Malus
'**Candied Apple**'

*Weeping Candied
Apple Crabapple
Flowers: 1½ in. wide
Fruits: ⅜ in. wide*

p. 358

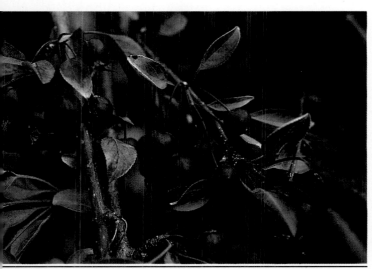

Malus
'**Makamik**'

*Makamik Crabapple
Height at 15 years:
18 ft.
At 40 years: 35 ft.
At maturity: 40 ft.
Zones 4–8*

*Blooms in spring
Flowers: 2 in. wide
Fruit in fall
Fruits: ¾ in. long
p. 360*

Malus 'Coralburst'

Coralburst Crabapple
Height at 15 years:
6 ft.
•At 40 years: 8 ft.
At maturity: 14 ft.
Zones 4–8

Blooms in spring

Malus 'Liset'

Liset Crabapple
•Height at 15 years:
12 ft.
At 40 years: 18 ft.
At maturity: 20 ft.
Zones 4–8

Blooms in spring
Flowers: 1½ in. wide
Fruit in fall
Fruits: ⅝ in. wide
p. 360

| *Malus* | *Coralburst Crabapple* | *p. 358* |
| 'Coralburst' | *Flowers: ³/₄ in. wide* | |

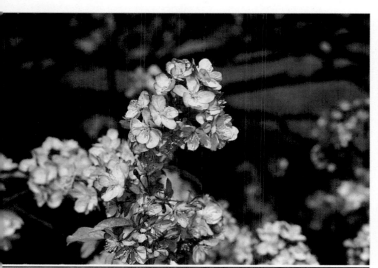

Malus	*Indian Magic*	*Blooms in spring*
'Indian Magic'	*Crabapple*	*Flowers: 1¹/₂ in. wide*
	Height at 15 years:	*Fruit fall to winter*
	12 ft.	*Fruits: ¹/₂ in. wide*
	At 40 years: 18 ft.	*p. 359*
	At maturity: 20 ft.	
	Zones 4–8	

Malus floribunda	*Japanese Crabapple*	*Blooms in spring*
	•*Height at 15 years:*	*Flowers: 1½ in. wide*
	12 ft.	*Fruit in fall*
	At 40 years: 20 ft.	*Fruits: ⅜ in. wide*
	At maturity: 25 ft.	*p. 359*
	Zones 4–8	

Malus	*Donald Wyman*	*Blooms in spring*
'Donald Wyman'	*Crabapple*	*Fruit fall to winter*
	Height at 15 years:	
	10 ft.	
	At 40 years: 15 ft.	
	•*At maturity: 20 ft.*	
	Zones 4–8	

Malus 'Bob White'	*Bob White Crabapple* Height at 15 years: 12 ft. At 40 years: 18 ft. At maturity: 20 ft. Zones 4–8	*Blooms in spring* Flowers: 1 in. wide Fruit fall to winter Fruits: ⅝ in. wide p. 358

Malus 'Donald Wyman'	*Donald Wyman Crabapple* Flowers: 1¾ in. wide Fruits: ⅜ in. wide	p. 359

Malus sargentii
Sargent Crabapple
Height at 15 years:
6 ft.
•At 40 years: 8 ft.
At maturity: 14 ft.
Zones 4–8

Blooms in spring
Fruit late summer to
early winter

Malus
'Mary Potter'

Mary Potter Crabapple
•Height at 15 years:
10 ft.
At 40 years: 15 ft.
At maturity: 17 ft.
Zones 4–8

Blooms in spring
Fruit in fall

Malus sargentii   *Sargent Crabapple*   *p. 360*
                             Flowers: 1 in. wide
                             Fruits: ³⁄₈ in. wide

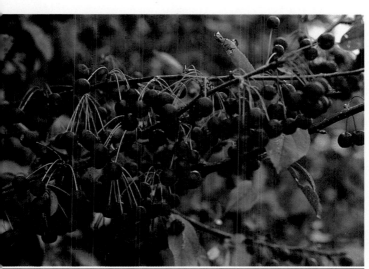

Malus   *Mary Potter Crabapple*   *p. 360*
'Mary Potter'   *Flowers: 1 in. wide*
                             Fruits: ³⁄₈ in. wide

**Malus
'White Angel'**

White Angel
Crabapple
•Height at 15 years:
12 ft.
At 40 years: 20 ft.
At maturity: 25 ft.
Zones 4–8

Blooms in spring
Fruit fall to winter

Cornus nuttallii

Pacific Dogwood
Height at 15 years:
10 ft.
At 40 years: 40 ft.
•At maturity: 75 ft.
Zones 7–9

Blooms in spring
Fruit summer to fall

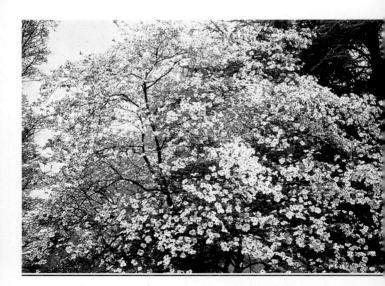

Malus   White Angel   p. 362
'White Angel'   Crabapple
                   Flowers: 1 in. wide
                   Fruits: ½ in. wide

Cornus nuttallii   Pacific Dogwood   Fall color
                         Flowers: 4 in. wide   p. 322
                         Fruits: ⅖ in. long

Cornus kousa   Kousa Dogwood   Blooms in spring
                    Height at 15 years: Fruit in fall
                    12 ft.
                    At 40 years: 20 ft.
                    •At maturity: 30 ft.
                    Zones 5–8

Cornus kousa   Kousa Dogwood
                    In summer

Cornus kousa   *Kousa Dogwood*   *Fall color*
                      Flowers: 2 in. wide   *p. 321*

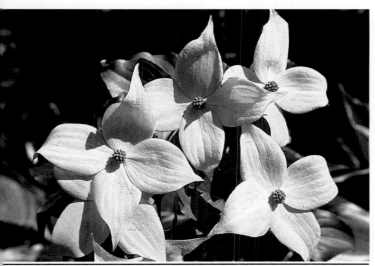

Cornus kousa   *Kousa Dogwood*   *p. 321*
                      Fruits: 1 in. wide

Cornus florida   *Flowering Dogwood*   *Blooms in spring*
Height at 15 years: *Fruit in fall*
15 ft.   *Requires acid soil*
At 40 years: 25 ft.
•*At maturity: 30 ft.*
Zones 5–9

Cornus florida   *Flowering Dogwood*
In summer

Cornus florida   _Flowering Dogwood   Fall color_
Flowers: 3–4 in. wide   p. 321

Cornus florida   _Double-flowering   Fall color_
'Pleniflora'   _Dogwood   p. 321_
Flowers: 3–4 in. wide

**Cornus florida
var. *rubra***

*Red Flowering
Dogwood
In spring*

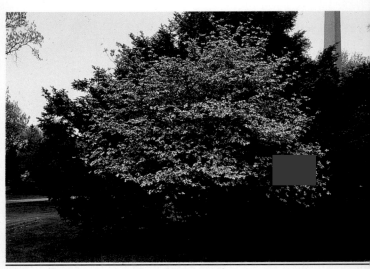

Cornus florida

*Flowering Dogwood
In fall*

Cornus florida
var. rubra

Red Flowering
Dogwood
Flowers: 3–4 in. wide

Fall color
p. 321

Cornus florida

Flowering Dogwood
Fruits: ³⁄₈ in. long

p. 321

Melia azedarach   *Chinaberry*   *Blooms in spring*
Height at 15 years: *Fruit in fall*
20 ft.   *Tolerates drought, wet*
At 40 years: 40 ft.
•At maturity: 50 ft.
Zones 7–10

Cornus mas   *Cornelian Cherry*   *Blooms in spring*
Height at 15 years: *Fruit in summer*
10 ft.
•At 40 years: 20 ft.
At maturity: 25 ft.
Zones 5–7

Melia azedarach   *Chinaberry*   *p. 353*
                       Flowers: ¾ in. wide
                       Clusters: 8–16 in.
                       long
                       Fruits: ¾ in. wide
                       Fragrant

Cornus mas   *Cornelian Cherry*   *Fall color*
                       Flowers: ⅙ in. wide   *p. 322*
                       Clusters: ¾ in. wide
                       Fruits: ⅝ in. long

Fagus sylvatica
'Pendula'

*Weeping European
Beech
Height at 15 years:
12 ft.*
•*At 40 years: 30 ft.
At maturity: 60 ft.
Zones 5–8*

Requires acid soil

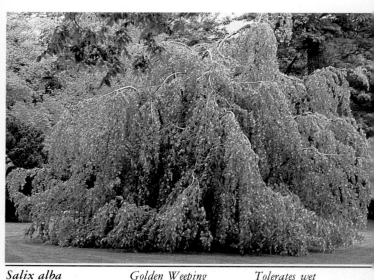

Salix alba
var. *tristis*

*Golden Weeping
Willow
Height at 15 years:
20 ft.*
•*At 40 years: 40 ft.
At maturity: 70 ft.
Zones 3–9;
semihardy 2*

Tolerates wet

Fagus sylvatica 'Pendula'	*Weeping European Beech*	*Fall color* p. 336

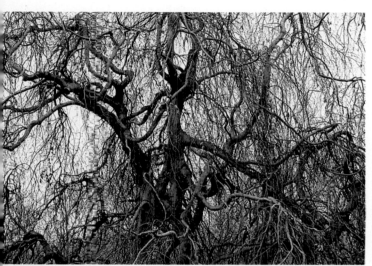

Salix alba* var. *tristis	*Golden Weeping Willow*	p. 392

Betula pendula | Purple-leaf European | Fruit in fall
'Purpurea' | Birch
Height at 15 years:
18 ft.
•At 40 years: 40 ft.
At maturity: 50 ft.
Zones 3–9

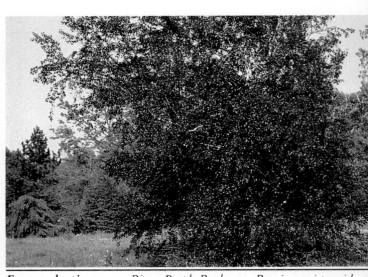

Fagus sylvatica | Rivers Purple Beech | Requires moist, acid
'Riversii' | Height at 15 years: | soil
15 ft.
At 40 years: 35 ft.
•At maturity: 75 ft.
Zones 5–8

Betula pendula *Purple-leaf European* p. 3C7
'Purpurea' *Birch*
Clusters: 1 in. long

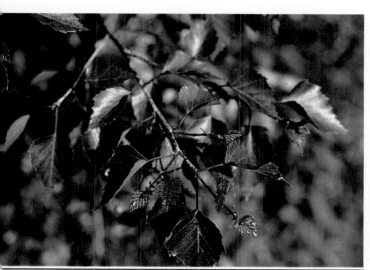

Fagus sylvatica *Tricolor Beech* *Fall color*
'Tricolor' p. 336

Prunus virginiana
'Schubert'

Schubert Chokecherry
•*Height at 15 years:*
18 ft.
At 40 years: 25 ft.
At maturity: 30 ft.
Zones 3–5

Blooms in spring

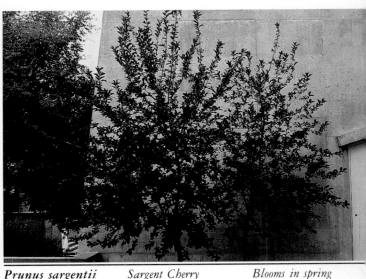

Prunus sargentii

Sargent Cherry
Height at 15 years:
15 ft.
•*At 40 years: 35 ft.*
At maturity: 50 ft.
Zones 5–8

Blooms in spring

Prunus virginiana
'Schubert'

Schubert Chokecherry   *p. 384*
Flowers: ⅓ in. wide
Clusters: 3–6 in. wide

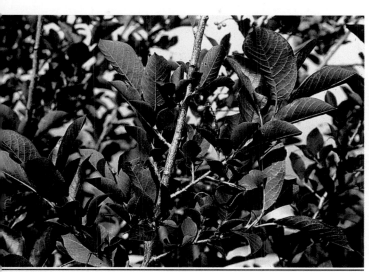

Prunus sargentii

Sargent Cherry   Fall color
Flowers: 1½ in. wide   p. 383
Clusters: 3 in. wide

Acer griseum   Paperbark Maple
Height at 15 years:
8 ft.
At 40 years: 20 ft.
•At maturity: 25 ft.
Zones 5–8

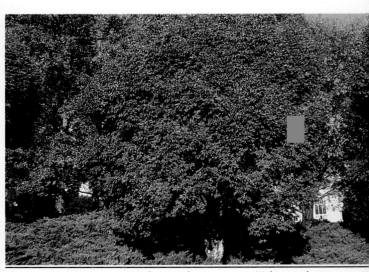

Acer campestre   Hedge Maple   Tolerates dry,
Height at 15 years: compacted soil
12 ft.
At 40 years: 25 ft.
•At maturity: 35 ft.
Zones 5–8

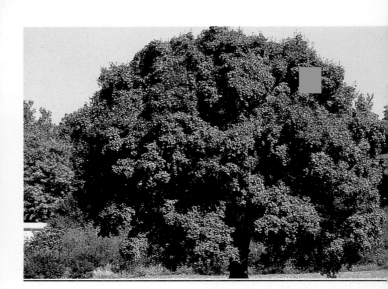

Acer griseum   *Paperbark Maple*   Fall color
                                         p. 294

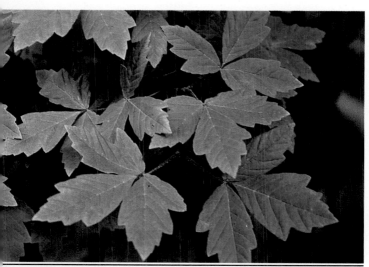

Acer campestre   *Hedge Maple*   Fall color
                                       p. 294

Amelanchier laevis Allegheny Serviceberry Blooms in spring
•Height at 15 years: Fruit in summer
15 ft. Requires moist soil
At 40 years: 28 ft. Tolerates shade
At maturity: 35 ft.
Zones 4–8;
semihardy 3

Amelanchier × Apple Serviceberry Blooms in spring
grandiflora Height at 15 years: Fruit in summer
13 ft. Requires moist soil
•At 40 years: 20 ft. Tolerates shade
At maturity: 25 ft.
Zones 4–8;
semihardy 3

Amelanchier laevis *Allegheny Serviceberry* *Fall color*
Flowers: ½ in. wide *p. 300*
Clusters: 3 in. long
Fruits: ⅓ in. long

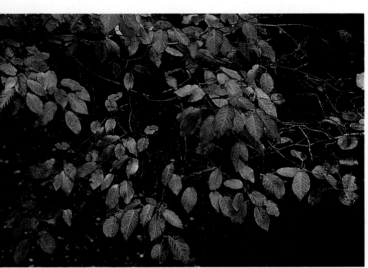

***Amelanchier* ×** *Apple Serviceberry* *Fall color*
grandiflora *Flowers: 1¼ in. wide* *p. 300*
Clusters: 3 in. long
Fruits: ⅓ in. long

Sorbus alnifolia   Korean Mountain Ash   Blooms in spring
Height at 15 years: Fruits in fall
15 ft.
•At 40 years: 30 ft.
At maturity: 50 ft.
Zones 4–7

Sorbus aucuparia   European Mountain   Blooms in spring
Ash   Fruit in fall
•Height at 15 years: Requires acid soil
15 ft.
At 40 years: 35 ft.
At maturity: 50 ft.
Zones 3–7

Sorbus alnifolia   Korean Mountain Ash   Fall color
                        Flowers: ¾ in. wide   p. 397
                        Clusters: 2–3 in. wide
                        Fruits: ½ in. wide

Sorbus aucuparia   European Mountain   Fall color
                        Ash   p. 397
                        Flowers: ⅓ in. wide
                        Clusters: 4–6 in. wide
                        Fruits: ¼ in. wide

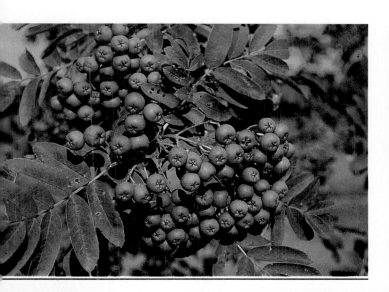

Pyrus calleryana
'Bradford'

Bradford Pear
Height at 15 years:
20 ft.
•At 40 years: 35 ft.
At maturity: 50 ft.
Zones 5–9

Blooms in spring

Oxydendrum
arboreum

Sourwood
Height at 15 years:
15 ft.
•At 40 years: 30 ft.
At maturity: 50 ft.
Zones 5–9

Blooms in summer
Fruit fall to winter
Requires acid soil

Pyrus calleryana
'Bradford'

Bradford Pear
Flowers: ⅓ in. wide
Clusters: 3 in. wide

Fall color
p. 386

Oxydendrum
arboreum

Sourwood
Flowers: ⅓ in. long
Clusters: 8–10 in.
long
Fruits: ⅕ in. wide,
8–10 in. clusters
Fragrant

Fall color
p. 368

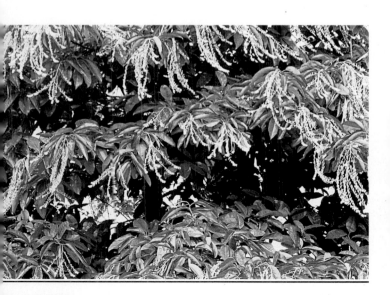

Carpinus betulus
'Fastigiata'

Upright European
Hornbeam
Height at 15 years:
20 ft.
At 40 years: 40 ft.
•At maturity: 50 ft.
Zones 5–9

Blooms winter to spring
Fruit in fall
Tolerates acid,
alkaline soil

Quercus robur
'Fastigiata'

Upright English Oak
Height at 15 years:
12 ft.
•At 40 years: 30 ft.
At maturity: 80 ft.
Zones 5–8

Carpinus betulus 'Fastigiata'	Upright European Hornbeam Flowers: minute Clusters: 1½ in. long Fruits: 2–3 in. long	Fall color p. 311

Quercus robur 'Fastigiata'	Upright English Oak	p. 390

Quercus palustris   *Pin Oak*   *Requires acid soil*
                          Height at 15 years: *Tolerates wet*
                          20 ft.
                          •At 40 years: 40 ft.
                          At maturity: 100 ft.
                          Zones 5–9

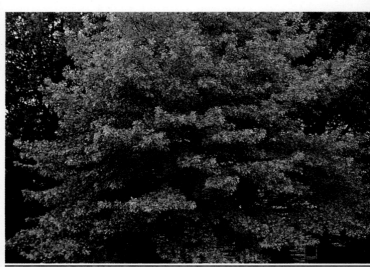

Taxodium   *Bald Cypress*   *Requires acid soil*
distichum   *•Height at 15 years:*   *Tolerates wet*
                          25 ft.
                          At 40 years: 50 ft.
                          At maturity: 100 ft.
                          Zones 5–10

Quercus palustris   *Pin Oak*   *Fall color*
p. 390

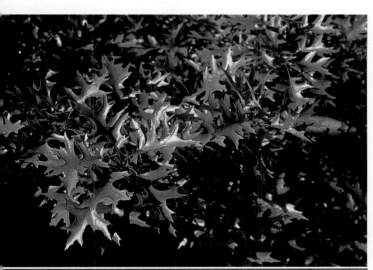

**Taxodium
distichum**   *Bald Cypress*   *Fall color*
p. 398

Larix kaempferi

Japanese Larch
•Height at 15 years:
20 ft.
At 40 years: 50 ft.
At maturity: 90 ft.
Zones 4–6

Cones fall to winter
Requires moist, acid
soil

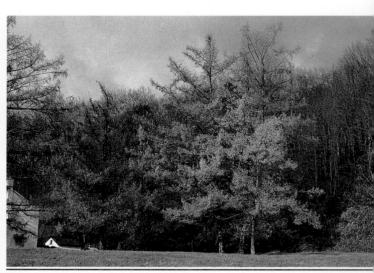

Metasequoia
glyptostroboides

Dawn Redwood
Height at 15 years:
20 ft.
•At 40 years: 60 ft.
At maturity: 100 ft.
Zones 5–8

Requires moist, acid
soil

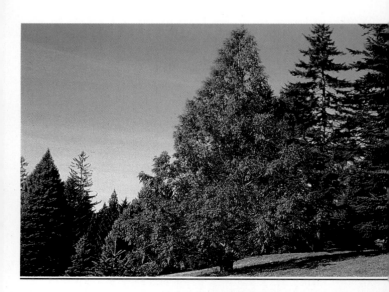

Larix kaempferi *Japanese Larch* *Fall color*
  Cones: 1 in. long *p. 351*

Metasequoia *Dawn Redwood* *Fall color*
glyptostroboides *p. 364*

*Deciduous Shade
Trees*

You can plant these trees to provide a canopy of cooling summer shade. Nearly all are spreading and massive at maturity, but remember, decades may pass before some shade trees become truly effective. Several species turn a brilliant fall color before dropping their leaves.

Quercus kelloggii   *California Black Oak*
Height at 15 years:
15 ft.
At 40 years: 35 ft.
•At maturity: 80 ft.
Zones 8–10

Quercus lobata   *Valley Oak*
Height at 15 years:
25 ft.
At 40 years: 60 ft.
•At maturity: 100 ft.
Zones 7–10

Quercus kelloggii   *California Black Oak*   Fall color
p. 390

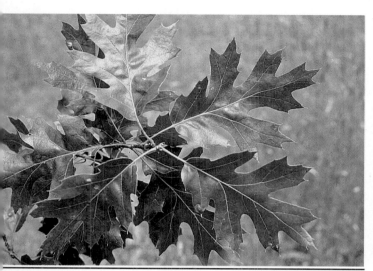

Quercus lobata   *Valley Oak*   p. 390

Quercus alba
White Oak
Height at 15 years:
12 ft.
At 40 years: 35 ft.
•At maturity: 80 ft.
Zones 4–9

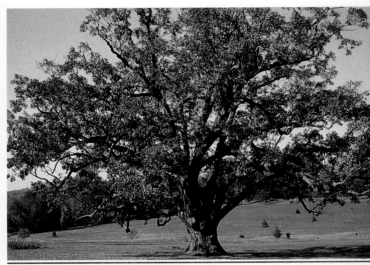

Quercus rubra
Red Oak
Height at 15 years:
20 ft.
At 40 years: 50 ft.
•At maturity: 100 ft.
Zones 4–8

Quercus alba   *White Oak*   *Fall color*
                                               p. 389

Quercus rubra   *Red Oak*   *Fall color*
                                              p. 390

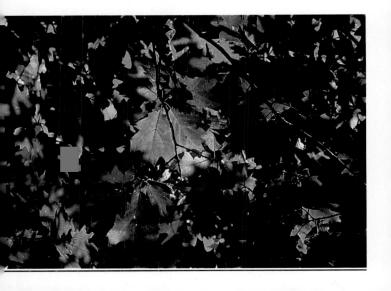

Quercus coccinea   *Scarlet Oak*   *Tolerates alkaline soil*
•Height at 15 years:
22 ft.
At 40 years: 45 ft.
At maturity: 80 ft.
Zones 5–9

Quercus imbricaria   *Shingle Oak*
Height at 15 years:
18 ft.
At 40 years: 40 ft.
•At maturity: 75 ft.
Zones 5–8

Quercus coccinea   Scarlet Oak   *Fall color*
p. 389

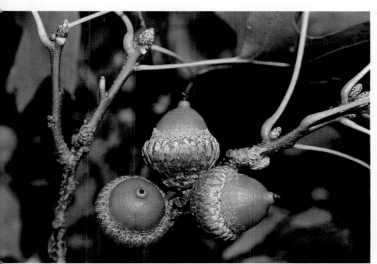

Quercus imbricaria   Shingle Oak   *p. 389*

Fagus grandifolia   American Beech
Height at 15 years: *Requires moist, acid*
15 ft.   *soil*
•At 40 years: 40 ft.
At maturity: 100 ft.
Zones 4–9

Fagus sylvatica   European Beech
•Height at 15 years: *Requires moist, acid*
15 ft.   *soil*
At 40 years: 40 ft.
At maturity: 100 ft.
Zones 5–8

Fagus grandifolia   *American Beech*   *Fall color*
                                                    p. 335

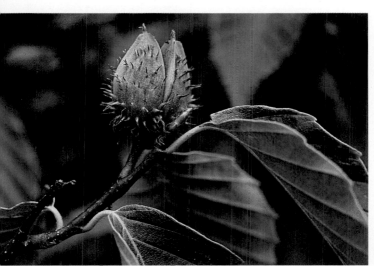

Fagus sylvatica   *European Beech*   *Fall color*
                                                    p. 335

Liquidambar
styraciflua

Sweet Gum
Height at 15 years:
20 ft.
•At 40 years: 45 ft.
At maturity: 75 ft.
Zones 5–9

Fruit fall to winter
Tolerates wet

Aesculus glabra

Ohio Buckeye
Height at 15 years:
15 ft.
At 40 years: 35 ft.
•At maturity: 60 ft.
Zones 4–8

Blooms in spring
Fruit summer to fall
Requires moist, acid
soil
Tolerates shade

| **Liquidambar styraciflua** | Sweet Gum
Fruits: 1½ in. wide | Fall color
p. 353 |

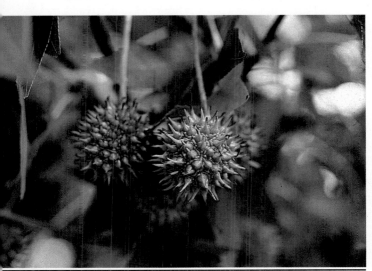

| **Aesculus glabra** | Ohio Buckeye
Flowers: ¾ in. long
Clusters: 4–6 in. long
Fruits: 1–2½ in.
wide | Fall color
p 297 |

Acer platanoides	Norway Maple •Height at 15 years: 20 ft. At 40 years: 40 ft. At maturity: 65 ft. Zones 4–7	Blooms in spring Tolerates air pollution

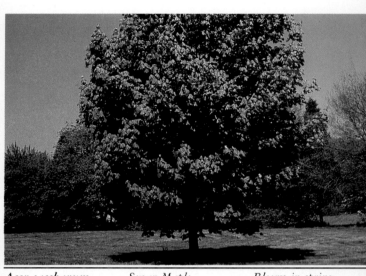

Acer saccharum	Sugar Maple Height at 15 years: 25 ft. At 40 years: 60 ft. •At maturity: 100 ft. Zones 4–8	Blooms in spring Requires moist, well- drained soil

Acer platanoides   Norway Maple   Fall color
                          Flowers: 1/3 in. wide   p. 294
                          Clusters: 1 1/2 in.
                          wide, drooping

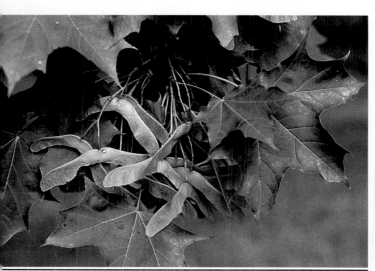

Acer saccharum   Sugar Maple   Fall color
                       Flowers: 1/4 in. wide   p. 296
                       Clusters: 2–3 in.
                       wide, drooping

Acer rubrum

Red Maple
Height at 15 years:
15 ft.
At 40 years: 40 ft.
•At maturity: 70 ft.
Zones 4–9

Blooms in spring
Tolerates drought, wet

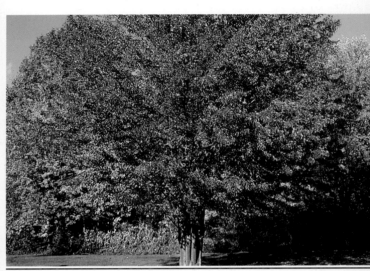

Acer saccharinum

Silver Maple
•Height at 15 years:
25 ft.
At 40 years: 70 ft.
At maturity: 100 ft.
Zones 3–9

Blooms in spring
Tolerates occasional
flooding, dry periods

Acer rubrum   Red Maple   Fall color
                   Flowers: 1/8 in. wide   p. 295
                   Clusters: 1 in. wide

Acer saccharinum   Silver Maple   Fall color
                        Flowers: 1/4 in. wide   p. 295
                        Clusters: 1 in. wide,
                        dense

Eucommia ulmoides   *Hardy Rubber Tree*   *Tolerates drought*
Height at 15 years:
15 ft.
At 40 years: 40 ft.
•At maturity: 60 ft.
Zones 5–7

Gymnocladus dioica   *Kentucky Coffee Tree*   *Fruit in fall*
•Height at 15 years: *Tolerates drought, air*
20 ft.   *pollution*
At 40 years: 50 ft.
At maturity: 90 ft.
Zones 5–8;
semihardy 4

Eucommia ulmoides   *Hardy Rubber Tree*   *p. 333*

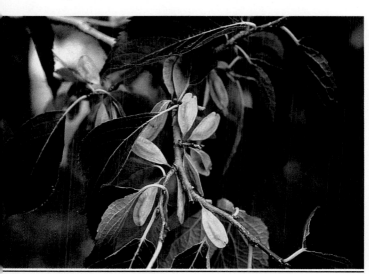

Gymnocladus dioica   *Kentucky Coffee Tree*   *Fall color*
                        Fruits: 5–10 in. long,   *p. 343*
                        2–3 in. wide

**Fraxinus
pennsylvanica**

*Green Ash
Height at 15 years:
20 ft.
At 40 years: 45 ft.
•At maturity: 65 ft.
Zones 3–8*

*Tolerates drought, wet,
salt*

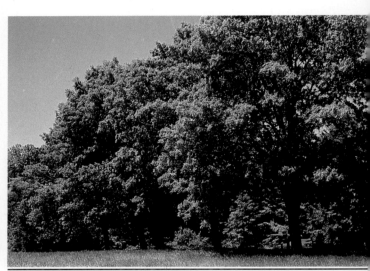

Fraxinus americana   *White Ash
Height at 15 years:
25 ft.
At 40 years: 55 ft.
•At maturity: 120 ft.
Zones 4–9*

Tolerates wet

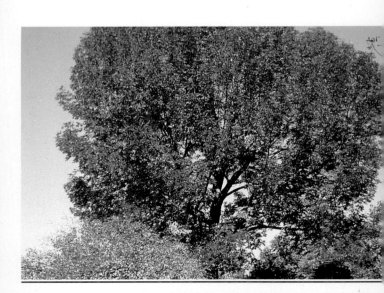

| **Fraxinus pennsylvanica** | Green Ash | Fall color p. 339 |

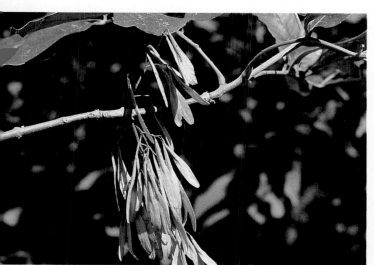

| **Fraxinus americana** | White Ash | Fall color p. 339 |

Fraxinus excelsior
'Aurea'

Yellow European Ash
•Height at 15 years:
20 ft.
At 40 years: 45 ft.
At maturity: 70 ft.
Zones 4–9

Pistacia chinensis

Chinese Pistache
Height at 15 years:
12 ft.
•At 40 years: 35 ft.
At maturity: 60 ft.
Zones 7–9

Fruit in fall
Tolerates drought

Fraxinus excelsior
'Aurea'
Yellow European Ash   p. 339

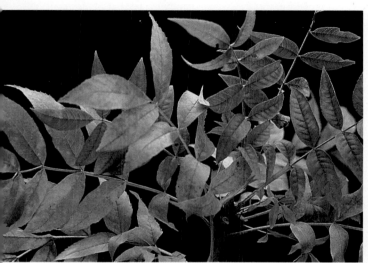

Pistacia chinensis
Chinese Pistache   *Fall color*
Fruits: ¼ *in. long*   p. 379

Gleditsia triacanthos var. *inermis*   Thornless Honey Locust   Tolerates drought, salt
•Height at 15 years:
25 ft.
At 40 years: 50 ft.
At maturity: 90 ft.
Zones 5–9;
semihardy 4

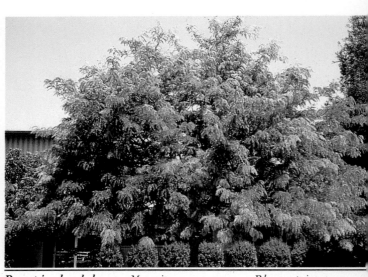

Prosopis glandulosa   Mesquite   Blooms spring to
Height at 15 years: summer
10 ft.   Fruit in winter
•At 40 years: 25 ft.   Tolerates drought
At maturity: 30 ft.
Zones 7–9

**Gleditsia
triacanthos
var. *inermis***   *Thornless Honey Locust*   Fall color
p. 342

Prosopis glandulosa   *Mesquite*   p. 381
Clusters: 2 in. long
Fruits: 2–6 in. long

Sapium sebiferum   *Chinese Tallow Tree*   *Fruit in fall*
Height at 15 years:
25 ft.
•At 40 years: 40 ft.
At maturity: 50 ft.
Zones 8–9

Alnus glutinosa   *European Alder*   *Blooms in spring*
•Height at 15 years: *Cones throughout year*
25 ft.   *Tolerates wet*
At 40 years: 55 ft.
At maturity: 80 ft.
Zones 3–9

Sapium sebiferum *Chinese Tallow Tree*   *Fall color*
Fruits: ½ in. wide   *p. 393*

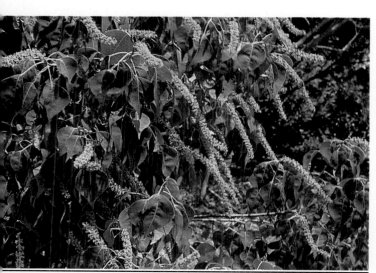

Alnus glutinosa *European Alder*   *p. 299*
Flowers: minute
Clusters: 2–3 in.
catkins
Cones: ½ in. long

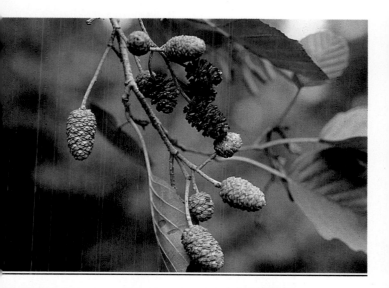

Alnus cordata

Italian Alder
Height at 15 years:
18 ft.
•At 40 years: 40 ft.
At maturity: 70 ft.
Zones 5–10

Blooms in spring
Cones throughout year
Tolerates wet, dry soil

Betula platyphylla

Asian White Birch
•Height at 15 years:
20 ft.
At 40 years: 40 ft.
At maturity: 60 ft.
Zones 5–7

Blooms winter to spring
Fruit in fall

Alnus cordata   *Italian Alder*   *p. 299*
          Flowers: minute
          Clusters: 2–3 in.
          catkins
          Cones: 1–1¼ in. long

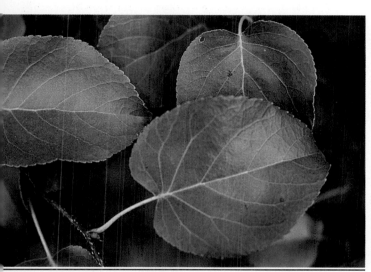

Betula platyphylla   *Asian White Birch*   *Fall color*
            Flowers: minute   *p. 308*
            Clusters: 1½ in. long
            Fruits: 1 in. long

Betula maximowicziana

Monarch Birch
Height at 15 years: 20 ft.
At 40 years: 45 ft.
•At maturity: 80 ft.
Zones 5–7

Blooms winter to spring
Fruit in fall
Requires moist soil

Betula papyrifera

Canoe Birch
Height at 15 years: 25 ft.
•At 40 years: 60 ft.
At maturity: 90 ft.
Zones 3–7

Blooms winter to spring
Fruit in fall
Requires moist, acid soil

Betula   Monarch Birch   Fall color
maximowicziana Flowers: minute   p. 306
                    Clusters: 4–5 in. long
                    Fruits: 2–2½ in. long

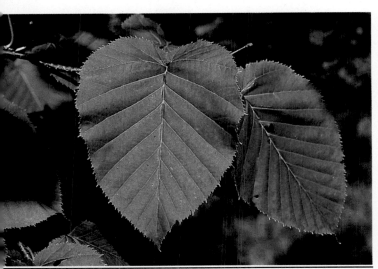

Betula papyrifera   Canoe Birch   Fall color
                        Flowers: minute   p. 307
                        Clusters: 3–4 in. long
                        Fruits: 1¼ in. long

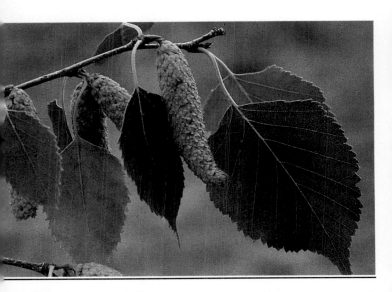

Betula lenta

Sweet Birch
Height at 15 years:
15 ft.
•At 40 years: 40 ft.
At maturity: 75 ft.
Zones 4–8

Blooms winter to spring
Fruit in fall
Requires moist, acid
soil
Tolerates shade

Betula nigra

River Birch
Height at 15 years:
25 ft.
•At 40 years: 60 ft.
At maturity: 80 ft.
Zones 5–10

Blooms winter to spring
Fruit in fall
Requires moist, acid
soil
Tolerates wet, shade

Betula lenta   Sweet Birch   Fall color
Flowers: *minute, in* p. 306
pendant catkins
Clusters: 2–3 in. long
Fruits: 1 in. long

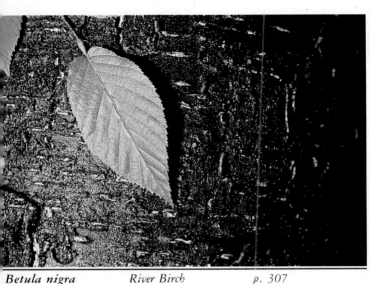

Betula nigra   River Birch   p. 307
Flowers: *minute, in*
pendant catkins
Clusters: 2–3 in. long
Fruits: 1¼ in. long

Celtis occidentalis   *Common Hackberry*   *Fruit in fall*
Height at 15 years: *Tolerates drought, wet,*
20 ft.   *acid, alkaline soil*
At 40 years: 60 ft.
•At maturity: 100 ft.
Zones 4–8

Pyrus ussuriensis   *Ussurian Pear*   *Blooms in spring*
Height at 15 years:
15 ft.
•At 40 years: 40 ft.
At maturity: 50 ft.
Zones 4–6

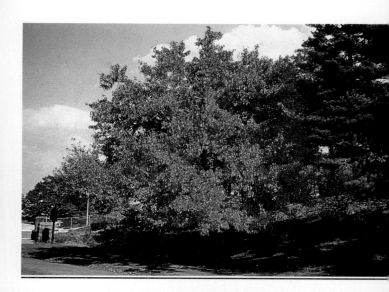

Celtis occidentalis   *Common Hackberry*   p. 314
Fruits: 1/3 in. long

Pyrus ussuriensis   *Ussurian Pear*   *Fall color*
Flowers: 1 1/3 in. wide   *p. 387*

Zelkova serrata
Japanese Zelkova
•*Height at 15 years:*
20 ft.
At 40 years: 35 ft.
At maturity: 70 ft.
Zones 5–8

Morus alba
'Fruitless'
Fruitless White
Mulberry
Height at 15 years:
15 ft.
•*At 40 years: 35 ft.*
At maturity: 40 ft.
Zones 5–9

Tolerates drought, salt

Zelkova serrata *Japanese Zelkova* *Fall color*
p. 409

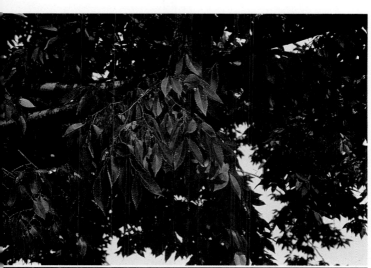

Morus alba *White Mulberry* *p 365*

Ulmus parvifolia *Chinese Elm* *Fruit in fall*
Height at 15 years:
15 ft.
•At 40 years: 35 ft.
At maturity: 60 ft.
Zones 5–10

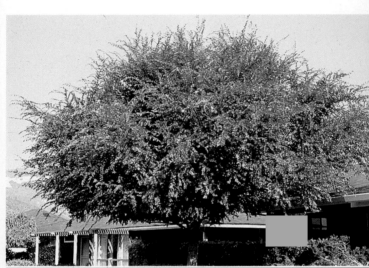

Ulmus carpinifolia *Globe Smoothleaf Elm*
'Umbraculifera' *Height at 15 years:*
15 ft.
•At 40 years: 25 ft.
At maturity: 35 ft.
Zones 5–8

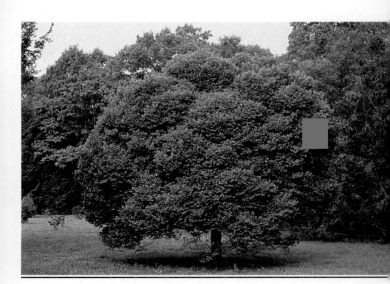

Ulmus parvifolia   Chinese Elm   Fall color
                       Fruits: ¼–½ in. long   p. 406

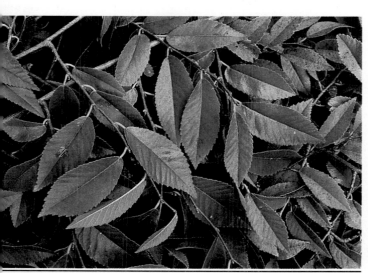

Ulmus carpinifolia   Smoothleaf Elm   p. 405
                         Height at 15 years:
                         15 ft.
                         At 40 years: 40 ft.
                         At maturity: 75 ft.
                         Zones 5–8

Tilia cordata
Little-leaf Linden
•Height at 15 years:
18 ft.
At 40 years: 40 ft.
At maturity: 90 ft.
Zones 3–8

Blooms spring to summer

Tilia tomentosa
Silver Linden
•Height at 15 years:
18 ft.
At 40 years: 40 ft.
At maturity: 90 ft.
Zones 5–8

Blooms in summer

Tilia cordata *Little-leaf Linden* *Fall color*
Flowers: ½ in. wide *p. 401*
Clusters: 2–3 in. long
Fragrant

Tilia tomentosa *Silver Linden* *p. 401*
Flowers: ³/₈ in. wide
Clusters: 2 in. long
Fragrant

Ulmus pumila   *Siberian Elm*   *Tolerates drought*
                    Height at 15 years:
                    25 ft.
                    At 40 years: 45 ft.
                    •At maturity: 75 ft.
                    Zones 3–9;
                    semihardy 2

Phellodendron   *Amur Corktree*   *Fruit in fall*
amurense   *Height at 15 years:*   *Tolerates drought*
                    15 ft.
                    At 40 years: 30 ft.
                    •At maturity: 50 ft.
                    Zones 4–7

Ulmus pumila   *Siberian Elm*   p. 406
'Coolshade'

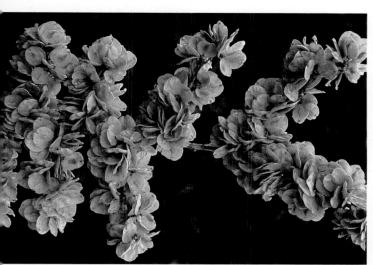

Phellodendron   *Amur Corktree*   p. 370
amurense   *Fruits: ½ in. wide,*
                        in loose clusters

Nyssa sylvatica

Sour Gum
Height at 15 years:
15 ft.
•At 40 years: 35 ft.
At maturity: 85 ft.
Zones 4–9

Requires acid soil
Tolerates wet, dry soil

Cercidiphyllum
japonicum

Katsura Tree
•Height at 15 years:
25 ft.
At 40 years: 50 ft.
At maturity: 100 ft.
Zones 5–8

Requires moist soil

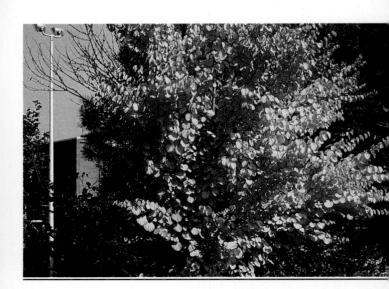

Nyssa sylvatica   *Sour Gum*   Fall color
p. 366

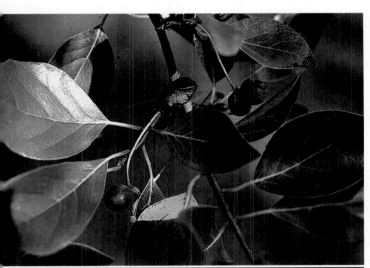

*Cercidiphyllum
japonicum*   *Katsura Tree*   Fall color
p. 316

Ginkgo biloba   *Ginkgo*   *Tolerates drought, wet,*
                     Height at 15 years: *salt*
                     18 ft.
                     •At 40 years: 40 ft.
                     At maturity: 125 ft.
                     Zones 5–9;
                     semihardy 4

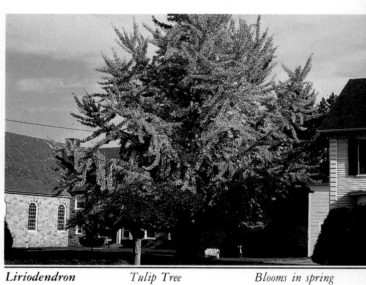

Liriodendron   *Tulip Tree*   *Blooms in spring*
tulipifera   *Height at 15 years:*   *Fruit fall to winter*
                    25 ft.
                    •At 40 years: 55 ft.
                    At maturity: 100 ft.
                    Zones 5–9

Ginkgo biloba   *Ginkgo*   *Fall color*
p. 341

Liriodendron   *Tulip Tree*   *Fall color*
tulipifera   *Flowers: 2½ in. wide*   *p 354*
    Fruits: 2–3 in. long,
    conelike

The Broadleaf

Evergreens

If you want year-round greenery and showy flowers or fruits, consider the trees in this group. Most are native to warmer climates, notably the highly decorative but quite frost-sensitive palms.

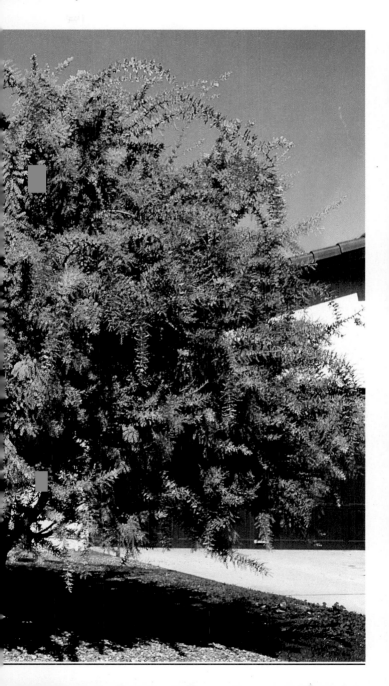

Washingtonia robusta

Mexican Fan Palm
•Height at 15 years: 18 ft.
At 40 years: 45 ft.
At maturity: 90 ft.
Zones 9–10

Tolerates drought

Trachycarpus fortunei

Windmill Palm
Height at 15 years: 8 ft.
•At 40 years: 20 ft.
At maturity: 30 ft.
Zones 8–10; semihardy 7

Blooms spring to summer
Fruit summer to winter

Washingtonia robusta Mexican Fan Palm p. 408

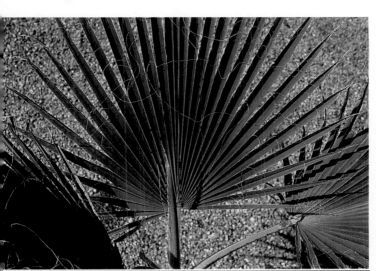

Trachycarpus fortunei Windmill Palm p. 402
Clusters: 18 in. long
Fruits: ½ in. wide

Washingtonia
filifera

California Fan Palm
•Height at 15 years:
10 ft.
At 40 years: 25 ft.
At maturity: 60 ft.
Zones 9–10

Brahea armata

Blue Palm
•Height at 15 years:
10 ft.
At 40 years: 30 ft.
At maturity: 40 ft.
Zones 9–10

Blooms summer to fall
Fruit fall to winter
Tolerates drought,
wind

Washingtonia filifera   *California Fan Palm*   *p. 408*

Brahea armata   *Blue Palm*   *p. 309*
Flowers: 4 in. wide
Clusters: 6–20 ft. long
Fruits: ¾ in. long

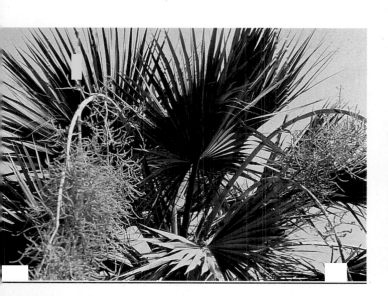

Butia capitata   *Pindo Palm*   *Blooms winter to*
                        •Height at 15 years: *summer*
                        8 ft.   *Fruit fall to winter*
                        At 40 years: 20 ft.
                        At maturity: 20 ft.
                        Zones 8–10

Phoenix canariensis   *Canary Islands Date*   *Fruit fall to winter*
                            Palm
                            •Height at 15 years:
                            15 ft.
                            At 40 years: 35 ft.
                            At maturity: 60 ft.
                            Zones 9–10

Butia capitata   *Pindo Palm*   *p. 310*
                      Flowers: ⅜ in. wide
                      Clusters: 3 ft. long
                      Fruits: 1 in. long, in
                      clusters

Phoenix canariensis   *Canary Islands Date*   *p. 371*
                          Palm
                          Fruits: ¾ in. long, in
                          3–8 ft. long clusters

Archontophoenix cunninghamiana

King Palm
•*Height at 15 years:*
20 ft.
At 40 years: 35 ft.
At maturity: 40 ft.
Zones 8–10

Blooms throughout year
Fruit throughout year
Requires moist soil
Tolerates shade, salt,
drought

Arecastrum romanzoffianum

Queen Palm
•*Height at 15 years:*
20 ft.
At 40 years: 40 ft.
At maturity: 50 ft.
Zones 10;
semihardy 9

Blooms throughout year
Fruit throughout year
Requires moist soil

Archontophoenix
cunninghamiana

King Palm
Flowers: ½ in. wide
Clusters: 4 ft. long
Fruits: ½ in. long

p. 303

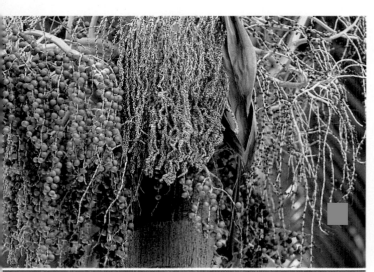

Arecastrum
romanzoffianum

Queen Palm
Flowers: ⅜ in. long
Clusters: 3–4 ft. long
Fruits: 1½ in. wide

p. 304

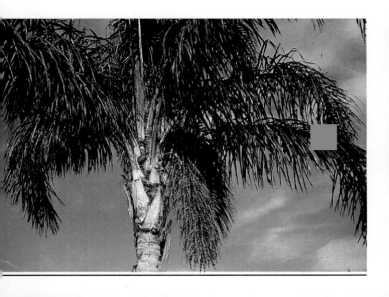

Ficus elastica   *Rubber Plant*   *Tolerates drought,*
Height at 15 years: *shade*
15 ft.
At 40 years: 25 ft.
•At maturity: 40 ft.
Zone 10

Ficus microcarpa   *Indian Laurel*
Height at 15 years:
20 ft.
At 40 years: 30 ft.
•At maturity: 40 ft.
Zones 10;
semihardy 9

Ficus elastica   *Rubber Plant*   *p. 337*
'Decora'

Ficus microcarpa   *Indian Laurel*   *p. 338*

| **Magnolia grandiflora** | Southern Magnolia
Height at 15 years:
18 ft.
At 40 years: 40 ft.
•At maturity: 80 ft.
Zones 7–9;
semihardy 6 | Blooms in spring
Fruit in fall
Requires moist soil
Tolerates wet, shade |

| **Magnolia virginiana** | Sweet Bay
•Height at 15 years:
12 ft.
At 40 years: 25 ft.
At maturity: 60 ft.
Zones 5–9 | Blooms spring to early
summer
Fruit summer to fall
Requires moist soil
Tolerates wet, shade |

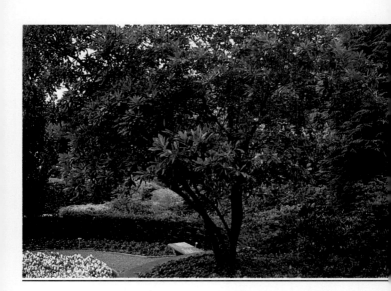

**Magnolia
grandiflora**

Southern Magnolia
Flowers: 6–8 in. wide
Fruits: 4 in. long
Fragrant

p. 355

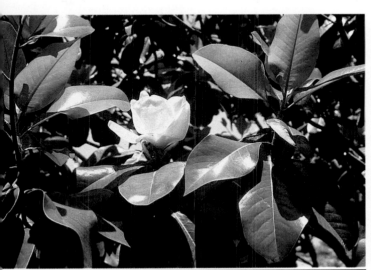

**Magnolia
virginiana**

Sweet Bay
Flowers: 2½ in. wide
Fruits: 2 in. long
Fragrant

p. 355

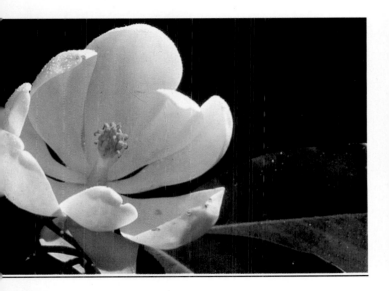

Arbutus unedo   Strawberry Tree   Blooms in fall
                     Height at 15 years: Fruit fall to winter
                     8 ft.   Tolerates drought
                    •At 40 years: 20 ft.
                     At maturity: 35 ft.
                     Zones 6–9

Pyrus kawakamii   Evergreen Pear   Blooms winter to spring
                       Height at 15 years:
                       12 ft.
                      •At 40 years: 20 ft.
                       At maturity: 30 ft.
                       Zones 8–10

Arbutus unedo Strawberry Tree *p. 302*
Flowers: ¼ in. wide
Clusters: 2 in. long
Fruits: ¾ in. wide

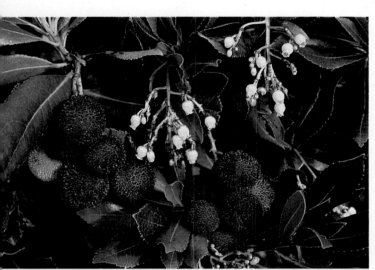

Pyrus kawakamii Evergreen Pear *p. 387*
Flowers: ½ in. wide
Fragrant

Laurus nobilis

Laurel
Height at 15 years:
8 ft.
•At 40 years: 20 ft.
At maturity: 40 ft.
Zones 8–10

Tolerates drought,
shade

Ilex opaca

American Holly
Height at 15 years:
12 ft.
•At 40 years: 28 ft.
At maturity: 50 ft.
Zones 5–9

Fruit fall to winter
Requires moist, acid
soil
Tolerates salt, shade

Laurus nobilis   *Laurel*   *p. 352*

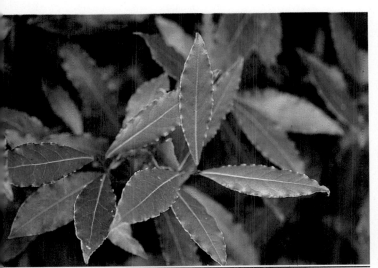

Ilex opaca   American Holly   p 345
                            Fruits: 1/4–1/3 *in. wide*

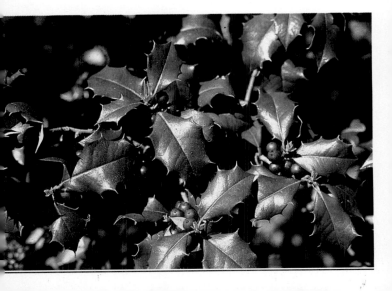

Prunus lusitanica   *Portugal Laurel*   *Blooms in spring*
•Height at 15 years: *Fruit in summer*
12 ft.
At 40 years: 30 ft.
At maturity: 40 ft.
Zones 7–10

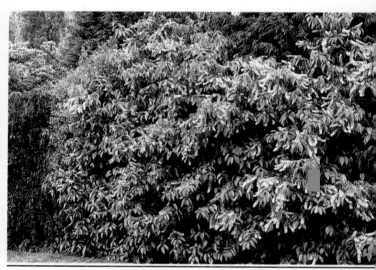

Eriobotrya japonica   *Loquat*   *Blooms in fall*
Height at 15 years: *Fruit in spring*
15 ft.   *Tolerates drought*
•At 40 years: 25 ft.
At maturity: 30 ft.
Zones 8–10

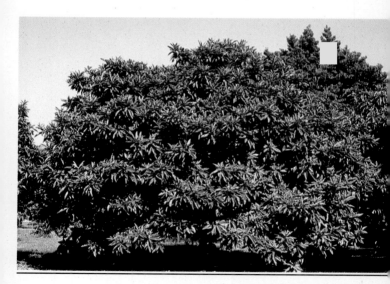

Prunus lusitanica   *Portugal Laurel*   *p. 382*
Flowers: minute
Clusters: 10 in. long
Fruits: ½ in. long

Eriobotrya japonica   *Loquat*   *p. 329*
Flowers: ½ in. wide
Clusters: 4–6 in. long
Fruits: 1–2 in. long
Fragrant

Arbutus menziesii Madrone
Height at 15 years:
20 ft.
•At 40 years: 50 ft.
At maturity: 100 ft.
Zones 6–9

Blooms in spring
Fruit fall to winter
Requires acid soil

Pittosporum
undulatum Victorian Box
Height at 15 years:
15 ft.
•At 40 years: 30 ft.
At maturity: 40 ft.
Zones 9–10

Blooms in spring
Fruit in fall

Arbutus menziesii   Madrone   p. 302
Flowers: ¼ in. long
Clusters: 6 in. long
Fruits: ½ in. long

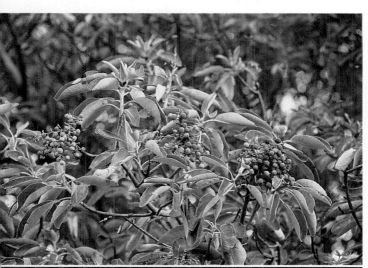

Pittosporum   Victorian Box   p. 379
undulatum   Flowers: ½ in. long
Clusters: 3 in. wide
Fruits: ½ in. long
Fragrant

Eucalyptus sideroxylon

Red Ironbark
Height at 15 years:
20 ft.
•At 40 years: 55 ft.
At maturity: 80 ft.
Zones 9–10

Blooms fall to spring
Fruit spring to summer
Tolerates drought

Olea europaea

Olive
Height at 15 years:
15 ft.
At 40 years: 22 ft.
•At maturity: 30 ft.
Zones 9–10;
semihardy 8

Fruit winter to spring
Tolerates drought

Eucalyptus
sideroxylon

Red Ironbark   *p. 333*
Flowers: 1 in. wide
Clusters: 8–20 in.
wide
Fruits: ½ in. wide
Fragrant

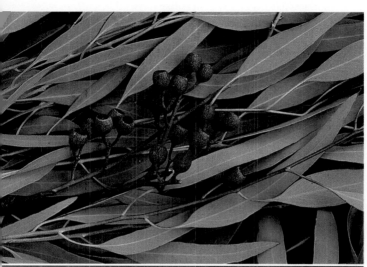

Olea europaea

Olive   *p. 367*
Fruits: 1½ in. long
Fragrant

Eucalyptus ficifolia
Red Flowering Gum
•Height at 15 years:
15 ft.
At 40 years: 35 ft.
At maturity: 40 ft.
Zones 9–10

Blooms in summer
Fruit in late summer
Tolerates drought

Melaleuca linariifolia
Flaxleaf Paperbark
Height at 15 years:
20 ft.
•At 40 years: 30 ft.
At maturity: 30 ft.
Zones 10;
semihardy 9

Blooms in late summer
Tolerates drought

Eucalyptus ficifolia   Red Flowering Gum   *p. 332*
Flowers: 1 in. wide
Clusters: to 12 in.
long
Fruits: ¹/₂ in. wide

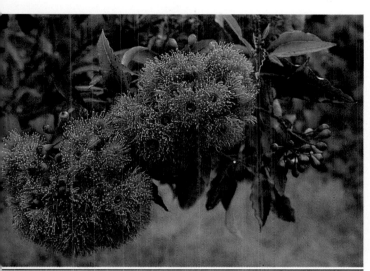

Melaleuca   Flaxleaf Paperbark   *p. 362*
linariifolia   *Flowers: ³/₄ in. long*
Clusters: 2 in. long

Podocarpus gracilior Fern Pine
Height at 15 years:
20 ft.
•At 40 years: 45 ft.
At maturity: 60 ft.
Zones 9–10

Podocarpus macrophyllus Yew Podocarpus
Height at 15 years:
10 ft.
•At 40 years: 25 ft.
At maturity: 40 ft.
Zones 8–10

Fruit in fall
Tolerates salt, shade

Podocarpus gracilior   Fern Pine   *p. 380*

Podocarpus   *Yew Podocarpus*   *p. 381*
macrophyllus   *Fruits: ¹/₂ in. long*

Acacia baileyana   Cootamundra Wattle   Blooms in winter
                     Height at 15 years: Tolerates drought
                     20 ft.
                     •At 40 years: 35 ft.
                     At maturity: 40 ft.
                     Zones 9–10

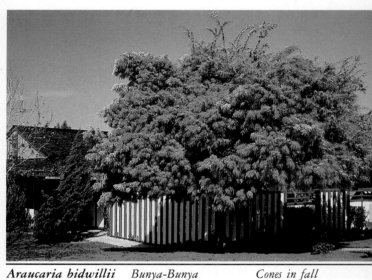

Araucaria bidwillii   Bunya-Bunya   Cones in fall
                        Height at 15 years: Tolerates shade
                        15 ft.
                        •At 40 years: 40 ft.
                        At maturity: 80 ft.
                        Zones 9–10;
                        semihardy 8

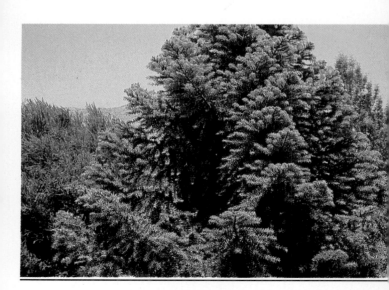

Acacia baileyana Cootamundra Wattle p. 292
Clusters: ¼ in. wide
Fragrant

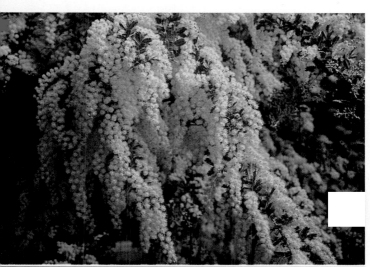

Araucaria bidwillii Bunya-Bunya p. 301
Cones: 7–10 in. long

The species pictured here are evergreen counterparts to the deciduous shade trees, and many have handsome, waxy leaves. Most reach a great size, making them invaluable for constant shade in semi-arid, tropical, or coastal regions.

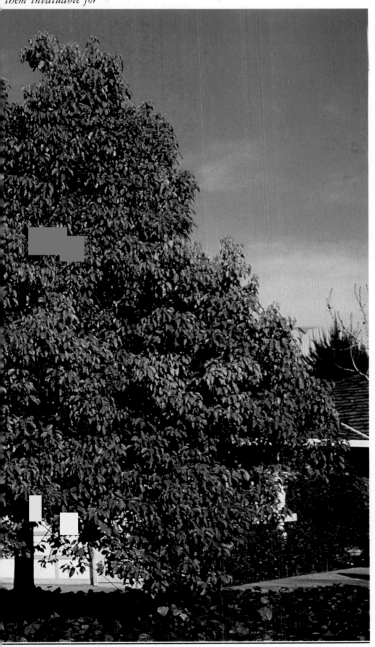

Acacia dealbata   *Silver Wattle*   *Blooms winter to spring*
                            Height at 15 years: *Tolerates drought*
                            25 ft.
                            •*At 40 years: 40 ft.*
                            At maturity: 50 ft.
                            Zones 9–10

Acacia melanoxylon   *Blackwood Acacia*   *Blooms in spring*
                            Height at 15 years: *Tolerates drought,*
                            20 ft.   *wind, poor soil*
                            •*At 40 years: 40 ft.*
                            At maturity: 50 ft.
                            Zones 8–10

Acacia dealbata   Silver Wattle   p. 292
Flowers: ¼ in. wide
Clusters: to 8 in. long
Fragrant

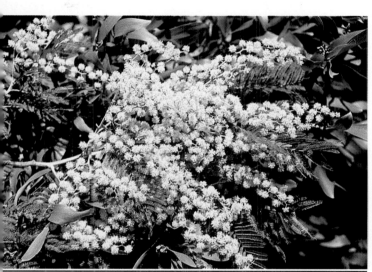

Acacia melanoxylon   Blackwood Acacia   p. 293
Flowers: ¼ in. wide
Clusters: 1 in. long

Grevillea robusta   *Silk Oak*   *Blooms in spring*
            •*Height at 15 years:*   *Tolerates drought*
            20 ft.
            At 40 years: 55 ft.
            At maturity: 150 ft.
            Zones 10;
            semihardy 9

Fraxinus uhdei   *Evergreen Ash*
            Height at 15 years:
            30 ft.
            •*At 40 years: 50 ft.*
            At maturity: 80 ft.
            Zones 9–10

Grevillea robusta   Silk Oak   p. 342
                        Clusters: 4–12 in.
                        long

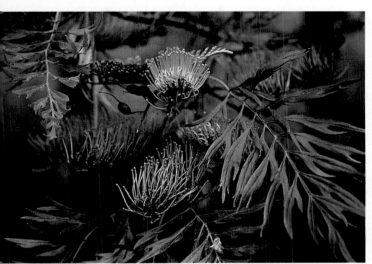

Fraxinus uhdei   Evergreen Ash   p. 340

Cinnamomum
camphora

Camphor Tree
Height at 15 years:
15 ft.
•At 40 years: 40 ft.
At maturity: 50 ft.
Zones 8–10

Ficus benjamina

Benjamin Fig
Height at 15 years:
15 ft.
•At 40 years: 30 ft.
At maturity: 40 ft.
Zone 10

Requires moist soil

Cinnamomum camphora *Camphor Tree* p. 319

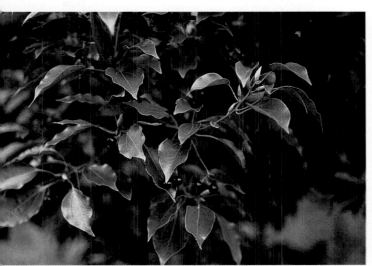

Ficus benjamina *Benjamin Fig* p. 337

Ficus macrophylla   *Moreton Bay Fig*   *Fruit in fall*
     Height at 15 years: *Requires moist soil*
     20 ft.
     At 40 years: 50 ft.
     •At maturity: 75 ft.
     Zones 9–10

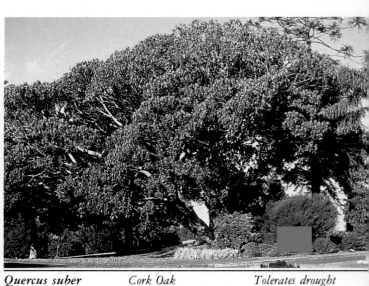

Quercus suber   *Cork Oak*   *Tolerates drought*
     Height at 15 years:
     12 ft.
     At 40 years: 30 ft.
     •At maturity: 60 ft.
     Zones 7–9

Ficus macrophylla   Moreton Bay Fig   p. 337
Fruits: 1 in. wide

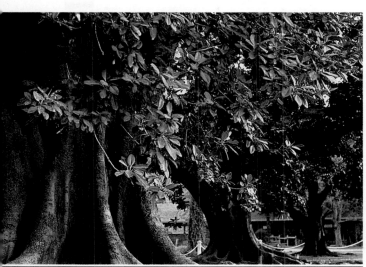

Quercus suber   Cork Oak   p. 391

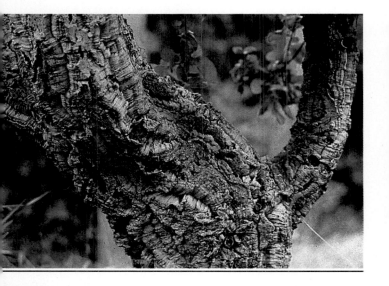

Quercus chrysolepis   *Canyon Live Oak*
Height at 15 years:
12 ft.
At 40 years: 30 ft.
•At maturity: 60 ft.
Zones 8–10;
semihardy 7

Quercus agrifolia   *California Live Oak*
Height at 15 years:
25 ft.
At 40 years: 60 ft.
•At maturity: 80 ft.
Zones 9–10

Quercus chrysolepis   *Canyon Live Oak*   p. 389

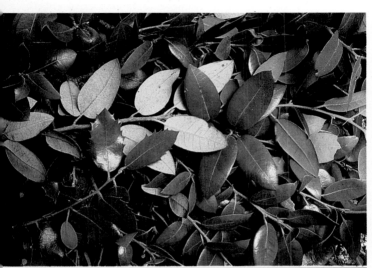

Quercus agrifolia   *California Live Oak*   p. 388

Quercus virginiana   Live Oak
Height at 15 years:
10 ft.
•At 40 years: 50 ft.
At maturity: 70 ft.
Zones 7–10

Ceratonia siliqua   Carob   Blooms in spring
Height at 15 years: Fruit in early fall
22 ft.   Tolerates drought
•At 40 years: 35 ft.
At maturity: 50 ft.
Zones 9–10

Quercus virginiana   Live Oak   p. 391

Ceratonia siliqua   Carob   p. 315
Flowers: 1/4 in. wide
Clusters: 6 in. long
Fruits: 4–12 in. long

Schinus terebinthifolius	Brazilian Pepper Tree	Fruit in winter

Schinus
terebinthifolius

Brazilian Pepper Tree
Height at 15 years:
10 ft.
•At 40 years: 25 ft.
At maturity: 30 ft.
Zones 9–10

Fruit in winter
Tolerates drought

Cupaniopsis
anacardioides

Carrot Wood
•Height at 15 years:
12 ft.
At 40 years: 30 ft.
At maturity: 40 ft.
Zones 10;
semihardy 9

Tolerates wet

| *Schinus*
terebinthifolius | Brazilian Pepper Tree
Fruits: ¼ in. wide, in
clusters | p. 393 |

| *Cupaniopsis*
anacardioides | Carrot Wood | p. 325 |

Erythrina caffra   *Kaffirboom Coral Tree*   *Blooms winter to spring*
Height at 15 years: *Tolerates salt*
20 ft.
•*At 40 years: 40 ft.*
At maturity: 60 ft.
Zones 9–10

Brachychiton   *Bottle Tree*   *Blooms in late spring*
populneus   *Height at 15 years:*   *Fruit summer to fall*
20 ft.   *Tolerates drought*
At 40 years: 30 ft.
•*At maturity: 50 ft.*
Zones 8–10

Erythrina caffra   *Kaffirboom Coral Tree*   *p. 330*
                         Flowers: 2 in. long
                         Clusters: 6–8 in. long

Brachychiton   *Bottle Tree*   *p. 308*
populneus   *Flowers: ½ in. wide*
                         Clusters: 3 in. long
                         Fruits: 2–3 in. long

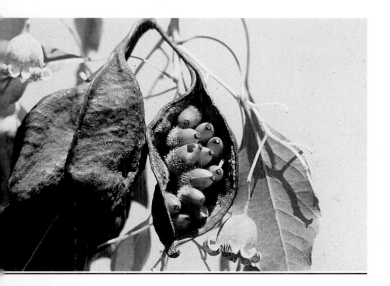

Eucalyptus camaldulensis

Red Gum
Height at 15 years: 40 ft.
At 40 years: 80 ft.
•At maturity: 125 ft.
Zones 9–10;
semihardy 8

Tolerates drought, wet
p. 331

Eucalyptus polyanthemos

Silver Dollar Gum
Height at 15 years: 20 ft.
•At 40 years: 40 ft.
At maturity: 60 ft.
Zones 8–10

Tolerates drought
p. 332

Eucalyptus gunnii	*Cider Gum*	*Blooms in spring*
	Height at 15 years:	*Flowers: ½ in. long*
	25 ft.	*Fragrant*
	At 40 years: 60 ft.	*p. 332*
	At maturity: 75 ft.	
	Zones 8–10;	
	semihardy 7	

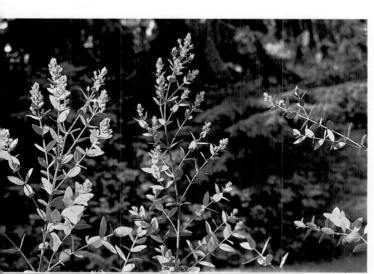

Eucalyptus citriodora	*Lemon-scented Gum*	*Tolerates drought, wet*
	Height at 15 years:	*Fragrant*
	25 ft.	*p. 332*
	At 40 years: 50 ft.	
	At maturity: 75 ft.	
	Zones 9–10	

Tristania conferta   Brisbane Box   Blooms in summer
                          Height at 15 years: Requires acid soil
                          20 ft.
                          At 40 years: 40 ft.
                          •At maturity: 50 ft.
                          Zones 9–10

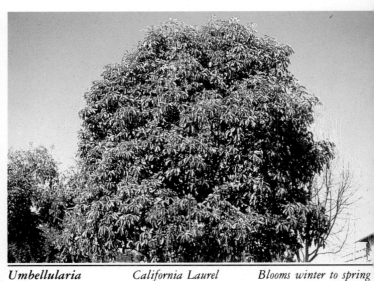

Umbellularia   California Laurel   Blooms winter to spring
californica   Height at 15 years: Fruit in spring
                         15 ft.   Tolerates shade, wind
                         At 40 years: 40 ft.
                         •At maturity: 75 ft.
                         Zones 7–10

Tristania conferta   *Brisbane Box*   *p. 403*
Flowers: ¾ in. wide
Clusters: 4 in. wide

Umbellularia   *California Laurel*   *p. 407*
californica   *Flowers: minute*
Clusters: ½ in. wide
Fruits: 1 in. long

The Needle-leaf

Evergreens

Use the distinctive
forms and foliage
textures of these
evergreens to create
year-round landscape
accents. Choices range
from narrowly
columnar species to
gracefully tiered ones.

***Cupressus sempervirens* 'Stricta Glauca'**	*Columnar Italian Cypress* •*Height at 15 years:* *18 ft.* *At 40 years: 50 ft.* *At maturity: 75 ft.* *Zones 8–10*	*Cones in fall*

Juniperus scopulorum	*Rocky Mountain Juniper* •*Height at 15 years:* *12 ft.* *At 40 years: 25 ft.* *At maturity: 40 ft.* *Zones 4–10*	*Fruit in fall* *Tolerates drought*

Cupressus   Columnar Italian   *p. 327*
sempervirens   Cypress
'Stricta'   *Cones: 1½ in. wide*

Juniperus   Rocky Mountain   *p. 348*
scopulorum   Juniper
                     Fruits: ⅓ in. wide

Juniperus virginiana	Red Cedar •Height at 15 years: 12 ft. At 40 years: 30 ft. At maturity: 75 ft. Zones 3–9	Fruit in fall Tolerates drought

Thuja occidentalis	American Arborvitae Height at 15 years: 15 ft. •At 40 years: 35 ft. At maturity: 60 ft. Zones 3–7; semihardy 8	Tolerates wet

Juniperus virginiana Red Cedar *p. 348*
Fruits: ⅓ in. long

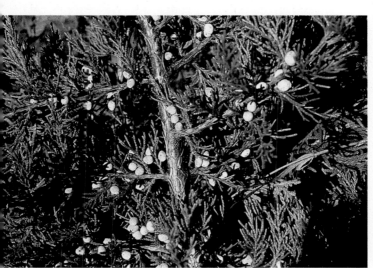

Thuja occidentalis *American Arborvitae* p 399

Thuja plicata

Giant Arborvitae
Height at 15 years:
30 ft.
•At 40 years: 80 ft.
At maturity: 100 ft.
Zones 5–7; semihardy
4 and 8

× *Cupressocyparis*
leylandii

Leyland Cypress
Height at 15 years:
30 ft.
•At 40 years: 65 ft.
At maturity: 100 ft.
Zones 6–10

Cones in fall
Tolerates salt

Thuja plicata   *Giant Arborvitae*   *p. 400*

× **Cupressocyparis**   *Leyland Cypress*   *p. 326*
leylandii   *Cones: ⅝ in. wide*

Sequoiadendron giganteum

Giant Sequoia
•Height at 15 years:
35 ft.
At 40 years: 80 ft.
At maturity: 250 ft.
Zones 7–9;
semihardy 6

Chamaecyparis nootkatensis 'Pendula'

Weeping Nootka False Cypress
Height at 15 years:
12 ft.
•At 40 years: 22 ft.
At maturity: 30 ft.
Zones 5–9

Cones in fall
Requires moist soil

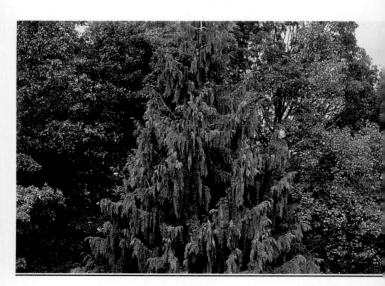

Sequoiadendron   *Giant Sequoia*   *p. 395*
giganteum

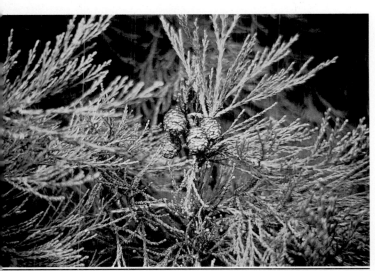

Chamaecyparis   *Weeping Nootka False*   *p. 318*
nootkatensis   *Cypress*
'Pendula'   *Cones:* 1/2 *in. wide*

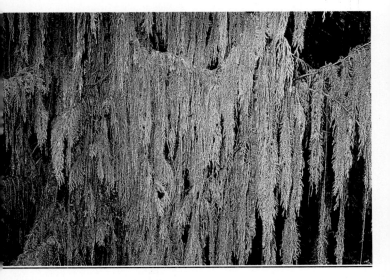

| *Cryptomeria japonica* | Japanese Cedar
•Height at 15 years: 15 ft.
At 40 years: 30 ft.
At maturity: 60 ft.
Zones 6–8 | Cones in fall
Requires moist, acid soil |

| *Sequoia sempervirens* | Redwood
Height at 15 years: 45 ft.
•At 40 years: 90 ft.
At maturity: 300 ft.
Zones 8–10;
semihardy 7 | |

| **Cryptomeria japonica** | Japanese Cedar
Cones: 1 in. wide | p. 325 |

| **Sequoia sempervirens** | Redwood | p. 394 |

Araucaria
heterophylla

Norfolk Island Pine
Height at 15 years:
18 ft.
•At 40 years: 45 ft.
At maturity: 100 ft.
Zone 10

Tolerates shade

Pinus canariensis

Canary Island Pine
Height at 15 years:
25 ft.
•At 40 years: 50 ft.
At maturity: 100 ft.
Zones 9–10;
semihardy 8

Cones fall to winter
Tolerates drought

Araucaria
heterophylla Norfolk Island Pine p. 301

Pinus canariensis *Canary Island Pine* p. 375
Cones: 6–9 in. long

Picea omorika   *Serbian Spruce*
•Height at 15 years:
17 ft.
At 40 years: 40 ft.
At maturity: 100 ft.
Zones 4–7

Picea abies   *Norway Spruce*   *Cones fall to winter*
Height at 15 years:
20 ft.
•At 40 years: 45 ft.
At maturity: 150 ft.
Zones 3–7

Picea omorika
'Pendula'

Weeping Serbian Spruce p. 373

Picea abies

Norway Spruce p. 372
Cones: 4–7 in. long

The conifers in this group are particularly well-suited for screen and background plantings. These trees vary in shape from tapering spires to picturesque masses, while their foliage ranges in color and texture from subtle and delicate to vibrant and rugged.

Pinus flexilis   Limber Pine   *Cones fall to winter*
                         Height at 15 years:
                         15 ft.
                         At 40 years: 30 ft.
                         •*At maturity: 75 ft.*
                         Zones 4–7

Pinus thunbergiana   Japanese Black Pine   *Cones fall to winter*
                         Height at 15 years: *Tolerates salt*
                         15 ft.
                         At 40 years: 35 ft.
                         •*At maturity: 90 ft.*
                         Zones 5–9

Pinus flexilis   *Limber Pine*   p. 376
Cones: 4–6 in. long

Pinus thunbergiana   *Japanese Black Pine*   p. 378
Cones: 2 in. long

Pinus densiflora
'Umbraculifera'

Tanyosho Pine
Height at 15 years:
15 ft.
•At 40 years: 20 ft.
At maturity: 30 ft.
Zones 5–8;
semihardy 4

Cones throughout year

Pinus halepensis

Aleppo Pine
Height at 15 years:
15 ft.
At 40 years: 30 ft.
•At maturity: 60 ft.
Zones 8–10

Cones fall to winter,
2 in. long
Tolerates: drought, salt
p. 376

Pinus densiflora   *Japanese Red Pine*   *Cones: 2 in. long*
Height at 15 years: *p. 375*
15 ft.
At 40 years: 35 ft.
At maturity: 100 ft.
Zones 5–8;
semihardy 4

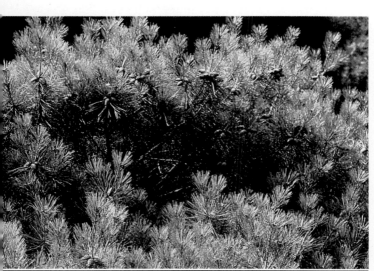

Pinus lambertiana   *Sugar Pine*   *Cones fall to winter,*
Height at 15 years: *10–20 in. long*
10 ft.   *p. 376*
At 40 years: 50 ft.
At maturity: 200 ft.
Zones 6–8

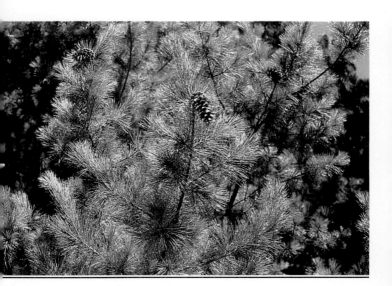

Pinus taeda   *Loblolly Pine*   *Cones fall to winter*
Height at 15 years:
20 ft.
At 40 years: 45 ft.
•At maturity: 90 ft.
Zones 7–9

Pinus resinosa   *Red Pine*   *Cones fall to winter*
Height at 15 years:
18 ft.
At 40 years: 50 ft.
•At maturity: 75 ft.
Zones 3–7

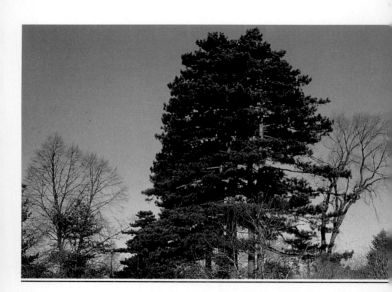

Pinus taeda   Loblolly Pine   p. 378
         Cones: 3–5 in. long

Pinus resinosa   Red Pine   p. 377
         Cones: 2 in. long

Pinus sylvestris   *Scotch Pine*   *Cones fall to winter*
                          Height at 15 years: *Tolerates drought*
                          15 ft.
                          •At 40 years: 45 ft.
                          At maturity: 90 ft.
                          Zones 3–8

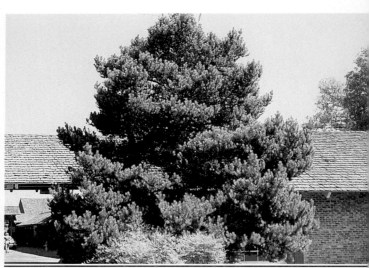

Pinus nigra   *Austrian Pine*   *Cones fall to winter*
                     •Height at 15 years:
                     15 ft.
                     At 40 years: 35 ft.
                     At maturity: 100 ft.
                     Zones 4–8

Pinus sylvestris   Scotch Pine   *p. 377*
Cones: 2½ in. long

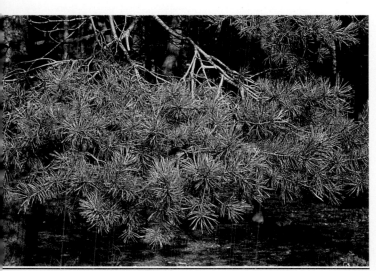

Pinus nigra   Austrian Pine   *p. 376*
Cones: 3 in. long

Pinus strobus
Eastern White Pine
•*Height at 15 years:*
15 ft.
At 40 years: 45 ft.
At maturity: 150 ft.
Zones 4–7

Cones fall to winter

Pinus contorta
Shore Pine
•*Height at 15 years:*
10 ft.
At 40 years: 25 ft.
At maturity: 30 ft.
Zones 7–10

Cones fall to winter

Pinus strobus   *Eastern White Pine*   *p. 377*
                           Cones: 4–8 in. long

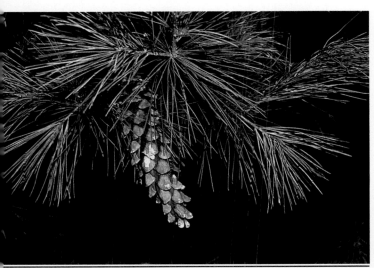

Pinus contorta   *Shore Pine*   *p. 375*
                           Cones: 2 in. long

Pinus bungeana   *Lacebark Pine*   *Cones fall to winter*
Height at 15 years:
12 ft.
•At 40 years: 30 ft.
At maturity: 75 ft.
Zones 5–8

Cedrus atlantica   *Blue Atlas Cedar*   *Cones throughout year*
'Glauca'   *Height at 15 years:*   *Tolerates drought*
10–15 ft.
•At 40 years: 35 ft.
At maturity: 60 ft.
Zones 6–9

Pinus bungeana *Lacebark Pine* *p. 375*
Cones: 2–3 in. long

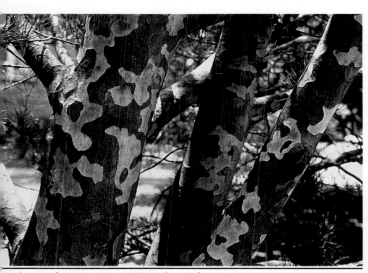

Cedrus atlantica *Blue Atlas Cedar* *p. 313*
Glauca' *Cones: 2–3 in. long*

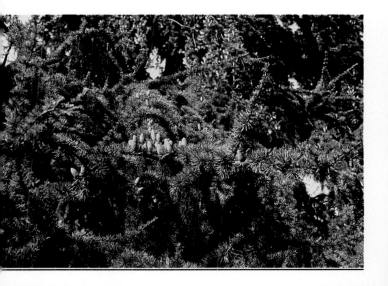

Cedrus deodara　　Deodar Cedar　　　　　*Cones throughout year*
Height at 15 years:
10–15 ft.
At 40 years: 55 ft.
•At maturity: 80 ft.
Zones 7–8

Cedrus libani　　Cedar-of-Lebanon　　*Cones throughout year*
Height at 15 years:　　　*Requires acid soil*
10–15 ft.
At 40 years: 40 ft.
•At maturity: 100 ft.
Zones 6–7

Cedrus deodara   *Deodar Cedar*   *p. 313*
                       Cones: 3–5 in. long

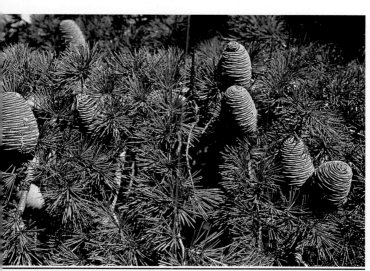

Cedrus libani   *Cedar-of-Lebanon*   *p. 314*
                       Cones: 3–4 in. long

Cupressus macrocarpa Monterey Cypress
Height at 15 years: 18 ft.
At 40 years: 50 ft.
•At maturity: 75 ft.
Zones 8–10

Cones in fall
Tolerates salt

Thuja orientalis Oriental Arborvitae
•Height at 15 years: 12 ft.
At 40 years: 25 ft.
At maturity: 40 ft.
Zones 6–9

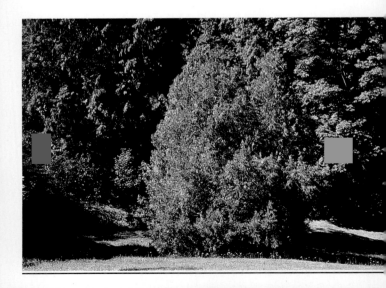

Cupressus
macrocarpa

Monterey Cypress   p. 527
Cones: 1½ in. wide

Thuja orientalis   Oriental Arborvitae   p. 400

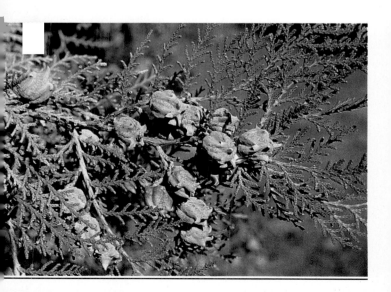

Tsuga heterophylla　　Western Hemlock　　Cones fall to winter
Height at 15 years:　　Requires moist soil
20 ft.
•At 40 years: 50 ft.
At maturity: 100 ft.
Zones 6–8

Tsuga canadensis　　Canada Hemlock　　Cones fall to winter
•Height at 15 years:　　Requires moist soil
18 ft.　　Tolerates shade
At 40 years: 50 ft.
At maturity: 90 ft.
Zones 4–7; semihardy
3 and 8

Tsuga heterophylla   Western Hemlock   p. 404
Cones: 1 in. long

Tsuga canadensis   Canada Hemlock   p. 404
Cones: ¾ in. long

Picea orientalis   Oriental Spruce   Cones fall to winter
Height at 15 years:
12 ft.
•At 40 years: 25 ft.
At maturity: 70 ft.
Zones 5–8

Pseudotsuga   Douglas-fir   Cones fall to winter
menziesii   •Height at 15 years:
15 ft.
At 40 years: 35 ft.
At maturity: 80 ft.
Zones 6–8;
semihardy 5

Picea orientalis   Oriental Spruce   p. 373
                       Cones: 2–4 in. long

Pseudotsuga   Douglas-fir   p. 385
menziesii   Cones: 3–4 in. long

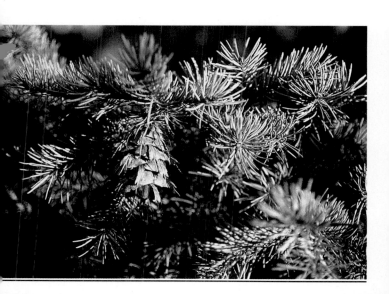

Picea pungens   Colorado Spruce   Cones fall to winter
                          •Height at 15 years:
                           15 ft.
                           At 40 years: 35 ft.
                           At maturity: 100 ft.
                           Zones 3–7

Picea glauca   White Spruce   Cones fall to winter
                           Height at 15 years: Tolerates drought
                           15 ft.
                          •At 40 years: 30 ft.
                           At maturity: 70 ft.
                           Zones 3–6

Picea pungens   *Hoops' Blue Colorado*   *p. 373*
'Hoopsii'   *Spruce*
                           Cones: 3–4 in. long

Picea glauca   *White Spruce*   *p. 372*
                          Cones: 2 in. long

Abies procera
'Glauca'

Noble Fir
•Height at 15 years:
20 ft.
At 40 years: 70 ft.
At maturity: 100 ft.
Zones 5–8

Cones summer to winter
Requires moist, acid
soil

Pinus parviflora

Japanese White Pine
•Height at 15 years:
12 ft.
At 40 years: 25 ft.
At maturity: 60 ft.
Zones 5–7

Cones fall to winter
Tolerates salt

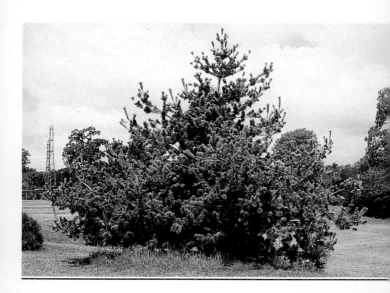

Abies procera   *Noble Fir*   *p. 291*
                           Cones. 6–9 in. long

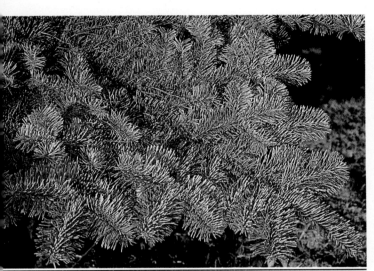

Pinus parviflora   *Japanese White Pine*   *p. 376*
                           Cones: 3 in. long

Abies concolor

White Fir
•Height at 15 years:
18 ft.
At 40 years: 45 ft.
At maturity: 65 ft.
Zones 4–7

Cones summer to winter
Requires moist, acid
soil

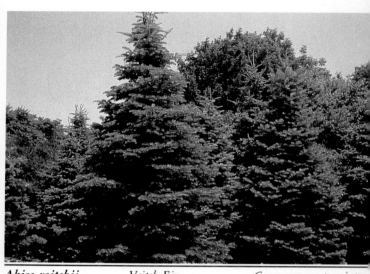

Abies veitchii

Veitch Fir
Height at 15 years:
15 ft.
•At 40 years: 40 ft.
At maturity: 60 ft.
Zones 4–6

Cones summer to winter
Requires moist, acid
soil

Abies concolor   White Fir   p. 290
                          Cones: 3–6 in. long

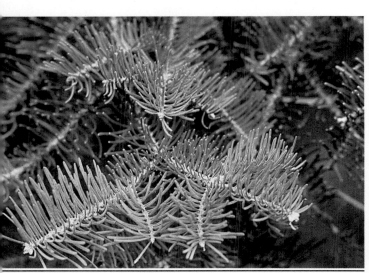

Abies veitchii   Veitch Fir   p. 291
                          Cones: 2–3 in. long

Abies homolepis   Nikko Fir
Height at 15 years:
12 ft.
•At 40 years: 35 ft.
At maturity: 60 ft.
Zones 5–6

Cones summer to winter
Requires moist, acid
soil

Abies koreana   Korean Fir
•Height at 15 years:
10 ft.
At 40 years: 18 ft.
At maturity: 35 ft.
Zones 5–6

Cones summer to winter
Requires moist, acid
soil

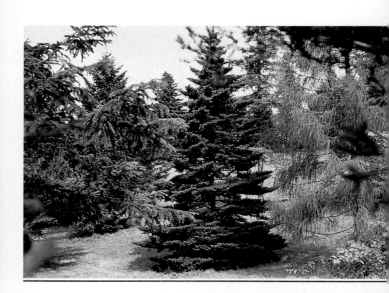

Abies homolepis   *Nikko Fir*   *p. 291*
                        Cones. 4 in. long

Abies koreana   *Korean Fir*   *p. 291*
                        Cones: 2 in. long

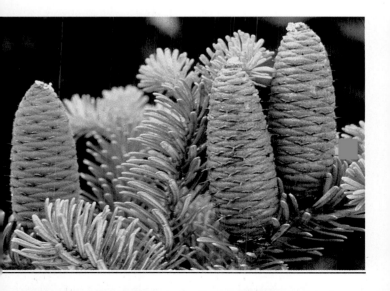

Abies
Pine family
Pinaceae

Ay'bees or ah'bi-ees. Fir. About 50 species of evergreen trees, all native to north temperate zones, handsomely distinctive in the landscape.

Description
Of stiffly conical habit, with whorls of horizontal branches. Leaves needle-like, constricted just above the circular base, flattened, and usually grooved, with 2 whitish bands below; often arranged as though 2-ranked, the spray of foliage hence flattened. Circular leaf scars on twigs after leaf drop are smooth. Cones erect during summer and fall, with scales falling at maturity.

How to Grow
Firs as a group are best suited to cool, humid conditions, like those in their mountainous native habitats. Plant firs in moist, well-drained acid soil. Rich soil is not essential, but be sure to mulch well with leaves, shredded bark, or wood chips. Firs tolerate light shade, but full sun is usually best.

Pruning is not necessary except to remove secondary leaders—upright stems that compete with the main leader—as soon as possible, and to remove dead or damaged branches. A branch, once removed, will not be replaced.

Few, if any, insects or diseases are troublesome to firs, unless trees suffer from environmental stress such as dry soil, excessive summer heat, and air pollution. Most firs are not suitable for city use; *A. concolor* is an exception.

concolor pp. 284, 285
White Fir; Colorado Fir. Reaches 40–65 ft. (12–20 m). Twigs bluish- or grayish-green, minutely hairy or smooth. Leaves 2 in. (5 cm) long, rounded or bluntly pointed at the tip, with 2 bluish-white bands on undersides. Cones greenish or purplish, 3–6 in. (7.5–15.0 cm) long. One of the most successful, as well as popular, of the cultivated firs; this species will endure more heat, drought, and air pollution than other firs. Oreg. to Baja Calif., eastward to Colo. and N. Mex. Cones summer to winter. Zones 4–7.

homolepis pp. 286, 287

Nikko Fir. To 60 ft. (18 m). Twigs
brownish, deeply grooved. Leaves 1 in.
(2.5 cm) long, rounded, pointed, or
notched at the tip, densely borne on twigs.
Cones purple, to 4 in. (10 cm) long.
Precisely spaced branches and dense, dark
green needles make this an especially
elegant fir, one of the best for the suburban
or rural eastern states. Japan. Cones summer
to winter. Zones 5–6.

koreana pp. 286, 287

Korean Fir. To 20–35 ft. (6.0–10.5 m).
Twigs at first yellowish and sparingly hairy,
becoming purplish and smooth. Leaves
½–1 in. (1.3–2.5 cm) long, rounded,
pointed, or notched at the tip, dark green,
whitish beneath. Cones purple, 2 in. (5 cm)
long, freely produced on young trees.
Because of its slow growth rate, this is a
good choice for smaller properties in cool
climates. South Korea. Cones summer to
winter. Zones 5–6.

procera pp. 282, 283

Noble Fir. To 100 ft. (30 m) or more.
Twigs brownish, minutely hairy. Leaves
1–1½ in. (2.5–4.0 cm) long, rounded or
notched at the tip; bluish green. Cones
purplish brown, large, 6–9 in. (15.0–
22.5 cm) long. Tolerates warmer climates
than most firs. Cultivar 'Glauca' has silvery
blue foliage as striking as that of the
Colorado Spruce, and grows more slowly
than the species. Wash. to extreme n. Calif.
Cones summer to winter. Zones 5–8.

veitchii pp. 284, 285

Veitch Fir. Reaches 30–60 ft. (9–18 m).
Twigs brown, minutely hairy. Leaves ½–
1 in. (1.3–2.5 cm) long, notched at the tip,
strikingly whitish on undersides. Cones
bluish purple, 2–3 in. (5.0–7.5 cm) long.
One of the winter-hardiest firs. Japan.
Cones summer to winter. Zones 4–6.

Acacia
Pea family
Leguminosae

A-kay'si-a; A-kay'sha. An enormous genus,
800 species of quick-growing shrubs and
trees found throughout the tropics and
subtropics. About 100 species have been

cultivated in America. Acacias are
attractive, free-flowering, and easy to grow
outdoors in warm climates. Most species,
once established, are drought resistant.
Those species described below are all
flowering broadleaf evergreen trees.

Description
Some acacias are thorny. Leaves are normally
twice-compound, the leaflets small and
numerous, but a few species often lack
leaves; instead there are modified, flattened
leafstalks that resemble lance-shaped leaves.
Flowers are very small but crowded into
dense finger-shaped or globular spikes or
racemes, all yellow in the species below.
The clusters may be solitary, but they are
more often arranged in variously branched
sprays, making handsome displays. Fruit
resembles a pea pod, but often becomes
woody and twisted in maturity.

How to Grow
Acacias tolerate a wide range of soils and,
once established, tolerate considerable
drought. Stake young plants until they are
well-rooted—usually one year. Water
infrequently but deeply, to discourage
surface rooting. Remove lower branches to
speed tree formation. As trees age, thin the
crown to admit sunlight and reduce wind
resistance. Always prune branches back to
the trunk or larger branches; do not leave
stubs. Acacias are notably short-lived
(30 years), but they reach tree size in 3 to 5
years and thus are quite useful for landscape
design.

baileyana pp. 216, 217
Cootamundra Wattle; Bailey Acacia. Showy
shrub or small tree, 30–40 ft. (9–12 m)
high, without spines and with beautiful,
feathery, bluish-gray foliage. Leaves twice-
compound, the ultimate leaflets scarcely
¼ in. (6 mm) long, numerous enough to
nearly hide the stem. Flower heads globular,
brilliant yellow, fragrant, ⅛ in. (3.2 mm)
across, borne abundantly in clusters ¼ in.
(6 mm) wide, longer than the leaves. Brown
fruit messy in late spring. Very popular in
California as a specimen tree. New South
Wales. Blooms in winter. Zones 9–10.

dealbata pp. 220, 221
Silver Wattle; Mimosa. To 50 ft. (15 m)
high. Leaves twice-compound, the ultimate
leaflets very numerous, ⅓ in. (8 mm) long,

silvery gray. Flowers ¼ in. (6 mm) across, highly fragrant, globular, golden yellow, and arranged in racemes.

Fast growing and longer-lived than most acacias. However, its roots are invasive, it reseeds readily, and its fruit is messy in late spring, so plant trees away from patios and walks. Also called *A. decurrens* var. *dealbata*. Australia. Blooms in late winter. Zones 9–10.

***melanoxylon** pp. 220, 221*
Blackwood Acacia; Black Acacia. A tall, unarmed tree, to 40–50 ft. (12–15 m). Flattened leafstalks more or less inverted lance-shaped, 4½ in. (11.5 cm) long and 1 in. (2.5 cm) wide. Sometimes there are also twice-compound leaves on young twigs. Flowers slightly fragrant, in dense globular heads ¼ in. (6 mm) across and 1 in. (2.5 cm) long, cream-yellow, not particularly showy.

Often planted as a street tree, but not very long-lived. Still, this species is so tolerant of wind, drought, and poor soil that it often serves well in landscapes in California's Central Valley. Australia. Blooms in spring. Zones 8–10.

Acer
Maple family
Aceraceae

A′sir. Maple. About 150 species native to north temperate zones, mostly deciduous trees and large shrubs. Many of the maples are grown as shade trees and for their attractive foliage, which often assumes brilliant hues in the fall. There are maples suitable for almost any kind of ornamental planting, coast to coast. They vary in height from 15 to 75 feet or more, and in habit from round to narrowly upright.

Description
Leaves opposite, simple and lobed, or compound. Flowers commonly unisexual, small, in panicles, corymbs, or clusters, often inconspicuous, in early to mid-spring. Fruit a pair of 2–winged keys, usually inconspicuous.

How to Grow
Maples will grow in any good soil, in areas with at least 30 inches of rainfall per year,

and are easily transplanted. With a few exceptions, maples require less than half shade and rich, moist but well-drained soil for best growth and health. To aid maples in heavy or poor soil, plant 3 or 4 inches higher than grade, and mulch from trunk to dripline with organic material—wood chips, shredded bark, or partially decomposed leaves—several inches thick. Heavy clay soils are improved by vertical mulching—drilling holes 1½–2 inches in diameter and 18 inches deep, 2 feet apart in root zone. During extended dry spells, irrigate deeply every two weeks or so. Fertilize maples annually with a high-nitrogen fertilizer. Start training maples while they are small. Prune to provide central leaders and wide branch angles; remove small internal branches that lack adequate sunlight. Give maples good soil conditions and they will thrive for many years.

campestre pp. 126, 127
Hedge Maple. A round-headed tree, to 35 ft. (10.5 m) high, the branches slightly corky. Leaves 3- to 5-lobed, 2–4 in. (5–10 cm) across, dull green above, soft-hairy beneath, usually turning yellow in fall. Flowers greenish, in erect, flat-topped corymbs. Fruit usually soft-hairy, with wings spreading horizontally. An attractive, dependable small tree that is tolerant of dry and compacted soil, withstands heavy pruning, and is usually pest-free. Eurasia. Zones 5–8.

griseum pp. 126, 127
Paperbark Maple. To 25 ft. (7.5 m) high, its papery, reddish-brown bark peels away in thin sheets, an arresting feature year-round. Leaves compound, the 3 leaflets elliptic or ovalish, 1½–4 in. (4–10 cm) long, coarsely toothed, sometimes turning red in fall. Flowers in short-stalked, hairy racemes. Fruit with wings spreading. China. Zones 5–8.

platanoides pp. 152, 153
Norway Maple. A smooth-barked, rounded tree, attaining 65 ft. (20 m) in height. Leaves 5–lobed, 4–7 in. (10.0–17.5 cm) across, bright green, with marginal teeth, turning yellow in fall. Flowers greenish yellow, in erect, many-flowered corymbs 1½ in. (4 cm) wide, surprisingly attractive, appearing before foliage. Fruit drooping, with horizontally spreading wings, not

ornamental.

Norway Maples are among the most widely planted trees in America—they are the fastest-growing maple species and provide quick shade and screens. However, they are shallow-rooted and cast such a dense shade that grass often fails beneath them. This species is subject to verticillium wilt more than most maples, and to frost cracking at its upper limits of hardiness, but it tolerates city air pollution and neglect quite well. Cultivars include 'Crimson King', with dark reddish-purple leaves; 'Summershade', with improved foliage; and 'Cleveland', 'Columnare', and others that are narrow and upright, and are widely grown as street trees. Europe to the Caucasus and Iran. Blooms in early spring. Zones 4–7.

rubrum pp. 154, 155

Red Maple. A large tree, to 70 ft. (21 m) high. Leaves 3– to 5–lobed, 2–4 in. (5–10 cm) long, shiny green above, with a bloom beneath, turning brilliant scarlet, sometimes yellow, in fall. Flowers red, in small showy clusters approximately 1 in. (2.5 cm) wide, appearing before leaves. Fruit bright red when young, smooth, on a slender stalk, wings spreading at a narrow angle. Valuable as an ornamental tree (though not as symmetrical as *A. saccharum*), as a shade tree, and as a street tree. Tolerant of both moderately wet and moderately dry sites. Many cultivars, such as 'Red Sunset', have excellent red fall color, and several, such as 'Armstrong', have narrow, upright growth habits. Newfoundland to Minn., south to Fla. and Tex. Blooms in early spring. Zones 4–9.

saccharinum pp. 154, 155

Silver Maple. A large, fast-growing tree, to 100 ft. (30 m) high. Leaves deeply 5–lobed, 3–6 in. (7.5–15.0 cm) across, lobes long-pointed, with marginal teeth, bright green above and silvery white beneath, turning yellow in fall. Flowers short-stalked, without petals, borne in dense clusters, 1 in. (2.5 cm) across, surrounding the twigs, greenish yellow or reddish, opening very early in spring and therefore of interest. Fruit soft-hairy when young, wings widely spread and sickle-shaped.

Silver Maples tolerate periods of flooding and drought. Branches and twigs are brittle, so trees can be hazardous in storms and are best planted in open areas away from streets, wires, and buildings. New Brunswick to Nebr., south to Fla. and Okla. Blooms in spring. Zones 3–9.

saccharum pp. 152, 153

Sugar Maple. A tall tree, to 100 ft. (30 m) high. Leaves 3- to 5-lobed, resembling the Norway Maple's, 4–6½ in. (10–16 cm) wide, turning red, scarlet, orange, or yellow in fall. Flowers light yellow, drooping in few-flowered clusters 2–3 in. (5.0–7.5 cm) long, before the leaves unfold. Fruit with widely divergent keys.

Though slower in growth than some others, this is an outstanding maple for displaying fall colors. It does need better soil conditions—moist but not soggy, well-drained, well-aerated—than most other maples. This tree is famous for its sap, which yields maple syrup and sugar.

A number of cultivars are available: 'Monumentale' and others are columnar; 'Bonfire' has bright red fall color; 'Green Mountain' has darker green foliage and endures dry soil better than the species. Newfoundland to S. Dak., south to Ga. and Tex. Blooms in spring. Zones 4–8.

Aesculus
Horsechestnut family
Hippocastanaceae

Es'kew-lus. Approximately 15 species of deciduous trees falling into two types— horsechestnuts and buckeyes—native to North America and Eurasia. Both types are ornamental, spring-flowering trees, some with fall color. Aesculus species cast dense shade; grass grows poorly beneath them. A buckeye seed in one's pocket is still considered to bring good luck in some parts of the U.S.

Description
Overall shape is oval to nearly round, precise in outline, resembling a stylized sketch, often low-branched. Horsechestnut buds are large with prominent scales and are sticky in winter. Leaflets are usually broadest near tips. Buckeye buds are not sticky and leaflets are broadest at mid-points. In both types long-petioled leaves are palmately compound with 5–9 leaflets. Showy flowers are white, yellow,

pink, or red in upright terminal panicles.
Fruit is a capsule, often spiny, with one or
more large brown seeds with a prominent
hilum, resembling the eye of a deer. If only
one seed occurs in a fruit, it is nearly round;
if several, they will have both rounded and
flat sides.

How to Grow
Aesculus species grow best in slightly acid,
moist but not wet soil, in sun or partial
shade. If your climate is dry, watch for leaf
scorch disease. Because these trees are not
easy to transplant, you should purchase
them as balled or container-grown plants.
Place them away from patios, entrances, and
other high-use areas because they do create
litter of leaves, spent flowers, and fruits.

× *carnea* 'Briottii' *pp. 76, 77*
Ruby Red Horsechestnut. Reaches 50 ft.
(15 m). Similar to *A. glabra,* but far more
spectacular in flower—bright red florets in
panicles up to 10 in. (25 cm) long and 3–
4 in. (7.5–10.0 cm) wide. Leaves with 5,
sometimes 7, leaflets, lustrous dark green.
A cultivar of the hybrid between *A. pavia*
and *A. hippocastanum.* Blooms in spring.
Fruit summer to fall. Zones 5–9.

glabra pp. 150, 151
Ohio Buckeye. A rounded, dense tree,
rarely taller than 35 ft. (10.5 m), but can
grow to 60 ft. (18 m). Flowers pale
greenish yellow, ¾ in. (19 mm) long, in
stiffish panicles 4–6 in. (10–15 cm) long.
Fruit egg-shaped, 1–2½ in. (2.5–6.0 cm) in
diameter. Leaflets 5, elliptic, 3–6 in.
(7.5–15.0 cm) long. One of the first trees
to leaf out in spring, suggesting tropical
foliage at that stage. Fall color is variable,
from none under stress, to pleasant yellow
or exciting orange when well-cultured.
Bark, when bruised or scratched, emits an
unpleasant odor. An ornamental shade tree
suitable for parks and larger residential lots.
Pa. to Ala. and west to Nebr. Blooms in
mid-spring. Fruit summer to fall. Zones
4–8.

Albizia
Pea family
Leguminosae

Al-bizz'ee-a. A genus of more than 100
species of tropical deciduous trees and
shrubs from cen. Asia. The species below is
hardier than most. Albizia closely resembles
and is related to Acacia.

Description
Leaves alternate, twice-compound, leaflets
small, numerous, and more or less oblique.
Flowers very small, congested in
globe-shaped heads; stamens long and
showy. Fruit a pod.

How to Grow
Albizia transplants with weedlike ease. Be
sure to give it sunshine and avoid wet
spots — little else matters. This tree endures
wind and drought, accepts soil reaction
from acid to alkaline, and shrugs off salty
conditions. Dead or crowded branches
should be pruned away in early spring.
Mimosa webworm is sometimes
troublesome, as is a wilt disease. The former
can be controlled with approved pesticides;
the latter may preclude the use of the tree
in some areas.

julibrissin 'Rosea' *pp. 80, 81*
Hardy Silk Tree. A medium-sized tree, not
over 30 ft. (9 m) high, but with a broad,
spreading crown, often wider than tall at
maturity. Compound leaves with 12–20
major divisions, each of which bears from
40–60 small oblique leaflets only ¼ in.
(6 mm) long. Flowers bright pink, 1 in.
(2.5 cm) long, in slender-stalked, compact
heads, 3 in. (7.5 cm) wide. Stamens, also
bright pink, are long, to 1¼ in. (3 cm),
and slender, lending a soft, fuzzy
appearance. Pod flat, 5–7 in.
(12.5–17.5 cm) long and 1 in. (2.5 cm)
wide, not particularly ornamental.
No other tree in temperate zones gives such
a spectacular tropical effect. It is especially
exciting when in flower and viewed from
above, as from a balcony. The tree is
sometimes incorrectly called mimosa. Some
experts consider another, similar cultivar,
'E.H. Wilson', to be identical; others
say 'E.H. Wilson' is separate and slightly
superior. Iran to cen. China. Blooms spring
to summer. Fruit in fall. Zones 6–9.

Alnus
Birch family
Betulaceae

Al'nus. Alder. About 30 species of
deciduous shrubs and trees grown as
specimens or in the shrub border, especially
in places too moist for other woody plants.
Catkins and cones are both present on twigs
in fall and winter, creating interesting
patterns against the sky and furnishing
attractive material for dried flower
arrangements.

Description
Alders have rather handsome, often
somewhat burnished or sticky, alternate
leaves. Flowers in catkins, the male and
female on the same plant, the latter
becoming small, scaly, woody cones. The
two species described below bloom before
the leaves unfold in spring.

How to Grow
Easy to grow in wet or moist places; alders
usually are not suitable for dry situations.
They need full sun or very little shade, and
seldom require pruning.

cordata pp. 166, 167
Italian Alder. A handsome tree, 70 ft.
(21 m) high, the foliage resembling a
pear's, the twigs reddish brown. Leaves
dark, shiny green, 2–4 in. (5–10 cm) long,
heart-shaped at the base, finely toothed.
Catkins 2–3 in. (5.0–7.5 cm) long; cones
1–1¼ in. (2.5–3.0 cm) long. An excellent
small tree for wet or moist soils that
tolerates drought as well; unfortunately rare
in the nursery trade. Corsica and Italy.
Blooms in spring. Cones throughout the
year. Zones 5–10.

glutinosa pp. 164, 165
European Alder; Black Alder. A tree, to
80 ft. (24 m), its twigs sticky. Leaves
dark green, nearly round or ovalish, 4 in.
(10 cm) long, coarsely toothed, the teeth
themselves also toothed. Catkins 2–3 in.
(5.0–7.5 cm) long; cones ½ in. (13 mm)
long. Often grown in a multi-stemmed style
similar to birches. There are several
horticultural varieties, such as a golden-
leaved form, one with much-cut leaves,
another with oaklike leaves, and a columnar
form. Most are uncommon. Quite hardy,
and will perform well in wet to moderately

dry soil. Eurasia. Blooms in spring. Cones throughout the year. Zones 3–9.

Amelanchier
Rose family
Rosaceae

Am-e-lang'ki-er. Serviceberry; Shadbush; Juneberry. About 25 species of deciduous shrubs or trees found in north temperate zones. Their profusion of white bloom is often called Shadblow on the East Coast, because the trees bloom with the onset of shad spawning runs up major eastern rivers.

Description
Leaves alternate, toothed. Buds prominently pointed. Flowers small, white, in profuse terminal racemes. Fruit a small, purplish, apple-like pome, sometimes used for jellies and attractive to birds, especially robins.

How to Grow
Serviceberries grow easily in ordinary garden soil, but perform poorly under drought conditions. You should mulch and irrigate during dry spells. They will grow well in moderate shade, but flowering and fall color will be reduced. You probably won't need to prune, and you may want to grow these trees with multiple trunks.

× *grandiflora* pp. 128, 129
Apple Serviceberry. A graceful small tree, reaching 25 ft. (7.5 m) in height. It differs little from its parents but has rather larger, sometimes pinkish flowers, 1¼ in. (3 cm) wide, in 3 in. (7.5 cm) racemes, produced in billowy profusion before the leaves unfold. Fruit a pome, ⅓ in. (8 mm) long, edible. Leaves turn pastel shades of yellow and orange in fall. A naturally-occurring hybrid of *A. canadensis* and *A. laevis*. Blooms in spring. Fruit in summer. Zones 4–8; semihardy 3.

laevis pp. 128, 129
Allegheny Serviceberry. A tree, to 35 ft. (10.5 m), rarely shrubby. Leaves purplish green when young, 3½ in. (9 cm) long, rounded or slightly heart-shaped at the base, ultimately bright green. Flowers, ½ in. (13 mm) wide, in slender nodding racemes, 3 in. (7.5 cm) long, appearing with or after

the unfolding of the leaves, making a
striking contrast with the early foliage.
Fruit a pome, ⅓ in. (8 mm) long, purplish
black, edible. Excellent fall color, ranging
from yellow-orange to pinkish red.
E. North America. Blooms in spring. Fruit
in summer. Zones 4–8; semihardy 3.

Araucaria
Araucaria family
Araucariaceae

Or-ro-cay'ri-a. Stately tropical evergreen
trees related to the pines, about 15 species.
All are natives of the southern hemisphere.

Description
Branches in symmetrical horizontal tiers.
Leaves evergreen, prickly and scale-like or
expanded into flat, thick, leathery blades,
always stiff. The flowers and seeds are borne
between the scales of large egg-shaped or
globelike cones, on mature trees.

How to Grow
Araucarias are popular as pot plants, outside
in mild weather, indoors anywhere. Soil
must be reasonably well-drained and
moisture should be abundant. Araucarias are
not demanding trees, but they do not
tolerate dry or soggy soils.

bidwillii pp. 216, 217
Bunya-Bunya. A tree, up to 150 ft. (45 m),
about 80 ft. (24 m) in cultivation. Leaves
glossy-green in distinct rows, sharp-pointed,
stiff, oblong-oval, 1½ in. (4 cm) long.
Edible seeds in large cones, 7–10 in.
(17.5–25.0 cm) long, that disintegrate at
maturity. Grown outdoors mostly in Calif.
and Fla. Tolerates shade. Australia. Cones
in fall. Zones 9–10; semihardy 8.

heterophylla pp. 254, 255
Norfolk Island Pine; Star Pine. Often grown
as a pot plant 2–10 ft. (0.6–3.0 m) high.
In landscapes, often grows 100 ft. (30 m)
tall. Branches 5–7, in a tier, thickly set
with sharp-pointed leaves that are ½ in.
(13 mm) long and curved at the tip. It
practically never flowers or fruits in
cultivation. Tolerates shade. Norfolk Island
in the Pacific Ocean. Zone 10.

Arbutus
Heath family
Ericaceae

Ar-bew'tus. A small genus, 14 species of
broadleaf evergreen trees grown in warmer
regions for their ornamental flowers and
striking bark. These plants and Trailing
Arbutus, *Epigaea repens,* are botanically
related, but dissimilar in appearance.

Description
Leaves alternate and stalked. Flowers white
or pinkish, urn-shaped, in loose terminal
panicles. Fruit fleshy, red or orange. Bark of
branches rough and shedding, usually
reddish.

How to Grow
Train arbutus species early to central leaders
to offset their tendency to become sprawly
and shrubby. Provide sandy, acid, well-
drained soil, protect plants from drying
winds, and irrigate during drought.
Madrone is fussier than Strawberry Tree
about its site requirements.

menziesii pp. *208, 209*
Madrone; Madrona; Laurelwood; Oregon
Laurel. A tall tree, 50–100 ft. (15–30 m).
Leaves oblongish, 4 in. (10 cm) long,
grayish green beneath, and without
marginal teeth. White flowers in terminal
panicles 6 in. (15 cm) long, each flower
¼ in. (6 mm) long. Fruit small, ⅖–½ in.
(10–13 mm) long, orange-red. Reddish-
brown bark peels in thin flakes. Madrone
pollen is an important source of honey for
California beekeepers.
Madrone is generally grown west of the
Rocky Mts., and requires acid soil. It is
difficult to transplant; start with young
small plants. Although a handsome tree, it
is messy, so plant it away from well-used
areas. British Columbia to Calif. Blooms in
spring. Fruit fall to winter. Zones 6–9.

unedo pp. *202, 203*
Strawberry Tree. Grows to 35 ft. (10.5 m),
less than half the height of Madrone.
Branches sticky-hairy. Leaves elliptic or
oblong, 3½ in. (9 cm) long, toothed, dark
green with red petioles. Flower panicles
drooping, 2 in. (5 cm) long, the white or
pink flowers ¼ in. (6 mm) in diameter,
occurring at same time as ¾ in. (19 mm)
diameter round fruit, orange-red, edible but

flavorless. Bark shreddy, rich red-brown.
Does not flourish in a humid climate.
To prevent shrublike growth, prune by
thinning stalks to induce tree form.
S. Europe. Blooms in fall. Fruit fall to
winter. Zones 6–9.

Archontophoenix
Palm family
Palmae

Ar-kon-toe-fee'nix. An Australian genus of
feather palms, the species below widely
planted in Calif. and Fla. as an ornamental.

Description
Noted for tall trunks crowned by a large
collection of compound leaves with
numerous, sometimes split, leaflets. Male
and female flowers are borne on separate
clusters considerably below the crown of the
leaves. Fruit is small, nearly round.

How to Grow
King Palms are difficult to transplant in
large sizes, though useful as houseplants.
They grow well in shade, even beneath
taller trees. Exposed young plants can be
killed by frost; mature trees endure 28° F
($-2°$ C). A breezy site naturally controls
aphids and honeydew.

cunninghamiana pp. 196, 197

King Palm. A stately palm, grows rapidly
when young, ultimately reaching 40 ft.
(12 m). Attractive urn-shaped flowers are
lilac or pinkish, ½ in. (13 mm) long. Both
male and female flowers bunched in tassle-
like clusters 4 ft. (120 cm) long at the base
of the crownshaft. Fruits are dark red,
small, ½ in. (13 mm) long. Compound
foliage fronds spread as much as 15 ft.
(4.5 m) in diameter on mature plants.
Tolerates light shade, moderate drought,
and salt winds. Also incorrectly known as
Seaforthia elegans. Australia. Blooms and
fruits intermittently throughout the year.
Zones 8–10.

Arecastrum
Palm family
Palmae

A-ree-kas′trum. A genus of South
American feather palms, one species widely
grown for ornament, both in greenhouses
and outdoors in Fla. and s. Calif., where it
is frequently grown as a fine avenue or street
tree. It is also effective in small clustered
groves with individuals of varied ages and
heights.

Description
They have smooth, light gray, ringed
trunks, glossy compound leaves with the
leaflets arranged feather-fashion, unisexual
yellow flowers borne in a cluster from the
leaf crown, and nearly round yellow fruits
1 in. (2.5 cm) in diameter.

How to Grow
Widely cultivated by florists for their
feathery ornamental foliage, Queen
Palms need a warm, moist-atmosphered
greenhouse and plenty of water.
Outdoors, they prefer full sun, and are
easily grown in ordinary soil. Spider mites
can be a problem; control by syringing
trees often. Trees are fast-growing, but
susceptible to cold.

romanzoffianum pp. 196, 197
Queen Palm; Plumy Coconut. A fine
ornamental; trunk straight, reaching 50 ft.
(15 m) in height, leaves bright green,
arching gracefully. Trunk ringed, often
clothed with a few dead but persistent
leaves in old specimens. Leaves in mature
plants 7–12 ft. (2.1–3.5 m) long, much
smaller in pot or tub specimens, the leaflets
very numerous, never more than 1 in.
(2.5 cm) wide. Flower clusters 3–4 ft. (90–
120 cm) long, creamy white to yellow,
emerge from a spathe, the female flowers
below the male and toward the tip. Fruits
numerous, yellow, not over 1½ in. (4 cm)
long, in large hanging clusters. Often
sold under the names of *Cocos plumosa,*
C. romanzoffiana, and *Syagrus romanzoffianum.*
S. Brazil to Argentina. Blooms and fruits
intermittently throughout the year. Zones
10; semihardy 9.

Bauhinia
Bean family
Leguminosae

Baw-hin'i-a. A large genus, some 300
species of tropical shrubs, trees, and woody
vines, a few species among the most
spectacular tropical flowering trees.

Description
Leaves compound, with 2 oblique leaflets,
or merely simple and with 2 oblique lobes,
much resembling the Redbud, to which it
is related. Flowers showy, not pealike, with
5 rather unequal petals, each narrowed into
a claw. Fruit a long flat pod, without viable
seeds.

How to Grow
Bauhinias are slow-growing, and bloom in
the winter and very early spring, after
which some species drop their leaves. They
need well-drained soil and moderate
moisture. No pests are serious, and they are
winter-hardy only in s. Calif. and Fla.

blakeana *pp. 78, 79*
Hong Kong Orchid Tree. A small, rounded
tree, to 25 ft. (7.5 m) high. Leaves 6–8 in.
(15–20 cm) wide, lobed less than half their
length. Flowers borne in racemes, to 6 in.
(15 cm) across, reddish purple, fragrant,
perhaps more flamboyant than any other
flowering tree. S. China. Blooms in winter.
Zone 10.

Betula
Birch family
Betulaceae

Bet'you-la. Birch. Medium or tall deciduous
trees, rarely shrubs, more often grown for
timber or aromatic properties than for
ornament, though several are widely
cultivated. There are 50 or 60 species,
mostly North American or Asiatic.
Unfortunately, birches are rather
short-lived. Grouped with evergreens, the
white-barked birches make beautiful winter
pictures. Weeping and cutleaved varieties
are also widely planted.

Description
Leaves alternate, always toothed and with
relatively straight veins. Male flowers

without petals, in early-blooming catkins;
female flowers in small, conelike, but leafy-
bracted clusters, the bracts 3–pointed and
dropping at maturity with the minute nut.

How to Grow
Most birches are not particular about soil,
but are balky about transplanting. Plant
balled or container-grown trees in early
spring for best results. Birches require
moist, well-drained soil for best growth.
Under moisture stress, several species are
subject to bronze birch borer, an insect
difficult to control that can kill a tree, and
birch leaf miner, which can ruin foliage by
late summer. Mulching and irrigating
reduce susceptibility. Prune birches in early
spring.

lenta pp. 170, 171
Sweet Birch; Cherry Birch; Black Birch.
Reaches 75 ft. (22.5 m) high. Leaves
oblong-oval, 3–5 in. (7.5–12.5 cm) long,
tapering at the tip and heart-shaped at the
base, double-toothed, an attractive yellow in
fall. Male catkins graceful in spring,
2–3 in. (5.0–7.5 cm) long. Female flower
cluster one-third as long as the leaf. An
aromatic tree: the bark of young twigs is
fragrant when bruised and wintergreen-
flavored when chewed. Mature bark is
handsome and resembles that of a cherry,
smooth and dark reddish brown. Soil should
be neither unusually wet nor dry; endures
considerable shade. Ontario to Ga. and
Tenn. Blooms winter to spring. Fruit in
fall. Zones 4–8.

maximowicziana pp. 168, 169
Monarch Birch. A vigorous species, reaching
80 ft. (24 m), with large, 6 in. (15 cm)
long, broad cordate leaves, coarsely double-
toothed, turning yellow in fall. Flowers are
minute, held in 4–5 in. (10.0–12.5 cm)
catkins in late winter and spring, followed
by 2–2½ in. (5–6 cm) conelike fruit in fall.
Bark reddish brown on young branches,
ochre or tawny gray on trunk and larger
branches, peeling away in long, wide papery
sheets. Prefers moist soil and is reputed to
be highly resistant to bronze birch borer.
Still uncommon, and some nurseries
have sold white-barked birches, perhaps
unknowingly, as Monarchs. Japan.
Blooms winter to spring. Fruit in fall.
Zones 5–7.

nigra pp. 170, 171

River Birch; Red Birch. A tree, 60–80 ft. (18–24 m) high, with attractive reddish-brown, ragged bark. Leaves somewhat ovalish, 1½–3½ in. (4–9 cm) long, double-toothed, whitish below when young. Female flower cluster about half as long as the leaves. Catkins in late winter and spring, 2–3 in. (5.0–7.5 cm) long, followed by 1¼ in. (3 cm) conelike fruit in fall. Tolerates moist or even wet sites, and will grow in average soils. Highly resistant to bronze birch borer. 'Heritage' is a cultivar with dark green leaves and salmon-white bark. Mass. to Fla. and westward, and hardy throughout the U.S. Blooms winter to spring. Fruit in fall. Zones 5–10.

papyrifera pp. 168, 169

Canoe Birch; Paper Birch. The white birch of e. North America. A tree, up to 90 ft. (27 m), with brilliantly white bark. Leaves more or less oval, but narrowed or wedge-shaped at the base, 3–5 in. (7.5–12.5 cm) long, double-toothed, turning clear yellow in fall. Female flower cluster one-third the leaf length. Pendant catkins in late winter and spring, 3–4 in. (7.5–10.0 cm) long, followed by small conelike fruits in fall. Not recommended for city use. Highly susceptible to bronze birch borer under drought conditions. Native in the cooler parts of North America. Blooms winter to spring. Fruit in fall. Zones 3–7.

pendula 'Purpurea' pp. 122, 123

Purple-leaf European Birch. A graceful tree resembling our Canoe, or Paper, Birch, but not as tall, to 50 ft. (15 m) high, and in old trees, with more or less drooping branches and resinous twigs. White bark gives way to black on old trunks. Leaves ovalish, mostly wedge-shaped at the base, double-toothed, 3–5 in. (7.5–12.5 cm) long, a deep reddish purple that contrasts dramatically with the white bark. Female flower cluster 1 in. (2.5 cm) long. This is a magnificent purple-leaved cultivar of the commonest white birch of cultivation, but not long-lived. Several other attractive cultivars exist, especially one with finely divided leaves and another with still more drooping branches that is nearly a weeping form. 'Purple Splendor' and 'Summer Glory' are other notable purple-leaved cultivars. Europe and Asia Minor.

Blooms winter to spring. Fruit in fall.
Zones 3–9.

platyphylla pp. *166, 167*

Asian White Birch. A handsome shade tree,
to 60 ft. (18 m). Tends to maintain a
central trunk, with graceful, slender
branches. Leaves bluish green, hold late in
fall, turning yellow. Flowers on catkins,
1½ in. (4 cm) long, blooming late winter to
spring, followed by 1 in. (2.5 cm) conelike
fruits in fall. Bark white. Borer resistance
good if mulched and irrigated when dry.
Two varieties are readily available,
B.p. szechuanica and *B.p. japonica;* the latter
is more ornamental. Manchuria and Korea.
Blooms winter to spring. Fruit in fall.
Zones 5–7.

Brachychiton
Chocolate family
Sterculiaceae

Brack-ee-ky'ton. The bottle trees, named
for the bottle-like swellings of their trunks,
are a small genus of Australian trees, most
deciduous, some species planted as
ornamentals in Fla. and Calif.

Description
They have alternate, and, in this species,
simple but variable leaves, some deeply
lobed. Flowers unisexual or polygamous,
blooming in very showy clusters or panicles
of scarlet or yellowish flowers. No petals,
but the calyx is bell-shaped and corolla-like.
Stamens 10–15, in a column surrounding
the pistil. Bloom in midsummer, after
which some species, but not *B. populneus,*
are briefly deciduous. Fruit woody, tardily
splitting.

How to Grow
Bottle trees are not particular about soil but
should be shaded by larger trees for at least
some of the day. They are quite tolerant of
drought.

populneus pp. *234, 235*

Bottle Tree; Kurrajong. A broadleaf
evergreen tree to 50 ft. (15 m) high, leaves
variable, scarcely more than 3 in. (7.5 cm)
long, lobed, or unlobed and ovalish,
shimmering in a breeze like aspen. Flowers
½ in. (13 mm) wide, held on 3 in.

(7.5 cm) panicles, yellowish white, reddish inside, and sometimes dark-spotted on the outside, hairy when young, not spectacular. Fruit 2–3 in. (5.0–7.5 cm) long, woody, causing messy litter. Often planted as a shade tree or windbreak. Blooming and fruiting seasons will vary with location. Often called *Sterculia diversifolia*. Australia. Blooms in late spring. Fruit summer to fall. Zones 8–10.

Brahea
Palm family
Palmae

Bra-he'a. A small genus of mostly Mexican, medium-sized ornamental fan palms.

Description
The stout trunks, toward the top, are usually covered with persistent but dead and drooping leaves, the lower part ringed and spineless. Leaves divided to the middle, or deeper, with many slender divisions.
Flowers in a cluster, appearing in the crown of leaves, branched and woolly. Sepals and petals 3 each. Stamens 6.

How to Grow
A tolerant genus, undemanding of soil conditions, but fares poorly in wet or shade. Withstands wind, heat, and drought.

armata pp. 192, 193
Blue Palm; Mexican Blue Palm. Not over 40 ft. (12 m) high, the trunk covered by the remains of withered leaf bases and their attendant shag. Leaves silvery blue, waxy, cut deeply into nearly 50 segments, the leafstalk spiny, up to 15 ft. (4.5 m) long. Flowering cluster 6–20 ft. (1.8–6.0 m) long, creamy white, spectacular, protruding beyond the crown of leaves and often to the ground. Fruit nearly round, fleshy, orange, ¾ in. (19 mm) long. Also known as *Glaucothea*. Lower Calif. Blooms summer to fall. Fruit fall to winter. Zones 9–10.

Butia
Palm family
Palmae

Bew'ti-a. A small group of tropical South
American feather palms, closely related to
the Coconut Palm. The species below is a
prominent avenue tree in s. Calif.

Description
Trunk stocky, solitary, not spiny, in nature
clothed with withered leaves or their scars.
Leaves rather stiff, arching gracefully beyond
the middle, the leaflets curving. Flower
cluster arising from between the lower
leaves, the male flowers with 6 stamens.
Fruit globelike or somewhat egg-shaped.

How to Grow
Butias are among the hardiest palms and
require no special culture, but should be
planted in enriched soil, especially in sandy
areas. Water abundantly during the growing
season for best foliage growth.

capitata pp. 194, 195
Pindo Palm. Trunk stout, to 20 ft. (6 m)
high, nearly 18 in. (45 cm) in diameter.
Leaves long and arching, the leaflets many,
2–12 ft. (0.6–3.5 m) long, and grayish
beneath. Clusters of small cream, pink, or
rarely maroon flowers protrude from a
spathe 3 ft. (90 cm) long, particularly in
midsummer. Fruit edible, nearly
egg-shaped, 1 in. (2.5 cm) long, in heavy
pendant clusters to 4 ft. (120 cm) long.
Also known as *Cocos australis.* Brazil.
Common in Fla. and Calif. Blooms winter
to summer. Fruit summer to fall. Zones
8–10.

Carpinus
Birch family
Betulaceae

Kar-py'nus. Hornbeam. Hard-wooded,
slow-growing, usually small deciduous trees
grown as specimen plants or large hedges.
Of the 35 known Eurasian and North
American species, only a few are of
horticultural interest, but they make
handsome small specimens or screen trees.

Description
Hornbeams have smooth, gray, close-fitting

bark and are twiggy enough, in the European cultivated species, to make hedges. Leaves alternate, but more or less 2-ranked, sharply toothed. Male and female flowers in different clusters on the same tree, both without sepals or petals, blooming before the leaves unfold. Male flowers in drooping, scaly catkins 2-forked at the tip. Between each scale are 3–13 stamens. Female catkins terminal. Fruit a ribbed nutlet, beneath and close to which is a flat, 3-lobed bract.

How to Grow
Most hornbeams will grow in ordinary garden soil, though they prefer some shade and protection from wind. They are hardy trees; practically no diseases or insects trouble them. They seldom need pruning but will withstand heavy pruning when used for tall hedges.

betulus 'Fastigiata' *pp. 134, 135*
Upright European Hornbeam. A handsome upright tree, to 50 ft. (15 m), often confused with the similar cultivar 'Columnaris', a more slender tree, in the nursery trade. Both are good candidates for screen planting, or as specimen plants in restricted areas. Leaves ovalish to oblong, birchlike, 3–4 in. (7.5–10.0 cm) long, yellow in fall. Female catkins 1½ in. (4 cm) long, the bract beneath each nutlet 2–3 in. (5.0–7.5 cm) long, the middle lobe much larger than the other two.
One of the finest trees for landscapes. Tolerates acid or alkaline soil, but must have good drainage. Best in full sun to light shade. Long-lived. Suited for hedges if trained for it. Europe to Iran. Blooms in winter to spring. Fruit in fall. Zones 5–9.

Catalpa
Trumpet-creeper family
Bignoniaceae

Ka-tal′pa. A genus of attractive deciduous trees, North American and Asiatic, valued for their rapid growth and spectacular spring flowers. Litter from catalpas is considerable: large leaves, florets, fruits, and branchlets. However, their bold foliage, spectacular flower display, and interesting winter pattern of long fruits hanging profusely from stout branches make catalpas good choices for parks, campus plantings, and as background trees on larger residential properties.

Description
Catalpas have long-stalked, opposite, and usually large leaves. Flowers showy, the corolla irregular and 2–lipped, the flowers grouped in handsome, branched, upright panicles. Fruit a long, cylindric, very narrow pod, the many seeds with a tuft of white hairs at each end.

How to Grow
Catalpas are easily grown in any ordinary garden soil, and young trees make an astonishing growth in a single season. Because they are soft-wooded trees that quickly reach maturity and then soon begin to fail, catalpas should be used with other, more permanent, trees in any mass planting. They tolerate both wet and drought conditions.

bignonioides pp. 90, 91
Southern Catalpa; Common Catalpa; Indian Bean. A round-headed tree with a short trunk, 30–40 ft. (9–12 m) high, often less in cultivation. Leaves broadly oval, 6–8 in. (15–20 cm) long, bad-smelling when crushed. Flower panicles 7–10 in. (17.5–25.0 cm) long, pyramidal, the flowers 1½ in. (4 cm) long, white, but yellow-striped inside, and spotted with purple-brown. Pod 9–14 in. (22.5–35.0 cm) long. Native from Ga. to Fla. and Miss., but naturalized in the ne. U.S. Cultivar 'Aurea' has yellow-tinted foliage. Blooms in spring. Fruit in fall. Zones 5–9.

speciosa pp. 90, 91
Northern Catalpa; Hardy Catalpa. Often up to 60 ft. (18 m), with a long trunk, the bark deep reddish brown. Leaves oval or oval-oblong, 8–12 in. (20–30 cm) long, densely hairy on the underside, not malodorous when crushed. Flower cluster rather sparse and open, 7 in. (17.5 cm) long panicles, the flowers 2 in. (5 cm) wide, white, but yellow-striped inside and inconspicuously spotted purple-brown. Pods 10–16 in. (25.0–40.5 cm) long. Blooms earlier than *C. bignonioides*. Cen. U.S. Blooms in spring. Fruit in fall. Zones 4–8.

Cedrus
Pine family
Pinaceae

See'drus. Cedar. A genus of 4 species of
handsome evergreens, the true cedars, 3 of
which are widely cultivated as screen and
background trees, as well as specimens for
lawns and parks.

Description
Leaves stiff, needle-like, 4–angled, scattered
or arranged in small, dense clusters. Flowers
unisexual, the male and female on the same
tree, wholly without petals or sepals. Cones
erect, their scales closely fitted, the seeds
between them triangular and broadly
winged. Cedars somewhat resemble larches
in the arrangement of their leaves, but,
unlike larches, they are true evergreens.

How to Grow
Cedars need open places and ordinary good
soil, preferably not too moist. They should
be transplanted as container-grown plants
for best chances of success, and perform well
when not exposed to drying winds, summer
or winter. Cedars have no serious pests or
diseases.

atlantica 'Glauca' *pp. 270, 271*
Blue Atlas Cedar. An upright tree, 40–
60 ft. (12–18 m) high, taller in native
habitat, with a main leader or trunk. Leaves
silvery blue, just under 1 in. (2.5 cm) long,
rigid. Cones 2–3 in. (5.0–7.5 cm) long,
light brown. A beautiful wide-spreading
evergreen tree, width about three-quarters of
height. Needs plenty of space for best
landscape use. Tolerates drought. N. Africa.
Cones throughout the year. Zones 6–9.

deodara *pp. 272, 273*
Deodar Cedar. A tree, up to 150 ft. (45 m)
high in nature, reaching 80 ft. (24 m) as
usually cultivated. Branch tips, including
the leader, generally pendulous. Leaves dark
bluish- or grayish-green, nearly 2 in. (5 cm)
long, not very rigid. Cones 3–5 in.
(7.5–12.5 cm) long, reddish brown. One of
the most graceful of all evergreens.
'Shalimar', 'Kingsville', and 'Kashmir' are
the hardier cultivars, possibly in descending
order. Himalayas. Cones throughout the
year. Zones 7–8.

libani pp. 272, 273
Cedar-of-Lebanon. A tree, up to 100 ft.
(30 m), usually less in cultivation, with a
single trunk or several trunk-like branches,
its leading shoot generally erect. Leaves dark
green, 1 in. (2.5 cm) long. Cones 3–4 in.
(7.5–10.0 cm) long, brown. The var.
stenocoma, from s. Turkey, is an erect tree
and is hardy in warmer sections of zone 5.
Asia Minor and Syria. Cones throughout the
year. Zones 6–7.

Celtis
Elm family
Ulmaceae

Sell'tis. Hackberry. Elmlike, but usually
medium-sized, round-headed deciduous
trees, only a few of the 70 widely
distributed species cultivated as shade and
background trees. Hackberries are not
highly ornamental, but are valuable trees for
difficult sites.

Description
Leaves alternate, stalked, more or less
oblique at the base, and 3–veined. Flowers
inconspicuous, unisexual or polygamous,
without petals and with a 4– to 5–lobed
calyx. Stamens 4–5. Fruit a greenish or
blackish, bony, egg-shaped or rounded
drupe, the pulp scanty, but often tasty.

How to Grow
Hackberries are remarkably tolerant of soil
conditions—acid or alkaline, somewhat wet
or very dry—and are highly resistant to
wind and city air pollution. Subject to
witches'-broom, a harmless bunching of
twigs, and to a harmless but disfiguring
insect that causes protuberances on the
leaves called nipple galls.

occidentalis pp. 172, 173
Common Hackberry. A tree up to 100 ft.
(30 m), usually lower and round-headed.
Leaves ovalish or oblongish, 3–5 in.
(7.5–12.5 cm) long, tapering at the tip,
but rounded at the base, usually toothed,
except toward the base. Fruit greenish
orange, but ultimately blackish purple,
nearly ⅓ in. (8 mm) long, somewhat pear-
shaped; thin pulp has a pleasant taste. In
maturity, assumes the appearance of
American Elm. A similar species, hardy in

zones 5–9, is *C. laevigata,* the Sugar
Hackberry. E. North America. Fruit in fall.
Zones 4–8.

Ceratonia
Pea family
Leguminosae

See-ra-tone'ee-a. Carob. One species,
a broadleaf evergreen tree from the
e. Mediterranean, cultivated since antiquity
for its pods, which contain a sweet edible
pulp. These are St. John's bread, the
"wild locusts" of John the Baptist.

Description
Leaves alternate, wavy, arranged feather-
fashion, usually 4 pairs on each branchlet.
Fruit a long leathery pod containing a
sweet pulp surrounding the seeds.

How to Grow
Cultivated outdoors in zone 9, and as a
slow-growing pot plant. Carob grows in any
well-drained soil, and tolerates drought.
Remove lower branches to hasten
establishment as a tree rather than a large
shrub. Small plants flower readily. Carob
needs room; width may equal height. Both
male and female trees must be planted to
ensure fruit.

siliqua pp. 230, 231
Carob. A rounded tree, 20–50 ft. (6–15 m)
high. Leaves compound, with 2–3 pairs of
broad, leathery leaflets that are 2–4 in.
(5–10 cm) long. Flowers red, unisexual,
not pealike, ¼ in. (6 mm) wide, without
petals, in racemes 6 in. (15 cm) long.
Dark brown pods 4–12 in. (10–30 cm)
long, slightly flattened, not splitting, the
seeds surrounded by a sweetish, nutritious
pulp. A densely-crowned broadleaf evergreen
tree, planted for its shade, flowers, and
fruit. E. Mediterranean. Blooms in spring.
Fruit in early fall. Zones 9–10.

Cercidiphyllum
Katsura family
Cercidiphyllaceae

Sir-sid-i-fil'lum. One species, an Asiatic
deciduous tree, commonly called the

Katsura Tree. A handsome upright ornamental planted as a specimen or shade tree.

Description
Leaves opposite, or nearly so, mostly borne on short spurs, the veins arranged finger-fashion. Male and female flowers on different trees. Flowers small, without petals, borne on the spurs as the leaves unfold. Fruit a splitting pod with many seeds. Both flowers and fruit are ornamentally unimportant.

How to Grow
Katsura Trees grow readily, though they prefer ample moisture, especially when young. Mulch and irrigate for best results. The species has no serious diseases or pests, but the bark is soft and easily damaged.

japonicum pp. 182, 183
Katsura Tree. Reaches 30–50 ft. (9–15 m) in cultivation, up to 100 ft. (30 m) in native habitats. Often divided into several trunks or stems. Leaves nearly round, heart-shaped at the base, 2–4½ in. (5.0–11.5 cm) long, shallowly and bluntly toothed, pale beneath. These are handsome foliage trees, the leaves purplish when unfolding, changing in the fall from green to yellow and scarlet. The var. *sinense* usually has a single trunk and longer-stalked leaves. Japan. Zones 5–8.

Cercis
Pea family
Leguminosae

Sir'sis. Redbud; Judas Tree. Very attractive shrubs or small deciduous trees, 4 of the 7 known species often grown for their showy flowers. Their very early bloom, usually about peach-blossom time, makes them useful landscape accents while many plants are still dormant.

Description
Flowers bloom in early spring, mostly before the leaves expand. Unlike most plants of the pea family, the leaves are not compound, but simple and usually roundish or heart-shaped, stalked, and with the veins arranged finger-fashion. Flowers small, but usually numerous, pealike or nearly so, rose-

pink, rose-purple, or white in the cultivated
forms. Stamens 10, not united. Fruit a flat,
thin, and narrowly winged legume, its seeds
flattened.

How to Grow
Redbuds are easy to grow in open, sandy
loams, but do not like heavy, moist sites
and are hard to move when mature. In some
parts of the country, a vascular wilt disease
or a canker disease can be troublesome.
Drought may increase chance of disease;
mulch and irrigate during dry spells.

canadensis pp. 86, 87
Eastern Redbud. A small, round-headed
tree, not usually over 35 ft. (10.5 m) high,
often half that height. Leaves broadly oval
or nearly round, heart-shaped at the base,
3–5 in. (7.5–12.5 cm) long, pointed at the
tip. Flowers ½ in. (13 mm) long, cerise-
pink, in clusters 1–2 in. (2.5–5.0 cm)
wide, very numerous, often borne on mature
trunks and branches. There are white- and
double-flowered cultivars. Pod 3 in.
(7.5 cm) long. Tolerant of acid or alkaline
soil, sun or partial shade. Cannot tolerate
wet soil. N.Y. and Ontario to Fla. and Tex.
Blooms in spring. Fruit in fall. Zones 5–8;
semihardy 4.

Chamaecyparis
Cypress family
Cupressaceae

Kam-ee-sip'ar-is. False Cypress. This genus
has 8 species of tall, columnar evergreen
trees, native to North America and Asia.
They are very valuable timber trees, and
their numerous horticultural cultivars are
perhaps the commonest evergreens in
cultivation. They are extremely effective in
mass evergreen plantings or as accents and
specimen trees; however, most of the false
cypresses offered by nurseries are shrubs,
not trees.

Description
Leaves in mature plants scale-like, minute,
closely pressed against the flattened, often
fanlike, branchlets. In the juvenile state, the
leaves are needle-like but softish, and stand
out from the twigs. In some cultivated
specimens both sorts of leaves will be found,
in others mature foliage may never form, and

juvenile foliage persists for the life of the
plant, even though it grows to a full-sized
tree. Such forms, with permanently juvenile
foliage, were formerly called Retinispora or
Retinospora, a name also applied to *Thuja*
cultivars with similar persistently juvenile
foliage. Flowers minute and inconspicuous.
Fruit round, the scales of the small cone
pointed or keeled in the middle, the cones
not showy, as in pines or firs, generally
maturing at the end of the first year.

How to Grow
These extremely popular evergreens are
grown throughout the U.S. except in the
dry, hot plains and deserts. They do best in
reasonably humid regions, and prefer acid
soils over neutral or alkaline ones. They
need moisture, and do not like hot, dry
winds. Mulch false cypress with wood chips
or shredded bark, as the cultivated form
below is shallow-rooted. Prune to keep
shapely; otherwise they are no more difficult
to grow than any other evergreen.

***nootkatensis* 'Pendula'** *pp. 250, 251*
Weeping Nootka False Cypress; Weeping
Alaska Cedar. Grows slowly and narrowly
to 30 ft. (9 m), graceful branches slightly
upturned, branchlets hang vertically.
Leaves flat and scale-like, dull, dark green
on both sides, rarely needle-like. Cones
½ in. (13 mm) thick or less, glaucous.
Grace and elegance combine in this
striking accent tree. Alaska to Oreg. Cones
in fall. Zones 5–9.

Chorisia
Silk-cotton tree family
Bombacaceae

Ko-ris′i-a. A small genus of South
American deciduous trees, one planted in
zones 9 and 10 for its highly ornamental
flowers.

Description
Chorisias have alternate, compound leaves,
the leaflets arranged fanwise, and large
solitary flowers. Fruit a capsule, the seeds
with a silky floss.

How to Grow
Chorisias require excellent drainage and
monthly deep watering for success. Reduce

watering in late summer for mature trees to encourage flowering.

speciosa pp. 78, 79

Floss Silk Tree. A tree, up to 60 ft. (18 m), planted for ornament in s. Fla. Heavy trunk, green when young, is studded with broad spines. Leaflets usually 5, stalked, more or less lance-shaped, and toothed. Flowers solitary in axils, nearly 3 in. (7.5 cm) wide, pink, purple, or white, appearing profusely just after leaves fall. New leaves sprout as flowers fade, so the tree is never completely bare. Brazil. Blooms in fall. Zones 9–10.

Cinnamomum
Laurel family
Lauraceae

Sin-na-mo'mum. A genus of commercially important, aromatic evergreen trees, mostly from tropical Asia, 3 of them widely grown as the source of camphor and cinnamon. The species below is a stately ornamental or shade tree grown in the southernmost states.

Description
Leaves often distinctly 3–veined from the base. Flowers small, not showy, without petals, the calyx 6–lobed. Stamens 9 or fewer, in 3 series together with a fourth series of sterile stamens. Fruit a berry, set in a cuplike receptacle.

How to Grow
Camphor Trees do well in a sandy loam or in a variety of other soils. They have a slow to moderate growth rate, but are massive and oaklike at maturity, and so are not suitable for small spaces. No serious insect pests are known, but verticillium wilt may strike. If so, prune out affected branches and use nitrogen fertilizer and deep watering to improve vigor.

camphora pp. 224, 225

Camphor Tree. Not over 40–50 ft. (12–15 m) high, and wide-spreading. Bark is dark, almost black when wet. Shiny green foliage, new growth with tints of pink or red. Leaves alternate, more or less elliptic, but tapering at the tip, 4–5 in. (10.0–12.5 cm) long, pale underneath. Flowers yellow, the clusters shorter than the leaves, not important. Bruised foliage is camphor-scented, and in Formosa the wood is the commercial source of camphor. A stately park tree in s. Calif. and in the Gulf Coast region, where it occasionally escapes. China and Japan. Zones 8–10.

Cladrastis
Pea family
Leguminosae

Kla-dras′tis. A small genus of decorative deciduous trees, the native Yellowwood often planted for its spring flowers.

Description
The genus has alternate, compound leaves, the leaflets arranged feather-fashion, with an odd one at the end. Flowers fragrant, white in cultivated species, pealike, in showy drooping panicles. Fruit a pod, oblongish and flattened.

How to Grow
Transplant balled or container-grown small plants. A well-drained soil is important, but pH is not. Prune while tree is young to eliminate narrow crotches that are likely to split in later years, as wood is brittle.

lutea pp. 94, 95
American Yellowwood. A smooth-barked tree, 30–50 ft. (9–15 m) high, its wood yellow. Attractive light green foliage. Fall color yellow but not outstanding. Leaflets 7–9, ovalish, and about 3–4 in. (7.5–10.0 cm) long. Flowers 1 in. (2.5 cm) long, the panicle 10–15 in. (25–38 cm) long and drooping. Pod 4–5 in. (10.0–12.5 cm) long. A deservedly popular tree that thrives in a wide variety of soils and produces a showy bloom. Ga. and N.C. to Ill. and Mo. Blooms in spring. Fruit summer to fall. Zones 4–8.

Cornus
Dogwood family
Cornaceae

Kor′nus. Dogwood. The dogwoods, sometimes called cornels, are an important genus of deciduous garden shrubs and trees, popular for their handsome flowers, often

brightly colored fruits, and, in some
species, for the winter effect of their colored
twigs. All the 45 known species are native
to the north temperate zones.

Description
Leaves generally opposite, without marginal
teeth. Flowers small, with 4 small petals
and 4 stamens. In many species these
flowers are white and grouped in flat-topped
or rounded cymes resembling viburnums. In
a few species the flowers are inconspicuous,
greenish, and set in the midst of several
colored bracts that are often mistakenly
called petals, as in the Flowering
Dogwood and the Japanese Dogwood.
Fruit fleshy.

How to Grow
Fortunately, dogwoods grow easily in any
good garden soil, the exceptions being
noted for each species.

florida pp. 114–117
Flowering Dogwood. A showy tree, up to
30 ft. (9 m), often spreading wider than
high. Leaves oval, 3–5 in. (7.5–12.5 cm)
long, consistently coloring red or purplish
for a magnificent autumn show. Flowers
small, greenish, set in the midst of 4 large
3–4 in. (7.5–10.0 cm) showy, white,
notched, and petal-like bracts in spring.
Buttonlike flower buds are held at terminals
of upturned twigs on horizontal branches.
Fruit scarlet, ⅜ in. (9 mm) long.
In its natural state, the Flowering Dogwood
is a tree of forest edges, the aristocrat of
native flowering trees. A very popular red-
or pink-bracted variety, *rubra,* commonly
called the Red Flowering Dogwood, has
been cultivated since 1731. Cultivars
include one with weeping branches, and
another with 6–8 large bracts (as though
double-flowered) named 'Pleniflora'. Others
sport variegated foliage or extra-large bracts.
Dogwoods need excellent drainage, but
cannot stand extended drought. Mulch and
water regularly. E. U.S. Blooms in spring.
Fruit in fall. Zones 5–9.

kousa pp. 112, 113

Kousa Dogwood; Japanese Dogwood. An
Asiatic counterpart of our Flowering
Dogwood. It is a lower tree, with smaller
leaves turning scarlet in fall. Blooms about
two weeks later with similar flowers and
pointed bracts 2 in. (5 cm) wide. Pinkish

fruits are in a headlike cluster of fused drupes, slightly resembling a strawberry or large raspberry, 1 in. (2.5 cm) wide. A variety from China, *C. kousa chinensis,* is nearly identical. Japan and Korea. Blooms in spring. Fruit in fall. Zones 5–8.

mas pp. 118, 119
Cornelian Cherry. A hardy shrub or small tree to 25 ft. (7.5 m) high, the naked twigs of which are crowded with short-stalked, small, ¾ in. (19 mm) wide, headlike umbels of minute yellow flowers in March or April. Leaves oval or elliptic, 3–4 in. (7.5–10.0 cm) long, reddish in fall. Fruit edible, the size of a cherry, ⅝ in. (16 mm) long, but acid; scarlet, ripening in late summer. It tolerates smoky atmosphere better than most trees. Pest-free. Eurasia. Blooms in spring. Fruit in summer. Zones 5–7.

nuttallii pp. 110, 111
Pacific Dogwood. A western species similar to Flowering Dogwood (*C. florida*), but a much taller tree, reaching 75 ft. (22.5 m), usually with 6 petal-like white or pinkish bracts instead of 4. Bracts 4 in. (10 cm) wide. Fruit red or orange, ⅖ in. (10 mm) long. Fall color yellow to red. Easily cultivated in the Pacific Northwest if given good drainage and frequent watering. British Columbia to s. Calif. Blooms in spring, frequently flowering again at the end of summer. Fruit summer to fall. Zones 7–9.

Crataegus
Rose family
Rosaceae

Kra-tee′gus. Hawthorn; Thorn; Thornapple. An enormous genus of perhaps 1000 species of thorny deciduous shrubs and trees, found in the north temperate zone but most common in e. North America. Less than 20 are landscape worthy, grown for their spring flowers and bright fall fruit, although any of the wild species enhance informal plantings, and all attract wildlife, especially birds.

Description
Leaves alternate, always toothed or lobed, none truly evergreen. Older specimens are round-topped with pleasingly horizontal

branching. Bark on twigs and younger
branches usually light gray, attractive in
winter. Flowers white—red or pink in some
horticultural forms—nearly always in small
corymbs. Sepals and petals 5, the stamens
5–25, sometimes the anthers pink or
purple. Fruit resembles a miniature apple,
nearly always brightly colored, a very
attractive fall feature of the group.

How to Grow

Although most of the species given below
will grow in ordinary garden soil, often in
poor soil, hawthorns prefer limestone
regions and an open, sandy loam. Because of
their thorns, impenetrable barriers can be
made of them, although they do not stand
being clipped for hedges.

A number of insects may bother
hawthorns—lace bugs, aphids, scale insects,
mites, leaf skeletonizers, tent caterpillars,
and borers. In some areas, fireblight and
cedar apple rust diseases are problems.
Frequent inspection and timely treatment
are important. Despite such pests,
hawthorns are a worthy genus of small
ornamental trees, withstanding drought and
weather fluctuations exceedingly well.

crus-galli pp. 98, 99

Cockspur Hawthorn. A large shrub or small
tree, up to 30 ft. (9 m) high, tolerant of
city conditions. The thorns are numerous,
slender and sharp, to 4 in. (10 cm) long.
Leaves lustrous-green, oblongish, wedge-
shaped at the base, to 3 in. (7.5 cm) long,
toothed in the upper part, bronze-red in
fall. Flowers ½ in. (13 mm) wide in 2–
3 in. (5.0–7.5 cm) corymbs. Fruit nearly
round, ½ in. (13 mm) in diameter. There is
a thornless variety, *C.c. inermis.* Tolerates
drought. Quebec to Mich. and S.C. Blooms
in spring. Fruit fall to winter. Zones 5–9.

× *lavallei* pp. 98, 99

Lavalle Hawthorn. A tree up to 25 ft.
(7.5 m) high, the thorns stout and 2 in.
(5 cm) long. Leaves elliptic or oblongish, to
4 in. (10 cm) long, unequally toothed,
purplish in fall. Flowers white, with a red
disk, ¾ in. (19 mm) wide, held in 3 in.
(7.5 cm) corymbs. Fruit persisting through
the winter, brick-red, ½ in. (13 mm) long.
A hybrid between *C. crus-galli* and *C.
pubescens.* Blooms in spring. Fruit fall to
winter. Zones 5–9.

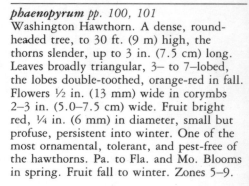

phaenopyrum *pp. 100, 101*
Washington Hawthorn. A dense, round-
headed tree, to 30 ft. (9 m) high, the
thorns slender, up to 3 in. (7.5 cm) long.
Leaves broadly triangular, 3– to 7–lobed,
the lobes double-toothed, orange-red in fall.
Flowers ½ in. (13 mm) wide in corymbs
2–3 in. (5.0–7.5 cm) wide. Fruit bright
red, ¼ in. (6 mm) in diameter, small but
profuse, persistent into winter. One of the
most ornamental, tolerant, and pest-free of
the hawthorns. Pa. to Fla. and Mo. Blooms
in spring. Fruit fall to winter. Zones 5–9.

viridis **'Winter King'** *pp. 100, 101*
Winter King Hawthorn. Introduced in
1955, so ultimate height is not known, but
probably not more than 30 ft. (9 m), since
older plants grow wide faster than tall.
Attractive glossy-green foliage, yellow fall
color. White flowers in spring, ¾ in.
(19 mm) wide in 2 in. (5 cm) corymbs.
Fruit bright red, ⅜ in. (9 mm) in diameter,
persisting well into winter. Bark silvery
gray, thorns sparse. Rather ungainly
branching at first, maturing into a round-
headed small tree. Quite tolerant of
drought. Blooms in spring. Fruit fall to
winter. Zones 5–7.

Cryptomeria
Bald cypress family
Taxodiaceae

Krip-to-meer′ri-a. Japanese Cedar. A single
species of evergreen tree from China and
Japan, much used there for the planting of
temple gardens and ceremonial avenues.

Description
A narrowly columnar tree, its evergreen
leaves small, awl-shaped, the tips always
curved inward, more or less completely
clothing the twigs, spirally arranged, and
keeled. Cones nearly globe-shaped, the
scales wedge-shaped but pointed at the tip.

How to Grow
Japanese Cedar is less particular about soil
than it is about climatic conditions. It
grows well near the seacoasts and in other
humid areas, but fails in regions of great
summer heat and sparse rainfall. For best
results, plant Japanese Cedars in moist, acid
soil and water during drought.

japonica pp. 252, 253

Japanese Cedar. A picturesque tree,
narrowly but irregularly columnar, to
160 ft. (48 m) in its native home, here
much lower, 60 ft. (18 m) tall. Hardy only
to zone 6, and often failing there, and
nearly always turning a bronzy color in
winter, but becoming green the following
season. Farther south it does much better.
Bark reddish brown and shreddy. Leaves
small, to ½ in. (13 mm) long, nearly
covering the twigs, bluish green, in spiral
patterns, keeled on both sides. Cones
globose, 1 in. (2.5 cm) wide, scales wedge-
shaped and pointed at tips. Usually sold as
C. japonica 'Lobbii', a compact glossy-green
cultivar, similar to the species. China and
Japan. Cones in fall. Zones 6–8.

Cupaniopsis
Soapberry family
Sapindaceae

Kew-pay-nee'op-sis. About 55 species of
woody plants, mostly from Australia and
New Caledonia. The species below is a
broadleaf evergreen grown as a shade tree in
frost-free areas.

Description
A genus of trees and shrubs with alternate,
pinnate leaves. Flowers in panicles, with 5
petals and 5 sepals. Fruit is typically a
brown, leathery 3–lobed capsule.

How to Grow
Forgiving and tolerant of wet and salt.
However, trees are susceptible to frost
damage in the colder areas of zone 9.

anacardioides pp. 232, 233

Carrot Wood. A tree of moderate growth,
taller than wide, reaching 40 ft. (12 m) in
height. Evergreen leaves are alternate,
pinnately compound, 6 in. (15 cm) long
with 6–10 leathery leaflets, each about 4 in.
(10 cm) long. Flowers and fruit
inconspicuous.
A relatively neat, clean tree casting fairly
dense shade. Brown bark-like fruits appear
on mature trees in late spring, producing
brief but abundant litter. Deep-rooting,
suitable for lawns and near paving, but not
drought-tolerant. Now one of the most
widely planted trees in zones 9 and 10,

particularly in Calif. Tolerates wet.
Australia. Zones 10; semihardy 9.

× *Cupressocyparis*
Cypress family
Cupressaceae

Kew-press-o-sip'aris. Leyland Cypress. A
fertile hybrid species found in the garden of
C.J. Leyland in Welshpool, England, in
1888, the offspring of *Chamaecyparis
nootkatensis* and *Cupressus macrocarpa*. Leyland
Cypress are valued as fast-growing screen
and specimen evergreens.

Description
Similar to *Chamaecyparis nootkatensis* in habit
and foliage, with branchlets or twigs in
fanlike growths, particularly toward the
upper part of the tree. Leaves flat and scale-
like, green on both sides, rarely needle-like.
Cones round, maturing the same year as the
minute flowers, the scales pointed or keeled
in the middle, usually 8, seeds usually 5 to
a scale.

How to Grow
Because their roots are stringy and difficult
to ball and burlap, plant container-grown
specimens. Almost any soil is acceptable
except soggy, extremely dry, or highly
alkaline ones. Plants need sun or partial
shade—to 75 percent of full sun. Pruning is
seldom necessary, other than to remove an
occasional wayward branch, but Leyland
Cypress responds well to shearing. Trees are
usually pest-free, but mites are sometimes
troublesome in the Southeast, borers in the
Southwest.

leylandii pp. 248, 249

Leyland Cypress. A fast-growing, narrowly
conical tree reaching 100 ft. (30 m) at
maturity, about one-fifth as wide as tall
when young, one-fourth as wide after 30–
40 years. Foliage blue-green on flat
spraylike branchlets, feathery. Cones
approximately ⅝ in. (16 mm) in diameter.
Often grows incredibly fast in youth.
Excellent for screens, windbreaks, hedges,
and large formal specimens. Cultivars
include 'Leighton Green', with grayish-
green foliage; 'Castewellan', yellow; and
'Naylor's Blue', soft bluish green. Tolerates
salt. Cones in fall. Zones 6–10.

Cupressus
Cypress family
Cupressaceae

Kew-pres'sus. Cypress. Magnificent
coniferous evergreens, mostly from the
warmer parts of the Old World, a few from
western North America, most unfortunately
not hardy for most of the U.S. Of the 12
known species, half are commonly grown
over most of the warmer sections of the
world. These are the true cypresses, and
make excellent accents, screens, and
specimens.

Description
Foliage aromatic, the branchlets densely
clothed with small, usually 4-angled leaves
pressed against the twigs. Leaves are very
small, opposite, and scale-like. Often young
plants or shoots sport longer, spreading
leaves; otherwise, leaves hug the twigs.
Cones nearly globe-shaped, composed of
6–12 woody scales, often nearly prickly at
the scale tip, each scale holding many
narrowly winged, flattened seeds. Cones
mature in 2 years.

How to Grow
Plant container-grown cypresses in full sun,
in well-drained soil. Irrigate during dry
spells in the first few years; older trees are
quite drought-tolerant. Mulching is
advisable. Prune unruly branches any time
to maintain neatness; other pruning is
unnecessary.

macrocarpa pp. *274, 275*
Monterey Cypress. A tree up to 75 ft.
(22.5 m) high, conical in youth, broad and
spreading with age. If grown at seaside,
winds give it an irregular, picturesque form.
Leaves blunt or 4–sided, dark green. Cones
nearly 1½ in. (4 cm) in diameter. Used as
specimens, screens, windbreaks, and clipped
hedges. Best grown in regions of cool ocean
breezes; in hot dry sites trees often develop
a fatal canker disease. There are several
cultivars, one with the young foliage
yellow. Calif., south of Monterey. Cones in
fall. Zones 8–10.

sempervirens 'Stricta' pp. *244, 245*
Columnar Italian Cypress. A narrowly
upright cultivar of the ancient
Mediterranean cypress. Grows to 75 ft.
(22.5 m) high, the branches erect,

branchlets or twigs flattened, the leaves dark green, blunt, 4–sided. Cones to 1½ in. (4 cm) in diameter. A strong formal element in the landscape, best used in rows or groups. Susceptible to mites. Cultivar 'Glauca' has bluish foliage. S. Eur. to Sw. Asia. Cones in fall. Zones 8–10.

Delonix
Bean family
Leguminosae

Dee-lon'icks. A genus of the Old World tropics, 3 deciduous tree species, the one described below widely planted in Fla. for its spectacular flowers and rapid growth.

Description
Alternate leaves, doubly pinnately compound. Flowers showy, in corymbose racemes; the petals clawlike. Fruit a large flat woody pod.

How to Grow
"Plant it and stand back," is only slightly exaggerated cultural advice for this spectacular flowering tree, commonly grown only in frost-free southern Fla. Almost any soil found there will suffice; it does need sunshine. Don't plant close to pavement because expanding roots can lift or break it.

regia pp. 80, 81
Royal Poinciana; Peacock Flower; Flamboyant. A broad-headed tree not over 50 ft. (15 m) high. Leaves twice-compound, 1–2 ft. (30–60 cm) long, composed of scores of small oblong leaflets. The tree is usually bare in spring. Flowers not pealike, 3–4 in. (7.5–10.0 cm) wide, the 5 long-clawed petals brilliant scarlet, or one of them yellow-striped, lending a yellow tinge to the overall scarlet. The flowers are in numerous racemes. A Royal Poinciana in flower is a memorable sight. Fruit a flat woody pod 2 in. (5 cm) wide and to 2 ft. (60 cm) long. This most gorgeous of cultivated trees will stand a variety of soils. Madagascar. Blooms in summer. Fruit fall to spring. Zone 10.

Eriobotrya
Rose family
Rosaceae

E-ri-o-bo′tri-a. A small genus of Asiatic evergreen trees and shrubs related to *Sorbus* and *Amelanchier*. One species, the Loquat, is widely grown in Fla. as an ornamental tree with edible fruit.

Description
Leaves nearly sessile, toothed. Flowers white in broad, usually woolly, panicles. Fruit a pome with one or several large seeds.

How to Grow
The Loquat is grown in Calif., the Gulf states, and Fla., but seldom fruits north of the citrus areas. The tree withstands temperatures of 10–15° F (−12.0 to −9.5° C) without material injury, but in midwinter the fruit or blossoms are damaged by a few degrees of frost. Plant in full sun, preferably in deep, well-drained soil. Mulch and water regularly, but do not plant in wet areas. Once established, Loquats will endure considerable drought. Fireblight is a problem in some areas; consult local authorities for a suitable resistant cultivar for your area.

japonica pp. 206, 207
Loquat; Japanese Plum; Japanese Medlar. A tree, up to 30 ft. (9 m) high, often as wide as high, the leaves nearly stalkless, leathery and crisp, nearly 1 ft. (30 cm) long, and rusty-hairy beneath. Foliage alone is attractive enough to warrant landscape use. Flowers fragrant, white, ½ in. (13 mm) wide, in hairy panicles 4–6 in. (10–15 cm) long. Petals 5, clawed. Stamens about 20. Flowers noticeable, but not particularly notable.
Fruit a 1–2 in. (2.5–5.0 cm) long fleshy pome, plum-shaped, 1- to 2–seeded, its yellow edible flesh agreeably acid, good for eating raw and for making jelly. Some of the improved cultivated varieties have fruits nearly 3 in. (7.5 cm) long. A variegated-leaved form is grown chiefly for ornament. Cen. China. Blooms in fall. Fruit in spring. Zones 8–10.

Erythrina
Pea family
Leguminosae

E-ry-thri'na. Coral Tree. A genus of about 100 species of handsome tropical shrubs and trees, both broadleaf evergreens and deciduous plants. They have many uses in the tropics, but are planted only as ornamentals in zone 10, where their usually showy flowers are mostly borne before or after, not with, the leaves. They are commonly called coral trees because of their striking flowers.

Description
Leaves compound, the leaflets usually only 3 and broad. Flowers almost pealike, very handsome, borne in large racemes. Pod long, somewhat woody, usually constricted between the seeds, which are usually brightly colored, hence sometimes called coral bean.

How to Grow
Coral trees appear to have no special soil preferences except that good drainage is necessary. Water regularly during dry spells.

caffra pp. 234, 235
Kaffirboom Coral Tree. A large, spreading tree, to 60 ft. (18 m) high, and equally wide if given room, the leaves semi-evergreen. Thorns on young trees disappear with age. Terminal leaflets broadly egg-shaped, to 7 in. (17.5 cm) long. Flowering as the new leaves expand. Flower clusters short, 6–8 in. (15–20 cm) long, the flowers bright red-orange, with the standard to 2 in. (5 cm) long in short racemes. Flowers last 4–6 weeks. Fruits to 4½ in. (11.5 cm) long, not ornamental. Seeds are red with a black spot. This is a good species for seashore planting. South Africa. Blooms late winter to early spring. Zones 9–10.

Eucalyptus
Myrtle family
Myrtaceae

You-ka-lip'tus. Gum Tree; Stringy-bark. An enormous genus of over 500 species of chiefly Australian, sometimes gigantic, mostly aromatic evergreen trees, widely planted in zones 9 and 10 for their striking flowers and foliage, but not usually hardy elsewhere. Eucalyptus are especially popular in Calif., where over 70 species are grown, all prized for their freedom from pests, and some as a source of bee pollen. The fruits and leafy branches are often colored and used in dried flower decorations.

Many valuable timber trees are not included here, although some are intensely cultivated for this purpose, since they grow quickly, to often incredible heights—200 ft. (60 m) or more. Some species, such as Blue Gum, *E. globulus,* are messy, brittle, and dangerous during storms; several better garden species are available. The following species are best for landscape use, though many other good or even excellent species are not mentioned here. See your local horticultural authorities for those best suited to your area.

Description
Leaves prevailingly alternate without marginal teeth, often very variable on the same plant. Flowers usually in the leaf axils, often in small umbels, but sometimes in branched clusters, white, yellow, or red. Calyx bell- or turban-shaped, the calyx lobes and petals forming a lid at flowering time, and separating from the calyx tube. Fruit a capsule opening at the top.

How to Grow
Eucalyptus grow easily in Calif., since they do well in a variety of soils. Most will stand periods of flooding and drought. Be sure to know the ultimate size of a species before planting, and choose a site with ample space.

Small plants, even from flats, are best for planting. Avoid plants with long leafless spaces on branches, those obviously heavily pruned, and those with pot-bound circling roots. If you find you have a root-crowded plant, wash the soil from the roots and spread them radially over a mound in a wide planting hole. Prune to shape and for strong crotch angles a year after planting and regularly thereafter to establish a good branch structure. Prune from spring to late summer.

camaldulensis p. 236
Red Gum. A slender, large tree, 80–125 ft. (24–38 m) high, with smooth tan and gray

mottled bark. Leaves lance-shaped, tapering to a point, thin. Flowers in groups of 5–10. Fruits to 5/16 in. (8.5 mm) long. Flowers and fruits unimportant. Grows best in alkaline soil. Tolerates wet and drought. Formerly called *E. rostrata*. Australia. Zones 9–10; semihardy 8.

citriodora p. 237

Lemon-scented Gum. A slender tree, 50–75 ft. (15.0–22.5 m) high. Bark smooth, tan, peeling to reveal cream-colored patches. Leaves lance-shaped, pendulous, strongly lemon-scented. Flowers in groups of 3–5. Fruits to 5/16 in. (8.5 mm) across. Flowers and fruits unimportant. Adaptable to varying amounts of moisture in soil. Young trees often need staking. Australia. Zones 9–10.

ficifolia pp. 212, 213

Red Flowering Gum. A tree, usually single-trunked, to 40 ft. (12 m), bark stringy, red to gray. Leaves leathery, 3–6 in. (7.5–15.0 cm) long, resembling those of the Rubber Tree. Flowers orange to red, sometimes pink or nearly white, 1 in. (2.5 cm) wide in spectacular clusters to 12 in. (30 cm) long. Fruit a 4–sided capsule, ½ in. (13 mm) wide, resembling dice cubes with swollen bottoms. Both flowers and fruit often occur sporadically outside of their normal seasons.
Best grown on the Pacific Coast, seldom successful inland. Responds poorly to regular irrigation, but is fairly drought-tolerant. Prune seed capsules from young trees to reduce weight on branches. Australia. Blooms in summer. Fruit in late summer. Zones 9–10.

gunnii p. 237

Cider Gum. A vertical tree, to 75 ft. (22.5 m) high, bark smooth, green and white. Leaves lance-shaped. Flowers to ½ in. (13 mm) long, in groups of 3. Creamy white in springtime. Fruits to ⅓ in. (8 mm) across, insignificant. One of the hardiest species. Australia. Blooms in spring. Zones 8–10; semihardy 7.

polyanthemos p. 236

Silver Dollar Gum; Red Box; Australian Beech. A slender upright tree, to 50–60 ft. (15–18 m) high, persistent mottled bark. Gray-green leaves oval or round when young, lance-shaped on mature plants. Flowers small, in a profuse, branched

cluster. Fruit ¼–½ in. (6–13 mm) wide.
Flowers and fruits not ornamental, but
young growth often used in flower
arrangements. Grows poorly in wet soil, but
tolerates drought. Australia. Zones 8–10.

sideroxylon pp. 210, 211
Red Ironbark. Not over 80 ft. (24 m) high,
the dark red or blackish rough bark
persistent. Leaves narrowly lance-shaped, the
young growth even narrower. Attractive
flowers 1 in. (2.5 cm) wide, light pink, in
umbels 8–20 in. (20–50 cm) wide. Fruit
½ in. (13 mm) in diameter. A variable
species with many forms: shorter, upright,
open, weeping, darker green or silvery
foliage, red or rose-colored flowers, and so
on. Drought tolerant. Australia. Blooms fall
to spring. Fruit spring to summer. Zones
9–10.

Eucommia
Eucommia family
Eucommiaceae

You-kom′mi-a. A single Chinese tree, of
interest as the only hardy deciduous plant
producing rubber. If the leaves are gently
torn apart, they remain connected by
strands of white latex in their veins. The
rubber is of no commercial importance.
Eucommias are vigorous and hardy, and
thrive where many other trees would fail.

Description
Leaves alternate, stalked and toothed,
elliptical or oblong. Unisexual flowers,
appearing before the leaves unfold, without
petals or sepals. The male flowers with red
anthers, the female consisting only of a
1–celled ovary. Fruit a stalked, 1–seeded
winged nutlet.

How to Grow
Plant in full sun, in almost any soil, except
soggy or extremely dry ones. Eucommia
endures city conditions nicely, and is hardy
and pest-free. Remove vertical water sprouts
from trunks and branches in early summer
and apply a sprout retardant to the wound.

ulmoides pp. 156, 157
Eucommia; Hardy Rubber Tree. A tree, to
60 ft. (18 m) high, narrow in outline when
young, smoothly rounded with age. Leaves

are alternate, stalked and toothed, elliptical
to oblong, 2–3 in. (5.0–7.5 cm) long.
Flowers and fruit are inconspicuous, but the
foliage is a dark lustrous-green, even in
droughts. A good tree for difficult sites and
in city conditions. No fall color. Cen.
China. Zones 5–7.

Fagus
Beech family
Fagaceae

Fay′gus. Beech. These deciduous trees,
constituting a genus of 10 species, grow in
temperate regions of the northern
hemisphere. The two species described
below are the only ones of interest to the
gardener, but they are among the most
decorative and hardy of all cultivated trees.
Perhaps no other trees better combine
majesty and grace than the beeches. Massive
trunks and major branches are clothed with
gray bark and enhanced by a delicate tracery
of downturned branchlets, slender twigs,
and long-pointed winter buds. The lustrous-
green, copper, or purple leaves make a
delightful contrast to the bark and turn
clear ochre or bronze in fall. Beech roots
often break through the soil surface,
creating mowing problems, but if lower
branches are not removed, they sweep the
ground and inhibit grass beneath.
Nuts are small, not ornamental, but tasty,
and once were important food sources for
native and domestic creatures, from the
now-extinct passenger pigeon to hogs.

Description
Leaves alternate and toothed in the species
given below. Male and female flowers in
separate clusters on the same tree. Male
flowers in slender-stalked heads, without
petals, but with 4- to 7–lobed calyx, and
8–16 stamens. Female flowers usually 2,
surrounded by many united bracts. Fruit a
triangular or egg-shaped nut in a woody,
4–valved, prickly covering.

How to Grow
Transplant beeches in spring, in sites with
plenty of space—trees are slow-growing, but
eventually massive, spreading if unimpeded
to 60 ft. (18 m) or more. Young plants
recover well, but larger trees are difficult to
transplant. Beeches prefer a moist but well-

drained soil, well-aerated and acid (pH
4.5–6.5). They grow poorly in wet or
compacted soil. Mulch and irrigate deeply
when rain is less than 1 in. (2.5 cm)
weekly.

Growth and foliage are best in full sun, but
beeches will adapt to dappled shade. Prune
young trees to a strong central trunk and
well-spaced branches. European Beech is
more tolerant than American, but neither
withstands city conditions. When
well-grown, both species are hardy and
pest- and insect-free.

grandifolia pp. 148, 149

American Beech. A tree, to 100 ft. (30 m)
high, with smooth, light gray bark, often
sadly attractive to initial-carving vandals.
Leaves oblong-oval, broadly wedge-shaped
at the base, coarsely toothed, 4–7 in.
(10.0–17.5 cm) long, with 9–15 pairs of
veins, bluish green above, light green
beneath; beautifully silky when unfolding,
rich yellow-bronze in fall, often persisting
on lower portions throughout winter. Enjoys
a moist, acid soil. E. North America. Zones
4–9.

sylvatica pp. 148, 149

European Beech. A tree, to 100 ft. (30 m)
high, bark darker gray than *F. grandifolia*.
Leaves dark, lustrous-green, finely and
somewhat remotely toothed or nearly entire,
more or less elliptic-ovate, 3½–5 in.
(9.0–12.5 cm) long, with 5–9 pairs of
veins, beautifully delicate when first
appearing in spring, turning a rich bronze
in fall. When grown as a specimen tree, it
forms a huge, broad top with horizontal and
ascending branches extending from a
generally low, bulky trunk that sometimes
measures 6 ft. (1.8 m) in diameter. In
wooded areas the habit is less broad and the
trunk often clean for a height of 40 ft.
(12 m).

American Beech has no cultivars, but
European Beech has spawned many beautiful
horticultural forms. Two are featured below.
Others, usually rare, are 'Roseo-marginata',
Rose Pink Beech, often confused in the
trade; 'Aspenifolia', Fernleaf Beech;
'Fastigiata', Upright Beech; 'Atropunicea',
similar to 'Riversii'; and others. Europe.
Zones 5–8.

sylvatica 'Pendula' *pp. 120, 121*

Weeping European Beech. A tree of fairy
tale quality, to 60 ft. (18 m) at maturity
with undisciplined weeping branches, often
spreading at first, then arching earthward
with abandon. To stand beneath or to
climb, a mature Weeping European
Beech is a treasure and a delight. Prefers
acid soil.

A combination of the pendulous-branched
and purple-leaved forms is known as *F.
sylvatica* 'Purpurea Pendula'. It combines the
characters of both forms, but is rather slow-
growing and seldom exceeds 40 ft. (12 m)
in height. Zones 5–8.

sylvatica 'Riversii' *pp. 122, 123*

Rivers Purple Beech. A large tree, to 75 ft.
(22.5 m) high, and wide-spreading.
Spectacular deep purple foliage gradually
fades as the season progresses. Best and
longest leaf color in full sun. In bright
sunshine, this tree will draw a gasp from
all. Similar cultivars and selections are
'Atropunicea', the Purple Beech; 'Cuprea',
the Copper Beech; 'Purpurea', another
Purple Beech cultivar; and 'Tricolor', the
Tricolor Beech, with variegated pink,
purple, and white leaves, among the slowest
growing of the Purple Beech cultivars.
Zones 5–8.

Ficus
Mulberry family
Moraceae

Fy'kus. Fig. A huge genus of over 800
species of chiefly tropical broadleaf evergreen
trees, shrubs, or vines, one of which is the
Common Fig, but also including many
ornamentals, like the Banyan and the much-
domesticated Rubber Plant.

Many fig species begin life as epiphytes.
Some remain epiphytes throughout their
lives, but others produce long, hanging
roots that eventually reach the ground and
take root. Such hanging roots sometimes (as
in the banyans) intertwine and graft onto
each other, forming a basketwork of roots
around the host plant, eventually strangling
it. In other species, the roots, formed from
the tree's branches, hang singly and, on
reaching the ground, form trunk-like
columns. Nearly all have a milky juice.
Ornamental figs are grown throughout zones

9 and 10, and a few species are
extraordinarily popular houseplants.

Description
Leaves alternate. Flowers and fruits minute,
borne on the inside face of a closed, fleshy
receptacle, which is edible in the Common
Fig, but in few others.

How to Grow
Given appropriately mild climates, figs are
easy to grow. Soils from sandy to heavy will
suffice, but figs need an occasional deep
watering during droughts. Prune for shape
or open character by cutting back to nodes
or main branches.

benjamina *pp. 224, 225*
Benjamin Fig; Chinese Banyan; Weeping
Fig; Java Fig. A large, perfectly smooth
tree, to 40 ft. (12 m), with spreading and
drooping branches. Popular outdoors in
frost-free climates and ubiquitous indoors in
malls, hotels, and atria. Leaves evergreen,
ovalish or oblong, 2–4 in. (5–10 cm) long,
the tip tapering; without marginal teeth,
and rather leathery. Fruit nearly round,
½ in. (13 mm) in diameter. Flowers and
fruits not ornamental. Grows best in
steadily moist but not wet soil. Fertilize
lightly, using half the recommended
strength, 2–3 times yearly. Needs plenty of
light, and responds poorly to overwatering.
Recently purchased or moved plants often
drop leaves until acclimated. Indo-Malaysia.
Zone 10.

elastica 'Decora' *pp. 198, 199*
Rubber Plant; Rubber Tree. The common
household Rubber Plant, in the tropics
forming a large tree, but is usually grown as
a pot plant. Leaves oblong-elliptic, 6–12 in.
(15–30 cm) long, green and glossy. Fruit
yellowish, ½ in. (13 mm) long,
inconspicuous. It was once an important
source of rubber, but not the true Rubber
Tree. Has an appealingly bold character,
looks indestructible, and comes close.
Tolerates low light, minimal water, and low
humidity. Popular outdoors in frost-free
areas, indoors everywhere as a pot plant.
Nepal to Assam. Zone 10.

macrophylla *pp. 226, 227*
Moreton Bay Fig. A large Australian tree,
50–75 ft. (15.0–22.5 m) high, spreading
twice as wide, very popular in Calif. It has
gray bark, bulging roots, and broadly

oblong leaves, nearly 12 in. (30 cm) long and brownish underneath. Fruit stalked, purplish but white-spotted, 1 in. (2.5 cm) in diameter. Needs ample water. Australia. Fruit in fall. Zones 9–10.

microcarpa pp. 198, 199

Indian Laurel; Laurel Fig. A tree, widely cultivated in the tropics in parks and along streets, to 40 ft. (12 m) high. Bark smooth and grayish. Long weeping branches; lower ones may be removed to display light gray trunk. Terminal buds to ½ in. (13 mm) long, smooth. Leaves with short petioles, elliptical to broadly elliptical, tip and base both blunt (or rounded), thick, 2½–3½ in. (6–9 cm) long and up to 1¼ in. (3 cm) wide, with 6–8 pairs of lateral veins. Figs globose, ½ in. (13 mm) in diameter, light green.

New leaves are rosy-chartreuse, produced throughout the growing season and contrasting markedly with mature green foliage. Foliage can be severely damaged by thrips. Monrovia Nursery in Azusa, Calif., claims to have bred an immune cultivar. *F. rubiginosa,* the Rustyleaf Fig, is more resistant to thrip infestation. Also known as *F. retusa.* Malaysia. Zones 10; semihardy 9.

Fraxinus
Olive family
Oleaceae

Frax'in-us. Ash. A group of 65 species of mostly deciduous trees of the north temperate zone, several important both as ornamental and timber trees. Ashes generally grow quickly but have strong wood, and thus endure storms better than many rapid-growing species. Their foliage and fall color are usually attractive.

Description
Handsome rounded or upright trees with compound, opposite leaves, and in cultivated species, 5 or more leaflets. Leaflets also opposite on the rachis, with an odd leaflet at the end. Flowers small, greenish or whitish, perfect or unisexual, without petals in most species. Fruit a small 1–seeded key with an elongated wing.

How to Grow

Ashes will grow in most ordinary garden soils, but are not suitable for very dry sites. Almost any pH is tolerable, except strongly alkaline soils. Ashes transplant easily; prune young trees early on to train to a single trunk. Water deeply during drought to keep trees vigorous and to reduce insect and disease problems. Easily propagated from seeds and often becomes a pest from profuse self-seeding.

americana pp. 158, 159

White Ash. A tree, 60–120 ft. (18–36 m) high, the young twigs lustrous-green. Leaflets mostly 7 (rarely 5 or 9), stalked, more or less oval, 3–5 in. (7.5–12.5 cm) long. Fruit oblong, 1½ in. (4 cm) long. White Ash is a vigorous, large tree with various insect and disease problems, better suited for parks and campuses than for the average homesite. Seeds are numerous, sprout readily, and can be troublesome in landscapes. Male nonfruiting cultivars such as 'Autumn Purple', 'Rosehill', and others are recommended over the species. Tolerates wetness. E. North America. Zones 4–9.

excelsior pp. 160, 161

European Ash. A tree, to 70 ft. (21 m) high, twigs smooth. Leaves not compound—simple and prominently toothed, shiny dark green. No fall color. Tolerant of almost any soil except highly alkaline or very dry ones. Usually grows with a straight trunk and rounded crown. Be sure to grow a male plant to avoid seeds. The best of several improved cultivars is 'Hessei', Hesse European Ash, valuable because of its darker green leaves and excellent pest—especially borer—resistance. 'Aurea', the Yellow European Ash, has yellow branchlets and a distinctly yellow cast to the bark; both are attractive winter features. Europe and Asia Minor. Zones 4–9.

pennsylvanica pp. 158, 159

Green Ash; Red Ash; River Ash. A tree much like *F. americana*, but not as large— to 65 ft. (20 m)—and growing more rapidly as a young plant. Leaflets usually 9, the lower ones, and sometimes the upper ones, with their stalks winged. Green Ash will grow in just about any soil in its hardiness range, and thus tends to be over-used. Plant male cultivars such as 'Marshall's Seedless'

340

to avoid nuisance seeds. Fall foliage yellow.
Nova Scotia to Alberta, south to n. Fla. and
e. Tex. Zones 3–8.

uhdei pp. 222, 223

Evergreen Ash; Shamel Ash. An evergreen
or semi-evergreen tree 50–80 ft. (15–24 m)
high; leaves drop after a frost. Leaves with
5–9 leaflets, each 4–6 in. (10–15 cm) long.
Flowers in large clusters but not particularly
ornamental. Keys to 1½ in. (4 cm) long.
Upright and narrow until maturity, when
crown broadens. Water deeply in droughts.
Cut back strong-growing branches in youth
to encourage compact habit. Mexico.
Zones 9–10.

Ginkgo
Ginkgo family
Ginkgoaceae

Gink'o; jin'ko. A remarkable deciduous
Chinese tree, the only species and only
genus of a nearly extinct family, once a
widely distributed group stretching back in
geologic time to the Carboniferous. Now
only this species survives, all the cultivated
specimens having been grown from trees
preserved around Chinese temples. Young
trees are often ungainly with clumsy
branching, but older trees always manage a
dignified appearance. Even forgetting its
astounding lineage, the Ginkgo or
Maidenhair Tree is one of the finest
street and specimen trees in the temperate
world.

Description
A resinous tree with deciduous fan-shaped
leaves. Male and female flowers on separate
trees, both without sepals or petals. The
male flowers consist of naked pairs of
anthers in catkinlike clusters. Female flowers
are naked ovules, which, uniquely among
trees, are fertilized by motile sperm cells, as
in the ferns. Fruit fleshy, drupelike, foul-
smelling, but the kernel is edible.

How to Grow
Only male trees should be planted, because
of the foul odor of the fruit. Ginkgos
require full sun; otherwise they are very
tolerant of soil conditions and air pollution.
Prune young trees when dormant to control
unruly branches. Ginkgo is practically

immune to all pests and stands street
conditions very well.

biloba pp. 184, 185

Ginkgo; Maidenhair Tree. A smooth tree,
up to 125 ft. (38 m). Leaves alternate, fan-
shaped, more or less cut at the broad tip,
wedge-shaped at the base, 2½–3½ in.
(6–9 cm) wide, resembling a segment of the
frond of a Maidenhair Fern. The foliage
turns a soft yellow in autumn; most leaves
fall at once, as if by command. Fruit
yellow, to 1 in. (2.5 cm) long, definitely
not ornamental. The cultivar 'Autumn
Gold' is more spreading than the species
and has rich yellow, fall foliage. Several
narrowly upright cultivars are excellent
choices for street plantings. China. Zones
5–9; semihardy 4.

Gleditsia
Pea family
Leguminosae

Gle-dit'see-a. Honey Locust. A genus of 12
species of thorny deciduous trees, mostly
Asiatic, but 2 in e. North America and 1
in South America. Honey locusts are
handsome, openly-branched trees that cast a
light, dappled shade, and so are excellent as
lawn plantings, but they do not compare
with the common locust in the beauty of
their flowers. Mesquite is often mistakenly
called honey locust.

Description
They are usually tall trees, the trunks
and branches of which are armed with
often-branched thorns. Leaves compound,
the leaflets arranged feather-fashion,
but with no odd one at the tip, and often
irregularly wavy-toothed. Flowers not
pealike; usually greenish, polygamous, and
mostly in racemes. Petals 3–5, nearly
equal. Fruit a large, usually flattened
pod, sometimes sickle-shaped and
twisted.

How to Grow
Honey locusts transplant easily and perform
well in a variety of soils, including alkaline,
dry, and salty. Plant in full sun. Because
ferny foliage casts light shade, grass grows
beneath them, but trees grow more
vigorously if mulched instead. Prune

anytime to remove low and crossing branches.

triacanthos var. *inermis* pp. 162, 163

Thornless Honey Locust. Although the species has perilously sharp thorns and flattened, twisted brown pods, var. *inermis* is thornless and fruitless for certain cultivars. Leaves are compound, some times doubly so, 6–8 in. (15–20 cm) long, with 20–30 small leaflets averaging only about 1 in. (2.5 cm) long. Leaves appear late in spring and drop early in fall, and are airy and lacy. Fall color pleasant yellow.

Form is usually broadly conical when young, rounded with age. Unfortunately, the tree has been over-used in some areas, causing the outbreak of a variety of troublesome pests and diseases that seldom kill a tree but often disfigure it. Cultivar 'Skyline' has performed well in the Midwest. Zones 5–9; semihardy 4.

Grevillea
Australian oak family
Proteaceae

Gre-vil'lee-a. About 250 species of Australasian broadleaf evergreen trees and shrubs, a few species often grown as shade or screen trees in warmer regions.

Description
Leaves alternate, sometimes small and heathlike, or much larger and divided or deeply parted, feather-fashion, into 5 segments. Flowers in close racemes or heads, without petals, but the calyx more or less tubular, the 4 lobes joined even after the flower has opened. Stamens 4. Fruit a woody follicle.

How to Grow
Grevilleas grow well in both rich and poor sandy soils, and tolerate drought very well. They also grow well in deep, rich soils, but need full sun. Because their wood is brittle and they litter the ground, plant specimens away from high-use areas.

robusta pp. 222, 223

Silk Oak. In outdoor cultivation, a tall narrow tree to 150 ft. (45 m) high, but only 3–10 ft. (0.9–3.0 m) high when grown as a pot plant. Leaves twice divided

into graceful, feathery, fernlike segments,
silvery beneath. Flowers orange, in 1–sided
racemes 4–12 in. (10–30 cm) long, and
borne on leafless branches. A popular street
tree in s. Calif., but always dropping parts
and littering the ground. Australia. Blooms
in spring. Zones 10; semihardy 9.

Gymnocladus
Pea family
Leguminosae

Jim-nock'lay-dus. A genus of 3 species
of deciduous trees, 2 in e. Asia and 1 in
e. North America. The last species, the
Kentucky Coffee Tree, is occasionally grown
for its striking winter appearance.
Gymnocladus is from the Greek for "naked
twigs," since the thick, conspicuous twigs
are bare in the winter.

Description
These trees have stout twigs, strong
asymmetrical branches, and large bipinnate
leaves. Flowers can be male or female, on
separate trees or on the same tree, or
polygamous. Fruit a large, thick-walled
legume.

How to Grow
Plant balled or container-grown plants in
spring in full sun. Deep rich soil with
adequate moisture and drainage is best, but
trees will endure dryness, acid or alkaline
soil, and city conditions. They have no
serious diseases or insect pests. Leaves and
fruits on female trees are messy in fall, but
this species is tidy the rest of the year.

dioica pp. 156, 157
Kentucky Coffee Tree. A tree to 90 ft.
(27 m) high, with twice-compound leaves,
the leaflets arranged feather-fashion, in 3–7
pairs, more or less ovalish, without teeth,
2–4 in. (5–10 cm) long. Leaves are large,
up to 3 ft. (90 cm) long and 2 ft. (60 cm)
wide, but have a demure texture because
leaflets are moderately spaced. Leaflets drop
in fall; twiglike midribs hang a few weeks
longer. Bold branches and twigs conform to
no pattern and create a picturesque winter
effect. Greenish white flowers in terminal
clusters, ornamentally unimportant. Fruit
a thick, flat, pulpy legume, 5–10 in.
(12.5–25.0 cm) long, 2–3 in. (5.0–7.5 cm)

wide, the seeds large and flattened.
Tolerates drought and pollution. N.Y. and
Pa. to Nebr., Okla., and Tenn. Fruit in
fall. Zones 5–8; semihardy 4.

Halesia
Storax family
Styracaceae

Ha-lee′zi-a. Five species of rather showy
medium-sized deciduous trees, one Chinese,
all the others from the se. U.S. and grown
for their spring flowers.

Description
Handsome, medium-textured trees with
white, bell-shaped flowers in axillary cymes
hanging gracefully along twigs of previous
year's growth, especially interesting when
viewed from below. Leaves alternate,
elliptic, finely toothed. Fruit an oblong,
nearly fleshless, winged drupe.

How to Grow
Halesias are best grown as woodland-edge
trees in partial shade, but they will tolerate
full sun. Give them an east exposure to
minimize wind damage. They prefer acid,
moist but well-drained soil; mulch if
possible. Hardy and pest-free.

carolina *pp. 88, 89*
Silver-Bell Tree; Snowdrop Tree. Not over
50 ft. (15 m) high, usually half that in
cultivation. Leaves ovalish or oblong, 2–
4 in. (5–10 cm) long, finely blunt-toothed,
yellow-green in fall. Flowers 2–5, in
pendulous cymose clusters, the stalks
¾ in. (19 mm) long. Corolla white, ¾ in.
(19 mm) long. Cymes loose; flowers usually
appear to be singly borne, but numerous
and eye-catching. Fruit oblong, to 1½ in.
(4 cm) long, 4–winged. Bark gray with
off-white stripes.
A fine, pest-resistant small tree, spectacular
against taller evergreens. Sometimes sold as
H. tetraptera. A similar, but larger, species
is *H. monticola,* Mountain Silver-Bell.
W.Va. to Fla. and Tex. Blooms in spring.
Fruit in fall. Zones 5–8.

Ilex
Holly family
Aquifoliaceae

Eye'lecks. Holly. Perhaps 400 species of mostly evergreen trees and shrubs widely scattered in temperate and tropical regions, several of which are among the most valuable of our broadleaf evergreens. A few deciduous species are grown for their showy fruits. Since the sexes of most hollies are borne on separate plants, it is essential to have male and female plants in reasonable proximity in order to ensure a crop of berries. Honeybees are the hollies' principal pollinators, and have been known to cause the fruiting of female plants as much as one-half mile from the nearest male, but don't rely on the chance of a male plant nearby.

Description
Hollies have alternate, sometimes spiny-toothed leaves and inconspicuous white or greenish flowers, usually in small clusters in the leaf axils. Sepals 3–6, and petals 4–5, both small. Fruit berrylike, often showy, actually a drupe with 2–5 stones.

How to Grow
American Holly is best suited to partial shade, in acid, loamy soils with good drainage and in a spot protected from wind. An east-facing hillside is often ideal. Plant balled and burlapped or container-grown plants in spring, placing the root ball no deeper than it grew before, higher in heavy soil. Mulch and top-dress moderately with a balanced fertilizer every year for a vigorous tree.

A disease called purple blotch can disfigure the foliage of plants under stress from dryness, high pH, or poor nutrition. Leafminer insects can decimate the foliage of even the healthiest American Hollies. Use the proper pesticide at blossom time, or at the first sign of leaf damage.

opaca pp. 204, 205
American Holly. Conical when young, later spreading, up to 50 ft. (15 m) high. Leaves leathery, evergreen, elliptic, 1½–4 in. (4–10 cm) long, dark but dull green above, pale green beneath, marginal teeth spiny. Fruit usually solitary, pea-sized, red on most cultivars, yellow on some. Tolerates salt, and enjoys shade and a moist, acid

soil. At least 1000 cultivars exist, varying
little to greatly in size, hardiness,
atmospheric and soil tolerances, and in
fruit. Check with local authorities for
cultivars recommended for your area and
needs. Mass. to Fla., west to Mo. and Tex.
Fruit fall to winter. Zones 5–9.

Jacaranda
Trumpet-vine family
Bignoniaceae

Jack-a-ran'da. Tropical American shrubs and
trees, comprising more than 50 deciduous
species. The species below is one of the
most widely planted of all tropical
ornamental trees, and highly valued for its
beautiful wysteria-colored blooms. The
valuable cabinet wood known as jacaranda,
which is rosewood, comes from timber trees
of the genus *Dahlbergia,* of the pea family.

Description
Leaves opposite, twice-compound, the
leaflets arranged feather-fashion, numerous,
the foliage handsome. Flowers showy, blue
or violet, in terminal panicles or on the leaf
axils. Corolla tubular, its limb slightly
2–lipped, the flower somewhat irregular,
resembling a foxglove. Stamens 4, often
with an odd sterile one. Fruit an oblong or
oval capsule.

How to Grow
Plant jacarandas in frost-free areas, or after
frost danger is past, in springtime. Stake
and prune young plants to establish a main
trunk. They do best in sandy soil, but
tolerate other soils if not extreme.
Jacarandas respond best to infrequent but
deep watering. They are not suitable for
frequently irrigated areas; too much water
encourages lush, tender growth. In zone 9,
jacarandas often grow only as a shrub, dying
back after frost, then recovering.

mimosifolia pp. 84, 85

Jacaranda. A tree, up to 50 ft. (15 m) high,
wide-spreading, holding its leaves until
early in the spring. Leaves hairy, fernlike,
delicately textured, with 16 or more pairs of
main divisions, each of these with 14–24
pairs of oblongish leaflets that are ½ in.
(13 mm) long. Flower cluster nearly 8 in.
(20 cm) long, the flowers strikingly bluish

lavender, corolla tube bent, 2 in. (5 cm) long. Bloom usually occurs on bare trees, but may overlap with young foliage. Fruit a rounded, flattened woody capsule, 1¼ in. (3 cm) in diameter, interesting. Often confused with *J. acutifolia*. Nw. Argentina. Blooms in spring; sporadically in fall. Fruit in fall. Zones 10; semihardy 9.

Juniperus
Cypress family
Cupressaceae

Jew-nip′er-us. Juniper. A genus of 70 species of evergreen trees and shrubs, widely distributed in the northern hemisphere from the arctic to the subtropics. Junipers vary in habit from low, prostrate shrubs to tall, slender trees, and are widely grown as background, specimen, and foundation plants. The tall, columnar types are conspicuous planted singly or in groups, and the low, spreading types are excellent for foundation plantings. An aromatic oil is obtained from the berries and branchlets of certain species; the wood is durable and usually fragrant.

Description
The leaves are of 2 types: needle-shaped, and usually borne in threes, and small, scale-like leaves that are opposite and pressed close to the twigs. On young plants and vigorous branches, the needle-shaped leaves predominate, whereas the scaly leaves are characteristic of adult growth. Both types often appear together on older plants, and many species and cultivars retain the needle-like leaves permanently.
Flowers insignificant; male flowers borne in small, oval catkins; female flowers composed of little scales in which the ovules are borne; these scales later become fleshy, growing together to form a berrylike fruit that takes 1–3 years to ripen. The fruit, on female plants only, is small but often bloomy blue and ornamental on some species.

How to Grow
Always plant junipers in well-drained soil in full sun. Many junipers do well in moist, aerated soil, most will endure dry, rocky sites, wind and drought, and air pollution; but none can grow in a soggy area.

Junipers take pruning well, hence are often sheared into hedges or stolid, boring shapes. The two tree-form species here need only an occasional pruning of wayward branches that spoil their outlines.

Avoid proximity to hawthorns, serviceberries, and native crabapples, or risk cedar apple rust, a dual-host disease that yellows the foliage of the deciduous hosts and forms grotesque growths on juniper twigs. Twig blight is a problem with some species, mites and bagworms with most. All the above problems are controllable with pesticides.

scopulorum pp. 244, 245

Rocky Mountain Juniper; Western Red Cedar. A usually low tree in the wild, but sometimes growing 30–40 ft. (9–12 m) high. Trunk short, often dividing near the ground; bark red-brown, shredding. Leaves of 2 types: mainly scale-like and opposite, pointed and closely pressed to stem; sometimes needle-like and spreading. Male flowers with 6 stamens. Fruit blue, bloomy, ⅓ in. (8 mm) across, ripening second year. The western representative of *J. virginiana*, from which it differs mainly in habit, bark, and nature of fruit. Stands dry and difficult situations. British Columbia and Alberta, south to Tex. and n. Ariz. Fruit in fall. Zones 4–10.

virginiana pp. 246, 247

Red Cedar. A tree, columnar or conical when young, becoming broader and spreading with age, usually growing 40–75 ft. (12.0–22.5 m) high. Bark red-brown, peeling off in long strips. Leaves of 2 types: needle-like, glaucous above, pointed, opposite or in threes on young plants and branches; on mature branches and plants, small and scale-like, pointed, overlapping, 1/16 in. (1.6 mm) long. Male flowers with usually 12 stamens. Fruit oval, ⅓ in. (8 mm) long, dark blue, slightly bloomy, ⅕–³⁄₁₀ in. (5.0–7.5 mm) in diameter. The wood is fragrant.

Easy to transplant, tolerant of a wide variety of soils—alkaline, acid, dry—but not wet or poorly drained ones. Needs full sun. Many cultivars with shape and foliage variations have been introduced. Consult local authorities for those best suited to your area. A common tree in dry, rocky fields from Canada to Fla., east of the Rockies. Fruit in fall. Zones 3–9.

Koelreuteria
Soapberry family
Sapindaceae

Kel-roo-teer'i-a. Golden-Rain Tree. A small genus of deciduous Asiatic trees often planted for their yellow summer-blooming flower clusters and fall seed pods. The trees have deep roots and are not invasive, and so are excellent for planting annuals or perennials beneath.

Description
Leaves alternate, compound, leaflets arranged feather-fashion with an odd leaflet at the end. Flowers in large terminal panicles, corolla somewhat irregular. Petals 4, with a claw and with 2 upward-pointing appendages to each. Stamens 8 or fewer. Fruit a bladderlike 3–valved capsule with black seeds.

How to Grow
Golden-Rain Trees do well in a variety of soils, and are better suited to open sunshine than to shade. Young plants may be harmed by winter temperatures, but mature trees withstand drought and grow well in acid to slightly alkaline soils. Stake and prune young trees to promote high branching, and prune out weaker crowded branches periodically.

bipinnata pp. 96, 97
Chinese Flame Tree. A rounded deciduous tree, to 60 ft. (18 m) high. Leaves twice-compound, to 18 in (45 cm) long, with 7–12 leaflets. Flowers yellow, in broad erect panicles up to 15 in. (38 cm) long. Capsule 2 in. (5 cm) long, rose-colored. Tolerates drought. Sw. China. Blooms in summer. Fruit in fall. Zones 8–10; semihardy 7.

paniculata pp. 94, 95
Golden-Rain Tree. A dome-shaped tree, not usually over 40 ft. (12 m) high. Leaves 9–18 in. (22.5–45.0 cm) long, the leaflets 7–15, ovalish-oblong, and coarsely toothed, sometimes deeply cut near the base. Flower cluster 12–15 in. (30–38 cm) long, showy, each flower with 4 petals, ½ in. (13 mm) wide. Pods 2 in. (5 cm) long, papery, brilliantly colored before dropping. Tolerates drought. E. Asia. Blooms in summer. Fruit fall to winter. Zones 5–8.

Lagerstroemia
Loosestrife family
Lythraceae

Lay-ger-stree′mi-a. A genus of about 55
species of decorative shrubs and trees,
mostly deciduous, all from warm regions of
the Old World. One, Crape Myrtle, is a
spectacular, summer-flowering deciduous
tree.

Description
Leaves opposite, the uppermost often
alternate, without marginal teeth. Flowers
in showy terminal panicles, pink, red,
purple, or white, the calyx turban-shaped.
Petals 6, usually with a long claw, crinkled
or fringed. Fruit a capsule.

How to Grow
Plant balled or container-grown specimens.
Crape Myrtles need full sun or nearly so,
and warm summers. Cool climates
encourage mildew on foliage, but some
cultivars are resistant. Soil should be rich in
organic matter, somewhat acid to neutral,
and neither too wet nor too dry. A mulch is
beneficial.
Since blossoms form on new growth, prune
before buds break in late winter or early
spring. Crape Myrtles respond well to
pruning, and may be cut almost to the
ground each spring for perpetual
shrubbiness, or trained to single trunks or
multiple-trunked small trees. Frequently a
second set of flowers will bloom in a single
season after cutting back branches as soon as
the first flowering is over.

indica pp. 76, 77

Crape Myrtle. A small tree, up to 30 ft.
(9 m), wider than high, bark exfoliates,
twigs 4–angled. Leaves nearly stalkless,
elliptic to oblong, 1–2 in. (2.5–5.0 cm)
long. Flowers with crinkly petals, white,
pink, red, lavender, or purple, 1¼ in.
(3 cm) wide, the cluster 6–8 in. (15–20 cm)
long. Blooms all summer, according to
variety.
Considered by many as the most
spectacularly showy deciduous, summer-
flowering shrub or small tree; also with fine
fall foliage, yellow, orange, and red.
Smooth gray bark flakes off, showing
varicolored underbark, especially attractive
during winter. Many cultivars are available
with various flower colors, growth habits,

and disease resistance. China. Blooms summer to fall. Zones 7–9.

Larix
Pine family
Pinaceae

Lar'icks. Larch. About 10 species of deciduous trees that have the typical pine habit. The larches are valuable timber trees and are widely grown for their attractive shape and handsome foliage.

Description
Cone-shaped head and more or less horizontal branches, with needle-shaped leaves that drop in the fall. Leaves are either spirally arranged on terminal shoots, or crowded into terminal clusters on short, lateral, spurlike growths. Male and female flowers are borne separately on the same tree; small cones have woody and persistent scales.

How to Grow
Give larches plenty of sunshine, moist acid soil, and plenty of space. These are not city trees. Mulch and water during drought. The species below prefers a moist, acid soil. They will wane in shade, alkaline soil, or polluted air. Because larches are large trees and are susceptible to a number of insects and diseases, it is wise to plant them sparingly.

kaempferi pp. 138, 139
Japanese Larch. A conical tree, up to 90 ft. (27 m) high, lower branches spreading to 40 ft. (12 m) wide. Scaly bark leaves red scars. Leaves flattened, ¾–1½ in. (2–4 cm) long, blunt, bluish green, white-banded below, glowing yellow in fall. Cones egg-shaped, 1 in. (2.5 cm) long. A very handsome, quick-growing tree. Formerly *L. leptolepis*. Japan. Cones fall to winter. Zones 4–6.

Laurus
Laurel family
Lauraceae

Law'rus. Laurel. A small but important genus of evergreen trees, native in the

Mediterranean region. There are only 2 species, and the cultivated one described below is probably the true Laurel of history and the poets, but is commonly called Bay or Sweet Bay—this last common name is also applied to *Magnolia virginiana*.
Outdoors it is a tree that casts dense shade, but it is also a popular tubbed evergreen, often trained to form standards, cones, pyramids, or other shapes, as it responds well to shearing.

Description
Laurel has stiff, alternate, oblongish leaves. Flowers small, inconspicuous, in umbels from the leaf axils. Fruit a berry.

How to Grow
Although the Laurel will stand considerable frost, it is not reliably hardy north of zone 8. Any ordinary soil is suitable if well-drained. Young trees should be watered in dry spells, but well-established Laurels endure quite a bit of drought. A site with afternoon shade is best in very hot climates.

nobilis *pp. 204, 205*
Laurel; Bay; Sweet Bay. A tree, broadly triangular in outline, to 40 ft. (12 m) high. Leaves elliptic to lance-shaped, to 4 in. (10 cm) long, dark green, aromatic. Flowers small, inconspicuous, yellowish green. Fruit a small black or purple berry. Laurels grow slowly; it takes many years to produce a specimen tree. Mediterranean region. Zones 8–10.

Liquidambar
Witch-hazel family
Hamamelidaceae

Liquid-am'bar. Sweet Gum. Few deciduous trees turn such a gorgeous fall color as the native Sweet Gum, the only commonly cultivated species of this small genus. Only 3 other species are known, all of them Asiatic. The name *Liquidambar* refers to the fragrant resin of an Asiatic species.

Description
Sweet Gums have lobed, maple-like leaves and unisexual flowers, the males in racemes or branching clusters, the females in globose heads. Fruit a pendant, spiny conglomerate ball.

How to Grow
Plant balled or container-grown plants in
good moist, acid soil. Mulch and water
deeply during drought; Sweet Gum is more
tolerant of poor drainage than of dryness.
Choose sunny sites removed from walks and
patios because the hard round fruits may
turn ankles.

styraciflua pp. 150, 151

Sweet Gum. A tree, up to 75 ft. (22.5 m)
high, its twigs and young branches
sometimes corky-winged. Leaves alternate,
starlike, stalked, much resembling a maple,
the 3–7 lobes toothed. Flowers small,
inconspicuous, mostly unisexual, and in
dense globe-shaped clusters. No petals.
Fruit a prickly globe-shaped conglomerate of
shining brown capsules, each tipped with a
spine, 1–1½ in. (2.5–4.0 cm) in diameter.
An extremely handsome tree, taller than
wide, its foliage brilliant yellow, scarlet, or
purple in the fall. The cultivar 'Moraine' is
recommended in colder areas of zone 5.
Conn. to Fla., Mo., Ill., and south to
Mexico. Fruit fall to winter. Zones 5–9.

Liriodendron
Magnolia family
Magnoliaceae

Lir-i-oh-den′dron. Tulip Tree. There are
only 2 species, both deciduous, one in
e. North America, the other in cen. China.
The native species is highly prized as a
magnificent lawn specimen or woods-edge
tree.

Description
Tulip Trees are recognized by their leaves,
which are long-petioled, seemingly cut off
at the tip, and slightly lobed, and by their
cone-shaped fruit, which consists of long
woody carpels.

How to Grow
Tulip Trees should be planted in spring as
balled or container-grown plants. Deep,
moist, well-drained, slightly acid soil is
best. They are not suitable for cities or areas
with restricted root space. Mulch, and water
deeply during extreme drought. Aphids can
be a problem, and Tulip Trees are easily
damaged by some lawn herbicides.
Otherwise, they are hardy and long-lived.

tulipifera pp. 184, 185
Tulip Tree; Whitewood; Yellow Poplar;
Tulip Poplar. A columnar or broadly
upright tree, to 100 ft. (30 m) high,
without branches on the lower part of the
trunk in forests, but often low-branched in
the open. Leaves alternate, broadly oval, or
saddle-shaped, the tip very blunt and deeply
notched, 3–5 in. (7.5–12.5 cm) long,
stalked, turning yellow in fall. Over each
leaf bud are 2 conspicuous stipules that are
long-persistent.
Flowers terminal, solitary, showy, tulip- or
lily-like, 2½ in. (6 cm) wide, the 6 petals
greenish white but with an orange band at
the base. The comely flowers open after
foliage forms, and are usually borne high on
the tree, hence often go unnoticed. Fruit a
conelike aggregate of keys, 2–3 in. (5.0–
7.5 cm) long. E. North America from
Ontario to Fla., Miss., and Wis. Fruit fall
to winter. Zones 5–9.

Magnolia
Magnolia family
Magnoliaceae

Mag-no'li-a. A genus of North American,
West Indian, Mexican, and Asiatic
evergreen or deciduous trees and shrubs,
comprising about 85 species, among them
several of the most beautiful spring-
flowering ornamental trees.
Magnolia species and varieties can be chosen
to produce flowers from early spring to
midsummer and, quite often, well into late
summer. The fruit ripens in late summer to
early fall and appears in the form of long,
often colorful, conelike formations that split
longitudinally at maturity, exposing scarlet-
colored seeds.

Description
Leaves alternate, without marginal teeth,
usually large. Flowers regular, solitary,
usually large and showy, commonly white,
yellow, rose, or purple, usually appearing
before the leaves of deciduous species, with
the leaves of evergreen species. Petals 6–20.
Sepals 3, often petal-like, the stamens
numerous. The fruit is a knobby aggregate
of carpels, brown, pink, or scarlet, the seeds
often orange or red, hanging by threadlike
cords when ripe.

How to Grow

Plant magnolias in spring, balled and
burlapped or container-grown, in acid to
nearly neutral soil, deep and moist. Cover
the root zone with mulch and avoid
disturbing the fleshy roots—even by
planting bulbs. Whenever possible, plants
should be left alone and not transplanted. In
the North, transplanting in spring is better
than in fall, and then only by the balled
and burlapped method.

Irrigate during drought. Prune after
flowering, only for form or maintenance.
Magnolias seldom have serious pests.

grandiflora pp. 200–201

Southern Magnolia; Bull Bay. A large
evergreen tree of noble proportions,
becoming 80 ft. (24 m) high. The
branchlets and buds are rusty-woolly when
young. Leaves 5–8 in. (12.5–20.0 cm)
long, somewhat oblong in shape, tapering
both ways, leathery, shining above, and
rusty-woolly beneath. Flowers cup-shaped,
coming out of great silky-hairy buds, 6–
8 in. (15–20 cm) across, creamy white,
richly fragrant. Petals usually 6 (rarely,
9–12), fleshy. Sepals 3, petal-like. Fruit
4 in. (10 cm) long, heavy, rusty-woolly,
exposing red seeds when ripe in fall. N.C.
to Fla. and Tex. Blooms in spring. Fruit in
fall. Zones 7–9; semihardy 6.

× *soulangiana* pp. 82, 83

Saucer Magnolia. A large shrub or small
tree, maximum size about 30 ft. (9 m) tall
and equally wide, often grown with several
trunks. Deciduous leaves broadly oval,
slightly soft-hairy beneath. Flowers appear
early, before the leaves, cup-shaped, 6 in.
(15 cm) across, purplish to white, scentless
or fragrant. Sepals usually petal-like,
sometimes small and greenish. This
beautiful small specimen tree, a pink to
lavender cloud when in bloom, originated in
1820. Tolerant of city air. May host scale
insects; control them with dormant oil
spray. There are numerous cultivars; consult
local authorities for the best in your area.
Blooms in spring. Zones 5–10.

virginiana pp. 200, 201

Sweet Bay; Beaver-Tree; White Bay; Swamp
Bay. Deciduous or semi-evergreen, growing
60 ft. (18 m) high in the South and
evergreen there, but maturing at 20 ft.
(6 m) and mostly deciduous in zone 5.

Branchlets smooth. Buds soft-hairy. Leaves oblong or elliptic, pointed or blunt, with a silvery bloom beneath, and at first silky soft-hairy; 3–5 in. (7.5–12.5 cm) long. Flowers appearing with the leaves, rounded, 2½ in. (6 cm) across, white, very fragrant, opening intermittently over a 6-week period in spring, often blooming into early summer. Petals 9–12. Sepals shorter and thinner, spreading. Fruit 2 in. (5 cm) long, red.

Grows well in wet places, and endures shade. Grows poorly in dry soil. Mass. to Fla. and Miss., near the coast. Blooms spring to early summer. Fruit summer to fall. Zones 5–9.

Malus
Rose family
Rosaceae

May'lus. Apple; Crabapple; Crabtree. A mostly deciduous genus of about 25 species of North American and Eurasian trees or shrubs. *Malus* rarely have spiny branches, but the spurs of wild or escaped species occasionally are thornlike. Some of our most beautiful and valuable ornamental trees belong to this genus, as well as important fruit trees. The cultivated apple is *M. pumila; Malus* is the ancient Latin name of the apple.

The growth habits of various crabapples are narrow-upright, upright-spreading, round, and weeping. Mature sizes range from shrubs to trees 40 ft. (12 m) high.

Description
Leaves alternate, elliptic, sometimes 3–lobed, folded or rolled in bud, with stipules, 1½–3½ in. (4–9 cm). Flowers usually in advance of foliage, regular, white to pink or carmine, in umbel-like terminal racemes. Petals 5, usually rounded, or broadly oval. Stamens 15–20 or more. All species bloom in early spring. Fruit a true pome, fleshy, often edible. Any member of the genus *Malus* bearing fruit 2 in. (5 cm) or less in diameter is considered a crabapple. Some types have fruit as small as ¼ in. (6 mm) in diameter, and fruit colors include purple, red, orange, and yellow.

How to Grow
Crabapples transplant easily; bare-rooted

when dormant, and at other times balled or container-grown. A well-drained soil is paramount; excessive moisture is deadly. Soil pH can vary from quite acid to somewhat alkaline. Established trees tolerate drought fairly well.

Pruning should begin in the first season and continue as needed to remove small crowded branches, crossing branches, maverick limbs that grow outside the desired outline, and suckers and water sprouts. Remove suckers and water sprouts in early summer to reduce resprouting, and apply a sprout-inhibiting product.

Crabapples, some species and cultivars more than others, host a variety of diseases. The most common diseases that disfigure or damage are apple scab, fireblight, powdery mildew, and cedar apple rust. The last can occur on trees within a mile of plantings of juniper (*Juniperus*) species and cultivars. Diseases are treatable by spraying and cultural practices, but select resistant cultivars when you plant. Insects that trouble crabapples—mites, aphids, fall webworms, and some others—are controlled with pesticides. The following crabapples resist diseases better than most others. Check with local authorities for those best suited to your area.

'Adams'

Adams Crabapple. To 22 ft. (6.5 m) tall, rounded. Leaves light green, 2–3 in. (5.0–7.5 cm) long, new leaves reddish tinged. Flowers carmine in bud, open pink, 1½ in. (4 cm) wide. Fruit red, ⅝ in. (16 mm) in diameter. Blooms in spring. Fruit in fall. Zones 4–8.

baccata 'Jackii'

Jack Crabapple. To 35 ft. (10.5 m) tall, upright-spreading. Leaves glossy dark green, 2–3 in. (5.0–7.5 cm) long. Flowers white, 1½ in. (4 cm) wide. Fruits purplish red, ½ in. (13 mm) wide. Blooms in spring. Fruit in fall. Zones 4–8.

'Beverly'

Beverly Crabapple. To 25 ft. (7.5 m) tall, upright-spreading. Light green leaves, less than 2 in. (5 cm) long. Buds dark red; flowers clear white, 1¼ in. (3 cm) wide. Fruit bright red, ½–¾ in. (13–19 mm) wide. Not for areas where fireblight is prevalent. Blooms in spring. Fruit in fall. Zones 4–8.

'Bob White' *p. 107*
Bob White Crabapple. To 20 ft. (6 m), densely rounded. Leaves light green, less than 2 in. (5 cm) long. Flowers pink in bud, open white, 1 in. (2.5 cm) wide. Fruit yellow, ⅝ in. (16 mm) wide, persisting into winter. Blooms in spring. Fruit fall to winter. Zones 4–8.

'Candied Apple' *pp. 102, 103*
Weeping Candied Apple Crabapple. To 20 ft. (6 m) high, weeping in an irregular fashion, picturesque. Leaves green, overcast with red. Buds red, flowers pink, 1½ in. (4 cm) wide. Fruit cherry-red, ⅝ in. (16 mm) wide, persistent. Blooms in spring. Fruit fall to winter. Zones 4–8.

'Coralburst' *pp. 104, 105*
Coralburst Crabapple. Ultimate height is about 14 ft. (4.3 m) as a shrub, correspondingly taller according to height at which grafted onto an upright or standard rootstock, making a small tree, horizontally oval in outline, slightly wider than high. Leaves small, 1½–2 in. (4–5 cm), a good green color and densely borne on branchlets, hiding the interior branch structure entirely. Flowers coral-pink in bud, opening to single or semidouble (many-petalled) rose-pink flowers ¾ in. (19 mm) across. Fruits, as with most double-flowered crabapples, are rare. When they do occur, fruits are ½ in. (13 mm), nondescriptly bronze-colored. Grafted onto standard, Coralburst is a striking patio or accent plant. Blooms in spring. Zones 5–7; semihardy 4.

'David'
David Crabapple. A new cultivar, height not yet known, with a formal, rounded habit. Leaves 2–3 in. (5.0–7.5 cm) long, dull green. Buds pink, flowers white, 1½ in. (4 cm) wide. Fruit scarlet, ½ in. (13 mm) wide. Quite resistant to diseases and a handsome, tightly branched tree. Blooms in spring. Fruit in fall. Zones 4–8.

'Dolgo' *p. 102*
Dolgo Crabapple. To 40 ft. (12 m) upright-spreading. Leaves medium green, 3 in. (7.5 cm) long or more. Flowers white, larger than most, up to 1¾ in. (4.5 cm) wide. Fruit egg-shaped, bright red, 1½ in. (4 cm) long, maturing into late summer, good for apple jelly. Tends to bloom and

fruit every other year. Blooms in spring. Fruit summer to fall. Zones 4–8.

'Donald Wyman' *pp. 106, 107*

Donald Wyman Crabapple. To 15–20 ft. (4.5–6.0 m), rounded. Leaves dark green. Buds pink, flowers white, large, 1¾ in. (4.5 cm) wide. Fruit bright red, ⅜ in. (9 mm) wide, persisting well into winter. Flowers abundantly and has good disease resistance. Blooms in spring. Fruit fall to winter. Zones 4–8.

floribunda p. 106

Japanese Crabapple. To 25 ft. (7.5 m) high, broadly rounded. Leaves dark green. Buds red, flowers pale pink, almost white, 1½ in. (4 cm) wide. Fruit red and yellow, ⅜ in. (9 mm) wide. Bears annually and has a dense, compact habit. A dependable tree. Blooms in spring. Fruit in fall. Zones 4–8.

'Gibbs Golden Gage'

Gibbs Golden Gage Crabapple. To 20 ft. (6 m) high, rounded. Buds pink, flowers white, 1¼–1½ in. (3–4 cm) wide. Fruit waxy-yellow, 1 in. (2.5 cm) wide, persistent, more noticeable than red-fruiting varieties. Among the oldest cultivars, and still highly prized. Blooms in spring. Fruit fall to winter. Zones 4–8.

'Indian Magic' *p. 105*

Indian Magic Crabapple. New; ultimate size unknown, but probably reaching 20 ft. (6 m) at maturity. Rounded habit. Leaves dark green. Flowers rose-pink, 1½ in. (4 cm) wide. Fruits ½ in. (13 mm) wide, glossy-red changing to orange in late fall, glossy-brown in winter, persistent. Sometimes suffers from apple scab, but does not defoliate as most cultivars do. Blooms in spring. Fruit fall to winter. Zones 4–8.

'Indian Summer'

Indian Summer Crabapple. New; ultimate size unknown. Rounded habit. Leaves 3 in. (7.5 cm) long, good fall color. Rose-red flowers, 1½ in. (4 cm) wide. Fruit bright red, ¾ in. (19 mm) wide. Has a greater resistance to apple scab than 'Indian Magic'. Blooms in spring. Fruit fall to winter. Zones 4–8.

'Liset' *p. 104*

Liset Crabapple. To 15–20 ft. (4.5–6.0 m) high, rounded. Leaves deep purplish green. Flowers rose-red, 1½ in. (4 cm) wide. Fruit glossy maroon-red, ⅝ in. (16 mm) wide. Flowers as a young tree. Blooms in spring. Fruit in fall. Zones 4–8.

'Makamik' *p. 103*

Makamik Crabapple. To 40 ft. (12 m) high, upright-rounded. Leaves dark green, turning bronzy in late summer. Flowers dark red in bud, opening to purplish red, changing to light red, 2 in. (5 cm) wide. Fruit abundant, carmine, ¾ in. (19 mm) wide. Flowers are among the largest of any crabapple, and appear annually. Blooms in spring. Fruit in fall. Zones 4–8.

'Mary Potter' *pp. 108, 109*

Mary Potter Crabapple. A rounded tree, broader than tall, to perhaps 17 ft. (5 m), compact and regular in outline with dense branching. Leaves cleanly green, reasonably resistant to diseases, 2–3 in. (5.0–7.5 cm) long or more. Flowers pink in bud, opening pure white with bright yellow stamens, 1 in. (2.5 cm) across. Fruits red, ⅜ in. (9 mm) in diameter, showy throughout the fall season. A hybrid between *M. sargentii* 'Rosea' and *M.* × *atrosanguinea*. Blooms in spring. Fruit in fall. Zones 5–7.

'Ormiston Roy'

Ormiston Roy Crabapple. To 25–30 ft. (7.5–9.0 m) high, upright when young, rounding with age. Flowers pale pink to white, 1½ in. (4 cm) wide. Fruit yellow, ⅜ in. (9 mm) wide, abundant and persistent through winter. Good disease resistance. Blooms in spring. Fruit fall to winter. Zones 4–8.

'Robinson'

Robinson Crabapple. To 25 ft. (7.5 m) high, upright-spreading. Leaves often 3-lobed, dark green with red veins, purplish overall, unusual and handsome. Flowers deep pink, 1½ in. (4 cm) wide. Fruit glossy dark red, ⅜ in. (9 mm) wide, lost in the foliage until leaf drop. Blooms in spring. Fruit summer to fall. Zones 4–8.

sargentii *pp. 108, 109*

Sargent Crabapple. Distinctly a shrub unless grafted onto an upright or standard rootstock, or pruned early into a small tree.

Matures at 12–14 ft. (3.5–4.3 m); may be
twice as broad as high. Branching is dense,
often criss-crossing. Leaves medium green,
2–3 in. (5.0–7.5 cm) long, of neat texture.
Flowers pink in bud, opening clean white,
fragrant, 1 in. (2.5 cm) across, sometimes
prolific in alternate years, sparse between.
Blooms later than many other crabapples.
Fruit small, to ⅜ in. (9 mm) across, shiny
dark red. Fruits form as early as late
summer and persist into early winter, when
they are often eaten by birds.
A fine species for small area specimens,
groupings, low screens, and bank plantings.
Unfortunately, some nurseries grow Sargent
Crabapple from seed, which results in
considerable variations in growth rate and
habit. The cultivar 'Rosea' has darker red
buds and taller growth. Blooms in spring.
Fruit late summer to early winter. Zones
5–7; semihardy 4 and 8.

'Sentinel'

Sentinel Crabapple. New; ultimate size
unknown. Narrow-upright habit. Flowers
pale pink, 1½ in. (4 cm) wide. Fruit bright
red, ½ in. (13 mm) wide colors in late
summer and persists into winter. The
unusual formal, upright habit makes it a
good choice for street planting. Blooms in
spring. Fruit late summer to winter. Zones
4–8.

'Silver Moon'

Silver Moon Crabapple. New; ultimate size
unknown. Narrow-upright habit. Leaves
glossy dark green. White flowers, 1½ in.
(4 cm) wide, late in spring after leaves, a
nice contrast. Fruit purplish red, small and
abundant. Blooms in late spring. Fruit in
fall. Zones 4–8.

'Snowdrift'

Snowdrift Crabapple. To 20 ft. (6 m) high,
densely rounded. Flowers white, profuse,
1¼ in. (3 cm) wide. Fruit orange-red, ⅜ in.
(9 mm) wide. Resistant to diseases except
fireblight; should not be used where that
disease is common. Blooms in spring. Fruit
fall to winter. Zones 4–8.

'Sugar Tyme'

Sugar Tyme Crabapple. To 20 ft. (6 m)
high or more, upright-oval to rounded.
Leaves green. Flowers pure white, 1¼ in.
(3 cm) wide. Fruit rich red, ½ in. (13 mm)
wide; holds color into midwinter and is still

reddish in spring. Blooms in spring. Fruit
fall to spring. Zones 4–8.

'White Angel' *pp. 110, 111*
White Angel Crabapple. To 20–25 ft.
(6.0–7.5 m) high, irregularly rounded-
spreading, giving trees an open, informal
appearance. Leaves glossy dark green.
Flowers white, 1 in. (2.5 cm) wide,
completely covering the tree in spring. Fruit
scarlet, ½ in. (13 mm) wide, persists into
midwinter. Good disease resistance. Blooms
in spring. Fruit fall to winter. Zones 4–8.

'Winter Gold'
Winter Gold Crabapple. To 20 ft. (6 m)
high, rounded. Carmine buds, white
flowers, 1¼ in. (3 cm) wide. Fruits
attractive, yellow, ½ in. (13 mm) wide,
hold color until a hard freeze. Blooms in
spring. Fruit in fall. Zones 4–8.

Melaleuca
Myrtle family
Myrtaceae

Mel-a-lew′ka. Bottle Brush; Tea Tree. A
genus of Australian broadleaf evergreen trees
and shrubs, more than 100 species, closely
related to the genus *Callistemon,* the
following a highly ornamental species grown
in zones 9 and 10 for its striking flowers,
foliage, and bark.

Description
Leaves mostly alternate, simple. Flowers
red, white, or yellow, in spikes or heads,
the stamens so protruding and prominent
that each flower resembles a bottle brush.
Fruit a capsule, often moderately decorative.

How to Grow
Bottle brushes grow in almost any soil and
will endure heat, wind, and drought. The
following species suffers somewhat from
seashore exposure and is better grown
inland. Young trunks are flexible; stake the
first season. Prune anytime to keep vigorous
branches in check.

linariifolia pp. 212, 213
Flaxleaf Paperbark. An umbrella-topped tree
to 30 ft. (9 m) tall; bark white, shedding
into paper-thin flakes. Leaves stiff, needle-
like, 1¼ in. (3 cm) long, bright green.

White flowers with protruding stamens to ¾ in. (19 mm) long in spikes 2 in. (5 cm) long, giving the appearance of fluffy snow on the branches. Tolerates drought. Australia. Blooms in late spring. Zones 10; semihardy 9.

Melia
Mahogany family
Meliaceae

Mee'lia. A genus of Asian or Australian deciduous or semi-evergreen trees. About a score have been described, but only one is common in this country, the Chinaberry, which has been cultivated since the sixteenth century and is naturalized in all warm-temperate and tropical regions around the world. It is grown throughout the southern states for its fragrant lilac-colored spring blossoms.

Description
Leaves alternate, pinnate or doubly pinnate, leaflets toothed or entire. Flowers in loose panicles, white or purple, produced from the leaf axils. Fruit a berry, often mistakenly called a drupe.

How to Grow
Chinaberry will grow almost anywhere with no care, tolerates wet and drought, and is pest-free.

azedarach pp. 118, 119
Chinaberry; Bead Tree; China Tree. A mostly deciduous tree of spreading habit, sometimes growing 50 ft. (15 m) high, with furrowed bark. Leaves alternate, compound, 12–24 in. (30–60 cm) long, the leaflets arranged feather-fashion and toothed, 1½–2 in. (4–5 cm) long. Flowers conspicuous, held in loose compound panicles from the axils of the leaves, lavender-lilac and fragrant. Florets ¾ in. (19 mm) wide, panicles 8–16 in. (20.0–40.5 cm) long, not outstanding. The fruit is nearly round, yellow, ¾ in. (19 mm) across, hanging on after the leaves fall, somewhat ornamental, poisonous. Chinaberry is fast-growing, weak-wooded, tolerant of most environmental extremes, and pest-free. Cultivar 'Umbraculiformis', Texas Umbrella Tree, has drooping foliage on erect, crowded branches that spread from

the trunk-like spokes, producing an umbrella-like effect. Himalayas and China. Blooms in spring. Fruit in fall. Zones 7–10.

Metasequoia
Bald cypress family
Taxodiaceae

Met-a-see-quoy'a. Dawn Redwood. An extraordinarily interesting genus of one deciduous coniferous species, previously known only through fossils estimated to be 30–50 million years old, and reputedly the ancestor of *Sequoia*. In 1946 it was discovered as a living tree near Mo-tao-chi in the province of Hupeh, China; young trees are now offered by many nurseries in this country.

Description
Leaves needle-like, deciduous, opposite, on lateral branchlets. Cones comprised of about 12 scales, with several winged seeds to each scale.

How to Grow
Dawn Redwood transplants easily and grows best in moist but well-drained, slightly acid soil, in full sun. Trees are subject to frost damage, so choose high or hillside sites rather than low spots, and avoid fall water and fertilizer. Pest- and disease-free.

glyptostroboides pp. 138, 139

Dawn Redwood. A tree, quite similar in aspect to our Southern Cypress, that loses its leaves each fall. Some small twigs are also deciduous. In its native habitat it is a tree up to 150 ft. (45 m), and many specimens now grow to 100 ft. (30 m) high. Leaves needle-like, opposite, arranged in flat sprays, the leaves ½–1½ in. (1.3–4.0 cm) long, soft and light green, delicate in texture, turning bronzy brown in fall. Cones inconspicuous, 1 in. (2.5 cm) long, comprising about 12 scales, the seeds winged. Dawn Redwood is a rapid-growing tree, rather narrowly conical; bark fissured and shredded and trunk buttressed on older specimens. Not for small properties. China. Zones 5–8.

Morus
Mulberry family
Moraceae

More′us. Mulberry. These fruit-bearing
deciduous trees, one of them widely grown
in the Far East as food for silkworms,
comprise 12 species, all the cultivated ones
Asiatic except for one native American.
Varieties of White Mulberry, the species
described below, were once widely planted
in the U.S. for their edible fruit and for
their foliage.

Description
Mulberries have alternate, often lobed
leaves, and small greenish flowers in
stalked, hanging catkins, the male and
female separate, sometimes on different
trees. Petals none, the sepals usually 4.
Fruit edible, berrylike, but actually an
aggregate fruit resembling a blackberry,
consisting of a dry fruit covered with the
fleshy sepals from several flowers.

How to Grow
Plant White Mulberry in almost any soil
except a swampy one. Trees withstand
drought, salt, and city conditions and need
little pruning except the occasional removal
of dead branches. A canker disease may kill
branches; if so, prune below the infested
area.

alba pp. *174, 175*
White Mulberry, nonfruiting cultivars. The
species is a tree to 60 ft. (18 m) tall,
producing very messy fruit. Fruitless
cultivars are generally less vigorous, forming
round-topped trees of 35–40 ft. (10.5–
12.0 m) high and wide. Leaves alternate,
simple, sometimes lobed, varying with
cultivar, 2–7 in. (5.0–17.5 cm) long, dark
green, with little or no fall color. Some
fruitless cultivars are 'Kingan', 'Chaparral'
(also weeping), 'Stribling', and 'Fruitless'.
China. Zones 5–9.

Nyssa
Tupelo family
Nyssaceae

Nis′sa. Tupelo; Sour Gum. A small genus
of 6 or 7 species of North American and
Asiatic deciduous shade trees, noted for

their fine fall foliage. The Sour Gum of
e. North America is the only widely planted
species.

Description
Leaves alternate, practically or wholly
without marginal teeth. Flowers small,
greenish, not showy, borne in small
headlike clusters, unisexual or polygamous.
Fruit an oblong, 1–seeded drupe, usually
black-purple, inconspicuous.

How to Grow
The species below is hard to transplant;
start with small trees, balled or container-
grown. Though often found growing
natively in swampy sites, it will grow in
most soil situations, and tolerates drought.
Light shade will lessen fall color, but not
growth. Insect and disease problems are
seldom serious. One taboo is polluted air—
Sour Gum is not a tree for cities.

sylvatica pp. 182, 183
Sour Gum; Pepperidge; Black Gum;
Tupelo. A tree, to 85 ft. (26 m) high,
occasionally taller in the wild, with
horizontal branches drooping gradually and
gracefully at the ends. Leaves 3–5 in.
(7.5–12.5 cm) long, somewhat broader
toward the pointed tip, mostly without any
marginal teeth. Fruit usually in clusters of
1–3, ⅔ in. (17 mm) long. One of the finest
native trees for moist sites, and will grow
well in dry soil. Sour Gum is one of the
earliest trees to show fall color, and its
brilliant scarlet hue is one of the brightest.
E. North America, Maine to Mich. to Fla.
and Tex. Zones 4–9.

Olea
Olive family
Oleaceae

O'lee-a. Olive. Evergreen shrubs and trees
of the Old World, a genus of 20 species,
one of which has been cultivated since
antiquity for its fruit, the olive. Picturesque
beauty qualifies it for landscape use as well.

Description
Olive is a tree with opposite leaves having
no marginal teeth. Flowers small, white.
Fruit a true drupe, the common olive being
the only edible one.

How to Grow

Plant olive trees in full sun, in well-drained soil, and you need worry about little else. Some authorities claim trees are more attractive in outline if soil is dry and nutrient poor. Olive trees may sucker from the base. To obtain a tree form, select one trunk, or several, and diligently remove all sucker growth and lower branches from the trunk. Early summer pruning will reduce resprouting. Problems are scale insects, which are easily controlled with dormant oil spray, and olive gall—prune off galls or infected branches and disinfect pruners after each cut.

europaea pp. *210, 211*

Olive. A ruggedly picturesque tree, to 30 ft. (9 m) high. Branches are thornless, but a wild thorny variety is known. Leaves elliptic or oblongish, 1–3 in. (2.5–7.5 cm) long, green above, silvery and somewhat scurfy beneath, giving a pleasant willowlike effect. Flowers small, white, fragrant, in 2 in. (5 cm) panicles. Fruit is the edible olive, 1½ in. (4 cm) long, green changing to purplish black.

Fruit stains walks, driveways, patios. For landscape use, the cultivar 'Fruitless', which has a few fruits, is best. Olives are soft-textured and attractive trees that assume the appearance of great antiquity, which in fact they often attain. Native throughout the Mediterranean region, but only its hottest parts. Zones 9–10; semihardy 8.

Oxydendrum
Heath family
Ericaceae

Ok-si-den'drum. Sourwood. A single species, a beautifully white-flowered deciduous tree, found wild in the eastern U.S. and grown for its flowers, fruit, and scarlet fall foliage.

Description

Leaves alternate, simple, and large. Flowers in drooping panicles, calyx 5–lobed, stamens 10. Fruit a 5–valved capsule.

How to Grow

Like rhododendrons, to which it is related, Sourwood needs an acid soil (pH 4.0–5.5 preferable), moist and well-drained. Full sun is best for flowers and fall color, but it will grow well in shade. Avoid disturbing soil in the root zone—Sourwood roots are shallow. Mulch, and water trees during drought during their first few seasons. Established plants endure dryness fairly well. Sourwood has no serious pests, but cannot endure polluted air.

arboreum p. 132, 133

Sourwood; Sorrel Tree. Grows 30–50 ft. (9–15 m) high, sometimes taller in the wild. Leaves alternate, stalked, bitter-tasting, oblongish, 6–8 in. (15–20 cm) long, brilliantly scarlet in the fall. Flowers small, not over ⅓ in. (8 mm) long, in drooping racemes 8–10 in. (20–25 cm) long, very handsome and fragrant. Fruit a gray-hairy capsule, for a time in fall almost as attractive as the flowers. Though the tree is hardy north of its wild range, it grows slowly, and few specimens reach the dimensions given. Pa. and Ill. to Fla. and La. Blooms in midsummer. Fruit fall to winter. Zones 5–9.

Paulownia
Foxglove family
Scrophulariaceae

Paul-ow′ni-a. Six species of deciduous Chinese trees. Paulownias are handsome trees when in bloom, and make good lawn specimens, but are not long-lived. The species below is prized for its spectacular spring flowers and rapid growth.

Description
Leaves similar to catalpa, opposite, variable in size and shape, sometimes lobed, usually entire. Flowers fragrant, tubular, resembling foxglove blossoms, white to violet and borne in terminal panicles before the leaves. Fruit an ovoid, pointed capsule containing a great many small winged seeds.

How to Grow
Transplant balled or container-grown plants in early spring. Paulownia grows best in rich, well-drained soil, neutral or acid, but tolerates a wide range of soil conditions, except soggy and very dry. Plant in either partial shade or full sun, but avoid windy areas.
Paulownia grows tall rapidly when young,

then rounds out; allow space for a tree up to
50 ft. (15 m) tall and equally wide. Plants
are sometimes cut to the ground in the
spring—especially if winter-damaged—to
encourage vigorous, large-leaved shoots, up
to 12 ft. (3.5 m) tall in one season. Few
insects or diseases bother them.

tomentosa pp. 84, 85
Empress Tree. Grows 30–50 ft. (9–15 m)
high, with thick, stiff branches, rather open
in habit and becoming round-topped. Leaves
hairy, more or less ovate, entire or lobed,
varying in size from 5–10 in. (12.5–
25.0 cm) on ordinary growth, to 2 ft.
(60 cm) or more on vigorous shoots. Flowers
pale violet, 2 in. (5 cm) long, in erect
panicles, 8–10 in. (20–25 cm) long.
Flower buds often killed by sub-zero
temperatures and are not reliably hardy
north of zone 6, but in bloom, it is one of
the most spectacular flowering trees in the
temperate zone. Flowers, leaves, and fruits
are litter problems when trees are planted
near high-use areas. China; escaped from
cultivation in the eastern states from N.Y.
to Ga. Blooms in spring. Zones 6–9.

Phellodendron
Citrus family
Rutaceae

Fell-o-den'dron. Corktree. A genus of 8
or 9 species of deciduous Asiatic trees.
Corktrees grow rapidly when young,
developing into shapely round-headed trees,
wide-spreading with age, that make good
lawn specimens. The foliage is dark green,
decorative, and turns yellow in the fall, but
drops soon after. Though the flowers are not
showy, they are followed by clusters of
black fruits that hang for several months
and are interesting in winter.

Description
Leaves opposite, compound, with leaflets
arranged feather-fashion. Leafstalks swollen
at the base and concealing the buds. Male
and female flowers in terminal clusters on
separate trees, greenish yellow, small and
inconspicuous. Fruit black, berrylike.

How to Grow
Amur Corktree transplants easily, needs
sun, and grows well in almost any type of

soil except soggy and very dry. However, once established, it endures drought nicely. Insects and diseases avoid this species. Prune to prevent ungainly shape during first 15 years; trees need little if any pruning thereafter.

***amurense** pp. 180, 181*
Amur Corktree. A tree to 40–50 ft. (12–15 m), with gray, deeply fissured, corky bark. Branches become massive and horizontal as tree ages. Leaves 10–15 in. (25–38 cm) long with 5–13 ovate or oval leaflets, 2–4 in. (5–10 cm) long, aromatic when bruised. Flowers yellow-green, small, in clusters 2–3 in. (5.0–7.5 cm) across, insignificant. Fruit black, berrylike, not highly ornamental. A pest-free species of picturesque form. Manchuria and n. China. Zones 4–7.

Phoenix
Palm family
Palmae

Fee'nix. An important genus of feather palms, including the Date Palm and several others widely grown ornamentally. There are 20 known African and Asiatic species, and 5 are horticulturally important.

Description
Trunks often spineless, except for the spinelike lower segments on the leaves of some species. Trunk not usually tall or woody, often consisting merely of the woody bases of old leaves. Leaflets or segments long and narrow, the midrib replaced by a ridge, along each side of which are 2 prominent veins. Male and female flowers on different plants, rarely blooming in cultivation, except on the Date Palm. Flowers small, yellowish, borne on long, drooping, branched stalks. Stamens 6. Fruit a fleshy drupe, its seed having a single groove.

How to Grow
Plant from a container in any season, in sun, and in rich well-drained soil. Irrigate regularly during dry weather, but don't overwater. Hose down leaves occasionally to discourage aphids. Old leaves dry and hang for a considerable time; remove them to improve a plant's appearance.

canariensis p. 194, 195
Canary Islands Date Palm. A handsome
ornamental palm, 50–60 ft. (15–18 m) high
at full maturity. Leaves handsome, good
green color, arching, 15–20 ft. (4.5–6.0 m)
long, the leaflets or segments very
numerous, standing at different angles from
the main leafstalk, narrow, long-pointed,
the lower ones spiny. Flowers insignificant.
Fruiting cluster often drooping, 3–8 ft.
(0.9–2.4 m) long, the fruit egg-shaped or
roundish, yellowish red, to ¾ in. (19 mm)
long. A deservedly popular palm, hardier
than many others and much used for avenue
planting in Calif. Canary Islands. Fruit fall
to winter. Zones 9–10.

Picea
Pine family
Pinaceae

Py-see'a or Py'see-a. Spruce. Usually
majestic, sometimes gigantic, needle-leaf
evergreen trees of great horticultural
importance; also widely used for timber and
in the making of paper pulp. Forty-five
species of spruce are known, all from the
northern hemisphere, generally from cool and
moist regions. Over 30 species and scores of
horticultural varieties are grown in the U.S.
The spruces are without doubt the most
versatile cultivated conifers and offer a wide
selection of material, ranging in size from
small shrubby plants to huge forest
specimens. Because of their dense habit,
spruces are excellent choices for protective
plantings such as hedges and windbreaks.
Below are the most representative and the
most readily available and generally hardy of
the cultivated species.

Description
Spruces normally have a single unbranched
trunk, with tiers or whorls of branches, and
often the outline of the tree is almost
exactly the shape of a candle flame. Leaves
small, very numerous, needle-like, each on a
tiny footlike stalk, from which it falls
readily when dry. The leaves are rarely flat,
generally being somewhat 4-sided in cross
section.
Male flowers composed only of naked
anthers, and the female of naked ovules
between the scales of what is ultimately the
cone. The cones are mostly drooping in

fruit, the scales becoming somewhat woody, but not as woody or prickly as in many pines. Two seeds under each scale, the seeds winged.

How to Grow
Spruces may be purchased bare root as seedlings and small transplants, and planted successfully if the roots are not exposed to air for more than a few moments. Larger plants should be balled or container-grown. The planting site should be in full sun or light shade. Avoid drying winds. Like most conifers, spruces are not fussy about soil, although a light, sandy loam is best. Requirements for moisture are far more exacting; neither a really dry soil nor a poorly drained one will do. Mulching retains moisture and protects the shallow roots.
Spruces seldom require pruning, other than the occasional removal of dead or diseased wood. Where some corrective shaping is desired, remove the terminal bud on branches that are growing out of place or are developing too fast. Spruce hedges should be much wider at the base than at the top, otherwise lower branches will die for lack of light. Always prune or shear spruces in late summer when dormant.

abies pp. 256, 257
Norway Spruce. Probably the most widely cultivated evergreen tree in America. A conical tree, up to 150 ft. (45 m) but usually less than 100 ft. (30 m) high, the mature bark reddish brown, branchlets picturesquely pendulous along the branches. Leaves ¾ in. (19 mm) long, glossy dark green. Cones 4–7 in. (10.0–17.5 cm) long. Though many horticultural forms of the typical tree exist, few but dwarf forms are common in the nursery trade. Sometimes known as *P. excelsa*. Europe. Cones fall to winter. Zones 3–7.

glauca pp. 280, 281
White Spruce. A tree, 60–70 ft. (18–21 m) high, the branches ascending, with drooping branchlets. Leaves ¾ in. (19 mm) long, bluish green. Cones cylindric, 1½–2 in. (4–5 cm) long. Withstands heat, wind, and dryness better than most spruces, but needs cold winters. N. North America. Cones fall to winter. Zones 3–6.

omorika pp. 256, 257

Serbian Spruce. An evergreen tree, up to
100 ft. (30 m) high, the upper branches
ascending. Very narrow for a spruce; width
at base only about one-quarter of height.
Leaves somewhat flattened, scarcely ½ in.
(13 mm) long. Dark green beneath, but
with 2 white bands above. Cones 2–2½ in.
(5–6 cm) long, not ornamental. Possibly the
most satisfactory spruce for the eastern
states. The cultivar 'Pendula' has gently
weeping branches, but maintains a narrowly
upright habit. S. Europe. Zones 4–7.

orientalis pp. 278, 279

Oriental Spruce. A magnificent evergreen,
slower growing than other spruces, reaching
120 ft. (36 m) in height in the wild, but
seldom more than 65–70 ft. (20–21 m) in
cultivation. Branches slightly ascending, the
branchlets often drooping in a graceful
effect. Leaves glossy-green, scarcely ½ in.
(13 mm) long, dense. Cones 2–4 in.
(5–10 cm) long. Will tolerate poor soils,
but not poorly drained ones. Windy, dry
winters cause browning of foliage, but new
growth soon covers. Caucasus and Asia
Minor. Cones fall to winter. Zones 5–8.

pungens pp. 280, 281

Colorado Spruce. A beautiful American
evergreen tree, often 150 ft. (45 m) high in
the wild, less in cultivation, to 100 ft.
(30 m) in a century. The whorls of
branches stiffly horizontal, leaves rigid,
stiff, prickle-pointed, nearly 1¼ in. (3 cm)
long, dull green to bluish. Cones 3–4 in.
(7.5–10.0 cm) long.
A commonly grown species, but sometimes
affected by canker, which kills the lower
branches. Lower branches are lost naturally
with age. Mites, bagworms, and other
insects can be serious problems, but are
easily controlled with proper treatments.
A number of cultivated forms are grown for
the color of their needles or for their growth
habit; blue-foliaged forms are called Blue
Colorado Spruce. *P. pungens* 'Hoopsii',
Hoops' Blue Colorado Spruce, has perhaps
the most silvery blue foliage of all the Blue
Colorado Spruce cultivars. It reaches 80 ft.
(24 m) at maturity, but is hardy only to
zone 4. Rocky Mts. Cones fall to winter.
Zones 3–7.

Pinus
Pine family
Pinaceae

Py'nus. Pine. Magnificent evergreen trees of
outstanding value as ornamental and timber
trees. Nearly all of the approximately 90
known species are from the north temperate
zone, a few in Mexico, the West Indies, and
Malaysia. Over 50 species of pine are in
cultivation in the U.S., many known only
to horticultural specialists. Those listed
below are readily available, easy to grow,
and make handsome screen or ornamental
plantings.

Description
In nearly all pines the trunk, barring injury,
is continuous, and has whorls or tiers of
branches, seldom with sporadic branches
outside the whorl. Leaves needle-like, borne
in sheathed clusters of 2–5, very rarely
solitary, the sheaths parchmentlike and
enclosing only the bases of the leaves. There
are also small scale-like leaves that drop
soon after new growth starts and are rarely
noticed.
Male flowers consist of naked, catkinlike or
conelike masses of anthers that produce
pollen—dusty clouds of it in some species.
Female flowers consist of naked ovules
between the bases of woody scales, the
collection of scales forming the familiar pine
cone. Scales of the cone, in some species,
tipped with a recurved prickle. Seeds,
usually winged, are edible in some species.
All are wind-pollinated.

How to Grow
Most pines will grow quite well in a rather
light soil. Drainage is by far the most
important consideration, because few pines
succeed in wet soil. Various pines have a
greater or lesser tolerance of drought, salt,
and air pollution than others—read
descriptions for details.
Exposure and winter sun are great enemies
of the pine. In the summer, a drying wind
will do far greater damage by turning
foliage brown than a dry soil. A warm
winter's sun, often from a direct southern
exposure, may cause a similar effect. Pine
roots cannot stand long exposure to the air,
so transplant trees with a ball of earth.
Prune by removing leading branches back to
side branches or to main trunks. Expanding
buds form long candles in spring; snapping

off part of a candle will reduce the length of the ensuing branch by the same ratio. Improve the shape of young pines by this method.

bungeana pp. 270, 271
Lacebark Pine. A tree, to 75 ft. (22.5 m) high. Bark on the trunk flaking off like a sycamore, leaving smooth patches that may be white or change through greenish to cream color. Needles 3, lustrous dark green, 2–4 in. (5–10 cm) long. Cones 2–3 in. (5.0–7.5 cm) long. Grows slowly. Often grown with several trunks and lower branches removed to showcase the attractive bark. China. Cones fall to winter. Zones 5–8.

canariensis pp. 254, 255
Canary Island Pine. A tree, up to 100 ft. (30 m) in the wild, much less as cultivated. Needles 3, bluish green when young, pale green in age, nearly 12 in. (30 cm) long, slender and graceful. Cones short-stalked, cylindric, 6–9 in. (15.0–22.5 cm) long, 3 in. (7.5 cm) wide, solitary or in small clusters. Grows fast; young plants are awkward, but mature trees are dense and round-topped. Canary Islands. Cones fall to winter. Zones 9–10; semihardy 8.

contorta pp. 268, 269
Shore Pine; Beach Pine. A round-headed, rather densely-branched tree, not over 30 ft. (9 m) high as cultivated, usually less. Needles 2, stiff, rigid and twisted, 1–3 in. (2.5–7.5 cm) long. Cones stalkless, ovoid, not over 2 in. (5 cm) long, the scales tipped by a slender prickle. A good small evergreen tree for Pacific coastal regions, not as well adapted to eastern climates. Var. *latifolia*, Lodgepole Pine, an inland form of the species, grows to 150 ft. (45 m) high. Alaska to Calif. Cones fall to winter. Zones 7–10.

densiflora pp. 262, 263
Japanese Red Pine. A round-headed tree with interesting irregular branching, up to 100 ft. (30 m) high, usually lower. Leaves bluish green, 3–5 in. (7.5–12.5 cm) long, 2 in each sheath. Cones oblongish, 2 in. (5 cm) long. Bark orangish red on branches and upper trunks, attractive the year around. There are several horticultural forms with white- or yellowish-tipped leaves, and the cultivar 'Umbraculifera', the Tanyosho

Pine, is a dwarf form with an umbrella-shaped head. Japan. Cones throughout the year. Zones 5–8; semihardy 4.

flexilis pp. 260, 261

Limber Pine. Grows slowly to 75 ft. (22.5 m) in height, usually less. Leaves stiff, dark green, 2–3 in. (5.0–7.5 cm) long, 5 in each sheath. Cones egg-shaped, 4–6 in.(10–15 cm) long. A doughty species that endures wind and dry soil better than most pines. Mts. of w. North America. Cones fall to winter. Zones 4–7.

halepensis p. 262

Aleppo Pine. An upright open tree, up to 60 ft. (18 m) high. Leaves light green, 3–4 in. (7.5–10.0 cm) long, 2, or rarely 3, in each sheath. Cones egg-shaped or conical, 3 in. (7.5 cm) long. Tolerant of drought, heat, wind, and salt. More attractive pines are available for good growing conditions. Mediterranean region. Cones fall to winter. Zones 8–10.

lambertiana p. 263

Sugar Pine. An immense forest tree, to 200 ft. (60 m) high. Leaves 3–4 in. (7.5–10.0 cm) long, 5 in each cluster, dark bluish green with silvery lines. Large cones cylindrical, 10–20 in. (25–50 cm) long, to 4 in. (10 cm) thick. Often planted as a shade or screen tree on large properties. Grows well in northwestern states; seldom planted east of the Rocky Mts. Oreg. to lower Calif. Cones fall to winter. Zones 6–8.

nigra pp. 266, 267

Austrian Pine. A broadly conical tree, up to 100 ft. (30 m) high, usually 60 ft. (18 m) or less. Leaves dark green, 4–6 in. (10–15 cm) long, 2 in each sheath. Cones egg-shaped or conical, 3 in. (7.5 cm) long. One of the most widely cultivated pines in the country, and, with *P. thunbergiana,* the best for city conditions. The dark, handsome foliage makes this a distinctive screen or background evergreen. In some areas, trees are subject to severe tip blight damage. S. and cen. Europe and Asia Minor. Cones fall to winter. Zones 4–8.

parviflora pp. 282, 283

Japanese White Pine. Seldom as tall as 60 ft. (18 m), with wide-spreading branches, width at base often equal to height. Leaves

1½ in. (4 cm) long, twisted, 5 in each sheath, usually crowded near ends of twigs, thus apparently in dense, small tufts, a fine-textured effect. Cones egg-shaped, 3 in. (7.5 cm) long. Salt tolerant. Trees are often ungainly when young, but mature gracefully into attractive small trees. The cultivar 'Glauca' has bluish needles, grows more slowly. Japan. Cones fall to winter. Zones 5–7.

resinosa pp. 264, 265

Red Pine; Norway Pine. Broadly conical; up to 100 ft. (30 m) high in native stands, seldom over 75 ft. (22.5 m) in cultivation. Leaves glossy-green, 4–6 in. (10–15 cm) long, 2 in each sheath, snapping when bent double. Cones egg-shaped or conical, 2 in. (5 cm) long.

The name Norway Pine is said to originate from Norway, Maine, where the tree is common. A very valuable, hardy, and quick-growing tree, useful for timber and as a screen or background tree in ornamental plantings. Newfoundland to Pa. and west to Minn. Cones fall to winter. Zones 3–7.

strobus pp. 268, 269

Eastern White Pine. One of the outstanding timber pines of North America and perhaps the most beautiful of all the eastern species; 50–150 ft. (15–45 m) high. Leaves soft, bluish green, 3–5 in. (7.5–12.5 cm) long, 5 in each sheath. Cones cylindric, 4–8 in. (10–20 cm) long. Not tolerant of inner-city air pollution, or of salt spray from highways or seashores. There are many horticultural forms of this most popular pine, some dwarf, others weeping, and one with a columnar, erect habit. E. North America. Cones fall to winter. Zones 4–7.

sylvestris pp. 266, 267

Scotch Pine. In age an irregular, round-topped tree, reaching 90 ft. (27 m) high, the bark cinnamon-brown. Leaves stiff, twisted, bluish green, 1–4 in. (2.5–10.0 cm) long, 2 in each sheath. Cones egg-shaped or conical, usually 2½ in. (6 cm) long. Tolerates drought. Useful as picturesque specimens. Mature trees are subject to a disfiguring and sometimes fatal fungal blight in some areas. There are several horticultural forms with variously colored foliage and various growth habits. A dwarf blue-foliaged form is sold under various names. 'Fastigiata' is a very narrow upright cultivar. Eurasia. Cones fall to winter. Zones 3–8.

taeda pp. 264, 265

Loblolly Pine. A rapidly growing evergreen tree, especially when young, reaching 90 ft. (27 m) at maturity. Conical in youth, losing lower branches and becoming round-headed with age. Reddish-brown bark. Bright green needles in clusters of 3, 6–9 in. (15.0–22.5 cm) long, bold in appearance. Cones 3–5 in. (7.5–12.5 cm) long, scales with sharp points. Not the most beautiful of the pines, but tolerant of a wide range of soil conditions, and seldom seriously affected by insects or diseases. N.J. to Tex. Cones fall to winter. Zones 7–9.

thunbergiana pp. 260, 261

Japanese Black Pine. Irregularly picturesque in outline, to 90 ft. (27 m) high, usually much shorter. Dark green rigid leaves 3–5 in. (7.5–12.5 cm) long or more, 2 in each sheath. Cones usually 2 in. (5 cm), not over 3 in. (7.5 cm) long. One of the most satisfactory of cultivated pines, especially in exposed, wind-swept places along the seacoast. Subject to browning of needles in severe zone 5 winters. Often called *P. thunbergii*. Japan. Cones fall to winter. Zones 5–9.

Pistacia
Sumac family
Anacardiaceae

Pis-tash′i-a. Pistachio. Aromatic shrubs or trees, deciduous and evergreen, most of the 10 species Eurasian, including the species below, which is a deciduous shade tree with handsome foliage and fruit. The species *P. vera* is the source of Pistachio nuts.

Description
Alternate, compound leaves, leaflets arranged feather-fashion, with or without an odd one at the end. Male and female flowers on separate plants, small, inconspicuous, without petals, and mostly in lateral panicles. Fruit a dry drupe.

How to Grow
Plant balled or container-grown trees. Needs full sun. Pistache grows best in good well-drained soil, but will grow quite well in

poor dry soil. Withstands wind and
drought, and has no serious pests. May need
early pruning to develop a symmetrical
rounded shape.

chinensis pp. 160, 161

Chinese Pistache. A rounded tree, up to
60 ft. (18 m) high, not evergreen. Leaflets
in 5–6 pairs, more or less lance-shaped.
Fruit (on female trees) flattened, ¼ in.
(6 mm) long, scarlet at first, ultimately
purplish. Foliage handsomely colored in the
fall, even under semidesert conditions. No
insect or disease problems. Excellent for
lawn or street planting. China. Fruit in fall.
Zones 7–9.

Pittosporum
Tobira family
Pittosporaceae

Pi-tos'po-rum or pit-o-spo'rum. Australian
Laurel. Over 100 species of Australasian
broadleaf evergreen shrubs and trees, several
grown in zones 9 and 10, especially in
s. Calif. The species below makes a fine
screen tree with attractive scented flowers.

Description
Australian laurels have alternate or whorled
leaves, wavy-margined and faintly toothed
or without teeth. Flowers in clusters or
solitary, usually terminal, but sometimes on
the leaf axils. Sepals 5, usually distinct.
Petals 5, mostly clawed and more or less
joined at the base, free above. Fruit a
capsule, its seed sticky.

How to Grow
Plant in full sun or partial shade, in
reasonably good soil. Grows best if watered
during droughts. Modest pruning maintains
a round-topped tree as wide as high, usually
with several trunks. Victorian Box may be
sheared regularly as a hedge or screen.
Watch for aphids and scale insects.

undulatum pp. 208, 209

Victorian Box; Cheesewood; Mock Orange.
A broadleaf evergreen tree, 30–40 ft.
(9–12 m) high. Leaves oblongish or
narrower, 4–6 in. (10–15 cm) long, wavy-
margined, tapering at the tip, shining
green. Flower clusters terminal, the corolla
sweetly fragrant, white, ½ in. (13 mm)

long in umbels 3 in. (7.5 cm) wide. Fruit
orange, ½ in. (13 mm) long, messy on
walks, etc. An attractive tree for lawn and
street planting, or as a screen. Australia.
Blooms in spring. Fruit in fall. Zones 9–10.

Podocarpus
Podocarpus family
Podocarpaceae

Po-do-kar′pus. Handsome evergreen trees or
shrubs, mostly from the southern
hemisphere north to the West Indies and
Japan, and chiefly from mountainous areas.
Of the 75 known species, only a few are
grown in the U.S., mostly in Calif., along
the Gulf Coast, and in Fla., and are useful
there as screen and background plantings,
and everywhere as specimens in tubs and
other planters. In the South, podocarpus are
commonly but incorrectly called Japanese
Yew.

Description
Leaves alternate, mostly narrow or ovalish,
but not scale-like or needle-like, and not
suggesting the foliage of a coniferous
evergreen. Male flowers consist of naked,
catkinlike masses of anthers, the female a
solitary naked ovule between 1 or 2 small
bracts. Fruit fleshy-stalked, mostly plumlike
or berrylike.

How to Grow
Podocarpus grow well in most soils, except
those that are alkaline, heavy, or wet. In
hot areas, some shade, especially in
afternoon, is advisable. Young plants need
staking and diligent pruning to develop a
tree form.

gracilior pp. 214, 215
Fern Pine. Slow-growing, may reach 60 ft.
(18 m) in time. Juvenile leaves glossy dark
green, 2–4 in. (5–10 cm) long. Mature
leaves grayish- or bluish-green, 1–2 in.
(2.5–5.0 cm) long, closely set on twigs.
Flowers insignificant. Fruit ⅝ in. (16 mm)
long, blue, ornamentally unimportant. A
tidy, pest-free tree, suitable for hedging and
many other landscape functions. Often
remains shrubby if not trained to a tree
form. E. Africa. Zones 9–10.

macrophyllus pp. 214, 215
Yew Podocarpus. Probably the most
common podocarpus in cultivation in the
U.S., a tree to 40 ft. (12 m) high. Leaves
lance-shaped, 3–4 in. (7.5–10.0 cm)
long, dark green above, paler beneath.
Fruit egg-shaped, ½ in. (13 mm) long,
greenish purple, the fleshy stalk purple. A
dependable and useful houseplant while
young, and often kept in a tub or large
flowerpot. Shrubby in zone 8; useful as a
rounded tree or for screening in zones 9 and
10. Tolerates salt and shade. Japan. Fruit in
fall. Zones 8–10.

Prosopis
Pea family
Leguminosae

Pro-soap'is. Mesquite. A genus of tropical
or subtropical thorny trees or shrubs,
comprising about 25 species. Mesquite is
usually a thorny shrub, only 3–10 ft.
(0.9–3.0 m) high in the desert, and is an
important forage plant throughout the
southwestern states. With proper care, they
can become effective screen and shade trees
for arid areas.

Description
Stems with or without spines. Leaves twice-
compound, leaflets small, not toothed.
Flower not pealike; greenish, small, in
roundish spikes, growing from the axils of
the leaves. Pod very narrow, leathery, not
splitting.

How to Grow
Mesquite needs a deep soil and regular
watering to become a tree, but tolerates
drought thereafter. Plants are also drought
tolerant when young, but will remain
shrubs if not irrigated. Remove lower
branches for headroom as trees develop.

glandulosa pp. 162, 163
Mesquite; Honey Mesquite; Western Honey
Mesquite. A shrub or small tree, to 30 ft.
(9 m) high, with the crown spreading an
equal distance or more. Twigs with sharp
thorns 1–2 in. (2.5–5.0 cm) long, especially
on young plants. Leaves twice-compound,
with 1–2 pairs of branchlets, each with
6–20 pairs of leaflets, bright green,
feathery. Flowers tiny, yellowish green, in

dense spike-like racemes about 2 in. (5 cm) long, attractive to bees. Fruit 2–6 in. (5–15 cm) long. Wide-spreading desert shade trees, also useful as screens and windbreaks, in the Southwest only. *P.g.* var. *torreyana* is a recommended variety. Ariz., s. Calif., Tex., and Mexico. Blooms spring to summer. Fruit in winter. Zones 7–9.

Prunus
Rose family
Rosaceae

Proo'nus. A large and immensely important genus of deciduous and broadleaf evergreen shrubs and trees, nearly all from the north temperate zone, a few reaching to the Andes. It comprises over 400 species and includes all the plums, cherries, apricots, peaches, and almonds. Besides the outstanding importance of the fruit trees, *Prunus* contains all the Japanese flowering cherries and many other superb flowering shrubs and trees, the fruit of which is generally inedible.

Description
Leaves alternate, nearly always sharply toothed, never compound. Flowers in corymbs or racemes, or sometimes few or only one; white, or pink, or red in some horticultural forms, typically with 5 sepals, 5 petals, and many stamens. Some horticultural forms have doubled petals and sometimes no functional stamens and no fruit. Fruit is typically a drupe—a fleshy fruit with a single stone.

How to Grow
Flowering cherries need full sun and reasonably moist, well-drained soil. Because stress of any sort increases susceptibility to various insects and diseases, cherries as a group are short-lived—about 30 years, unless coddled. Keep a circle of organic mulch beneath branch spread and water deeply and regularly during drought. Prune weak or crossing branches in early spring. Watch for insect and disease problems, and diagnose and treat them early.

lusitanica pp. 206, 207
Portugal Laurel. An evergreen tree to 40 ft. (12 m) or less. Leaves dark green, toothed, to 5 in. (12.5 cm) long on reddish

leafstalks. Small creamy white flowers in spring on racemes to 10 in. (25 cm) long. Fruit red, then purplish black, ½ in. (13 mm) long, maturing on the same racemes. Useful as a small tree, as an informal screen, or as a clipped hedge. Portugal, Spain. Blooms in spring. Fruit in summer. Zones 7–10.

padus pp. 92, 93

European Bird Cherry. A tree, up to 40 ft. (12 m) high, grown as a flowering shade tree; its fruit has no value. Leaves elliptic or oblongish, 3–5½ in. (7.5–14.0 cm) long, sharply toothed, grayish beneath. Flowers fragrant, white, ½ in. (13 mm) wide, in finger-shaped, hanging racemes 3–6 in. (7.5–15.0 cm) long. Fruit black, ½ in. (13 mm) in diameter. One of the first trees to leaf out in spring. Eurasia. Blooms in spring. Fruit in summer. Zones 4–7.

sargentii pp. 124, 125

Sargent Cherry. An extremely handsome tree, 50 ft. (15 m) high, with smooth reddish-brown bark. Leaves elliptic or broader, 2–5 in. (5.0–12.5 cm) long, purplish when unfolding, sharply toothed, orange-red in fall. Flowers rose-pink, 1½ in. (4 cm) wide, in stalkless umbels of 2–4, but very numerous. Fruit nearly round, ½ in. (13 mm) in diameter, purplish black, inconspicuous. Perhaps the best of the flowering cherries. Japan. Blooms in early spring. Zones 5–8.

serrulata 'Kwanzan' pp. 82, 83

Kwanzan Oriental Cherry. Vase-shaped, to 30 ft. (9 m) high. Sometimes grown with several trunks arising close to the ground, but usually grafted at a height of 4–6 ft. (1.2–1.8 m) on single trunks. Leaves double-toothed, 3–5 in. (7.5–12.5 cm) long. Leaves bronzy when unfolding, orange-bronze in fall. Flowers appear before leaves in spring, double (30 petals), deep pink, 2½ in. (6 cm) in diameter. 'Kwanzan' is one of the most popular of many cultivars. Japan. Blooms in spring. Zones 5–8.

subhirtella 'Pendula' pp. 86, 87

Weeping Higan Cherry. A very showy Japanese tree, 20–30 ft. (6–9 m) high, with graceful, slender, pendant branches. Leaves ovalish or oblong-oval, 1–3 in. (2.5–7.5 cm) long, often double-toothed, hairy on the veins beneath. Flowers 2–5 in a cluster, but very numerous, nearly 1 in. (2.5 cm) wide, light pink, the petals notched. Fruit ⅓ in. (8 mm) in diameter, black, not ornamental. This cultivar is commonly grafted onto a 6 ft (1.8 m) standard, resulting in a formal effect. Plants are also produced on own roots and from seeds. Both methods result in a more pleasing, irregular-fountain form; seed-grown trees vary considerably in their degree of weeping, growth rate, flower characteristics, and other features. Japan. Blooms in spring. Zones 6–8; semihardy 5.

***virginiana* 'Schubert'** *pp. 124, 125*
Schubert Chokecherry. A small deciduous tree, rounded in outline, rapid-growing while young, maturing at 25–30 ft. (7.5–9.0 m). Leaves usually elliptic, about 3 in. (7.5 cm) long, sharply toothed, green at first, turning reddish purple at maturity and for the balance of the season. Flowers white, ⅓ in. (8 mm) wide, in racemes 4–8 in. (10–15 cm) long. Fruit not ornamental, ¼ in. (6 mm) or more in diameter, red at first, turning almost purple, acid but edible and used for cookery.
An arresting subject as a summer accent specimen, for grouping, or for colorful screen planting. Keep a sharp eye out for leaf-eating insects. Wilted foliage is poisonous. Susceptible to diseases south of zone 5. An introduced variety of the native North American species; 'Canada Red' is a similar cultivar. Blooms in spring. Zones 3–5.

yedoensis *pp. 88, 89*
Yoshino Cherry. A very showy tree, up to 40 ft. (12 m) high, the young twigs slightly hairy. Leaves elliptic or broader toward the tip, 2–5 in. (5.0–12.5 cm) long, strongly double-toothed. Flowers 1¼ in. (3 cm) wide, 5–6 in a short and racemelike cluster, white or pink, faintly fragrant. Fruit black, inconsequential, often absent.
Unknown as a wild tree, but long cultivated in Japan and may have originated there by a crossing of *P. subhirtella* and *P. serrulata*. Many of the famous cherry trees of Washington, D.C. are this species. Widely cultivated in many named Japanese forms. Cultivar 'Akebono', also called 'Daybreak', has blush-pink flowers. Japan. Blooms in spring. Zones 6–8.

Pseudotsuga
Pine family
Pinaceae

Soo-doe-soo'ga. Six species of magnificent
evergreen trees from w. North America and
e. Asia, valuable as timber trees as well as
handsome screens and windbreaks.

Description
Branches irregularly whorled. Leaves needle-
like, flattened, and spirally arranged on
twigs, spreading usually into 2 opposite
ranks. Most easily recognized by their
cones, which resemble those of the spruces,
but have conspicuous 3–lobed bracts
protruding from between the scales.
Two-winged seeds under each scale.

How to Grow
Douglas-fir grows well in well-drained,
moist soils, neutral to moderately acid, in
full sun or very nearly so. Its enemies are
poor, dry soils, high winds, and dry
summer air. In lower areas with frost
pockets, new growth is often killed by
spring freezes, stunting and sometimes
malforming trees. Pests and diseases are
few, and usually unimportant.

menziesii *pp. 278, 279*
Douglas-fir. A handsome tree, valuable for
lumber, Christmas trees, and in landscaping
as screen plantings. Grows to 200 ft.
(60 m) and more in its native habitat, but
rarely more than 80 ft. (24 m) in
cultivation. Needle-like leaves about 1 in.
(2.5 cm) long, flattened, medium to dark or
bluish green with 2 white bands beneath.
Leaves aromatic and camphorlike when
bruised. Terminal buds unlike those of any
other conifer, narrow, pointed, ½ in.
(13 mm) or so long, with many scales.
Cones 3–4 in. (7.5–10.0 cm) long, with
3–pronged protruding bracts, usually
straight.
The Blue Douglas-fir, *P.m.* var. *glauca,* is
a slower-growing variety. Leaves usually
bluish green. Cones smaller, 3 in. (7.5 cm)
or less, with protruding bracts usually
recurved. Hardier, to zone 4, even into zone
3 for some strains from coldest parts of
the native range (Rocky Mts.). This variety,
even though usually grown from seed with
individual plants somewhat variable, is a
better choice for midwestern and
northeastern states.

Pacific Coast. Cones fall to winter. Zones 6–8; semihardy 5.

Pyrus
Rose family
Rosaceae

Py'rus. Pear. A mostly deciduous genus of about 20 species of trees and shrubs native to Eurasia and Africa. Pears are horticulturally important for their fruit, and a few species are among the most beautiful spring-flowering deciduous trees.

Description
Pears have alternate, stalked leaves and white flowers in umbel-like racemes with or before expanding leaves. Petals 5, nearly round, but narrowed to a claw. Stamens 20–30, the anthers red or dark-colored. Fruit a pome, technically differing from the closely related apples (*Malus* species) only in the numerous grit cells in the flesh of pears.

How to Grow
Pears are easily transplanted in spring if balled or container-grown. Most soils are adequate except wet, very dry, and highly alkaline ones. Full sun is paramount. Irrigate young plants in dry spells. Established trees will tolerate moderate drought. Prune in late winter or early spring to protect against the spread of fireblight disease; remove damaged, diseased, or crowded branches.

***calleryana* 'Bradford'** *pp. 132, 133*
Bradford Pear. The species is usually no taller than 30 ft. (9 m), broadly triangular in outline, showy when in bloom. The cultivar 'Bradford', selected in 1918, is taller, to 50 ft. (15 m), and more noticeably triangular in outline. Leaves ovalish or broader, 1–3 in. (2.5–7.5 cm) long, bluntly toothed, glossy-green, turning scarlet to purple in fall. Flowers profuse, white, in 3 in. (7.5 cm) corymbs. Fruits usually few, small, less than ½ in. (13 mm) wide, and thus not messy, but not ornamental. Resistant to fireblight disease, common on most pear species. Old trees tend to split in storms. China. Blooms in early spring. Zones 5–9.

***calleryana* 'Chanticleer'** *p. 92*
Chanticleer Pear. Maximum height as yet
unknown, but trees may reach 40 ft. (12 m)
in 40 years. Foliage resembles 'Bradford',
but fall color often runs to yellow more than
red. White flowers ⅓ in. (8 mm) wide, in
3 in. (7.5 cm) corymbs, profuse and
delicate. Fruit not ornamental. A better
choice for narrow spaces than 'Bradford'.
Also sold as 'Select' and 'Cleveland Select'.
A newer cultivar of *P. calleryana* than
'Bradford', much more narrow in outline
and somewhat hardier, to the warmer parts
of zone 4. Blooms in early spring. Zones
5–9.

kawakamii *pp. 202, 203*
Evergreen Pear. A semi-evergreen species
growing slowly to 30 ft. (9 m). Leaves
leathery, 2–4 in. (5–10 cm) long, on
petioles 1 in. (2.5 cm) long. Small but
conspicuous white flowers ½ in. (13 mm)
wide, massed in corymbs, often blooming
sporadically throughout the year, showy and
fragrant. Fruit about 1 in. (2.5 cm) in
diameter, green, not ornamental. Needs
staking and pruning in early years to form a
multi-trunked tree. Taiwan. Blooms winter
to spring. Zones 8–10.

ussuriensis *pp. 172, 173*
Ussurian Pear; Chinese Pear. A deciduous
tree, may reach 50 ft. (15 m). Leaves 2–
4 in. (5–10 cm) long, nearly as broad,
bristly-toothed, shiny green, turning
purplish red in fall. Flower buds often
tinged pink, flowers white, to 1⅓ in.
(3.3 cm) wide. Fruit 1½ in. (4 cm) in
diameter, yellowish green, inedible and not
ornamental, just big enough to be messy on
walks and driveways. The hardiest pear, to
zone 4 or into zone 3, but not for warm
climates. Resistant to fireblight. Ne. Asia.
Blooms in spring. Zones 4–6; semihardy 3.

Quercus
Beech family
Fagaceae

Kwer'kus. Oak. This genus includes the
finest hardwood timber trees in the
temperate world, and also many beautiful
species for planting on lawns, parks, and
streets. There are about 450 species of oaks,
nearly all from the north temperate zone, a

few in mountainous regions in the tropics.
Most oaks are evergreen, especially the
Asiatic species, and the group as a whole
just misses being evergreen in North
America, where many species have leaves,
usually withered, that persist over most of
the winter. Among the species described
below, however, only those whose leaves
stay green through the winter are designated
as evergreen.

Description
Leaves alternate, stalked, variously lobed,
toothed, or divided in most species, but
unlobed and without teeth in a few. Flowers
unisexual, but on the same tree, the male in
drooping catkins, the female in short spikes,
or solitary; both without petals. Most oaks
flower very early in the spring. Fruit a true
nut, the acorn, set in a cuplike involucre
which may surround the nut only at the
base, or partly or completely cover it; the
cup sometimes fringed. Acorns are
interesting fruits, but not ornamentally
important.

How to Grow
Oaks grow best in full sun, though most
will tolerate light partial shade. The oaks
like a rich, deep soil, without hardpan.
Mulch, but do not disturb an oak's root
zone. Trenching, grade changes, soil
compaction, and other similar activities in
the root zone—which may reach 3 times the
branch spread—can seriously harm or kill an
oak tree.
Some care is necessary in transplanting
certain species of oaks. *Q. alba* and
Q. coccinea are not easily moved except while
young, and where large specimens are
desired, *Q. rubra, Q. palustris,* and
Q. imbricaria are easier to transplant. Oaks
are excurrent trees; that is, they have a
single main trunk extending their entire
length. For this reason, you should restrict
pruning during transplanting to heading
back the lateral branches and removing any
competing upright shoots, while being
careful to preserve the main stem.

agrifolia pp. 228, 229
California Live Oak; Coast Live Oak;
Encina. A rounded evergreen tree, rarely to
80 ft. (24 m) high, rapid-growing. Leaves
with wavy, bristle-pointed teeth, generally
elliptic, 2–3 in. (5.0–7.5 cm) long. Cup of
acorn hairy. Calif. Zones 9–10.

alba pp. *144, 145*

White Oak. A magnificent round-headed
deciduous tree, 100 ft. (30 m) high, but
the species is slow-growing and not likely to
approach that height in cultivation—80 ft.
(24 m) is more realistic, and that in 100
years. Leaves broadest toward the tip,
bluntly 5– to 9–lobed, the lobes not bristle-
tipped. Unfolding leaves pinkish; fall foliage
color varies from brownish to purple. Cup
only one-quarter the length of acorn.
Probably the largest of all the native oaks,
the trunks of old specimens being over 20 ft.
(6 m) in circumference. Prefers a heavy,
damp clay soil. Best transplanted only when
young. E. North America. Zones 4–9.

chrysolepis pp. *228, 229*

Canyon Live Oak; Maul Oak. An evergreen
tree, seldom more than 60 ft. (18 m) high,
wide-spreading. Branchlets often pendulous.
Leaves elliptic, 2–4 in. (5–10 cm) long, the
margins rolled or toothed, but not lobed,
white-felty beneath. Cup of acorn felty, only
one-quarter the depth of nut. A beautiful
tree in its native area. Oreg. to lower Calif.
Zones 8–10; semihardy 7.

coccinea pp. *146, 147*

Scarlet Oak. An upright, roughly cylindric
tree, 50–80 ft. (15–24 m) high, more than
100 ft. (30 m) in the wild. Leaves
oblongish, 4–6 in. (10–15 cm) long,
shining green, sharply and deeply 7– to
9–lobed, the lobes bristle-tipped. Cup one-
third the length of nut. Foliage turns
brilliant scarlet in the fall. Similar to Pin
Oak, *Q. palustris,* but more tolerant of
alkaline soils. Prefers a light, sandy loam.
Transplant small sizes for best results.
E. North America. Zones 5–9.

imbricaria pp. *146, 147*

Shingle Oak; Laurel Oak. Broadly conical
when young, maturing to an open, rounded
tree, maximum height 75 ft. (22.5 m).
Leaves dark green, oblongish, 4–6 in.
(10–15 cm) long, without lobes, teeth, or
bristles; turning brown in fall, many
persisting all winter, and thus a good screen
or windbreak. Cup a little less than half the
length of acorn. Easy to transplant and a
durable tree. Prefers a light, sandy loam.
N.J. to Tenn. and westward. Zones 5–8.

kelloggii pp. 142, 143

California Black Oak. A medium-sized, globe-shaped tree, 30–80 ft. (9–24 m) high. Leaves oblongish, with 5–7 large, bristle-tipped lobes. Young leaves pinkish, mature leaves glossy-green, turning yellow to orange in fall. Cup one-third the length of acorn. Oreg. and Calif. Zones 8–10.

lobata pp. 142, 143

Valley Oak; California White Oak. A fast-growing tree, up to 100 ft. (30 m). Leaves 2½ in. (6 cm) long, with 7–11 blunt lobes, gray-felty beneath, the lobes not bristle-tipped. Cup one-third the length of acorn. A massive tree for California parks and other large areas, but does not grow well too close to the coast. Calif. Zones 7–10.

palustris pp. 136, 137

Pin Oak. A broadly conical tree that can reach 100 ft. (30 m), usually less in cultivation, upper branches ascending, middle branches horizontal, lower ones drooping, often sweeping the ground. Leaves more or less elliptic, 4–5 in. (10.0–12.5 cm) long, sharply and deeply 5– to 9–lobed, shining green, the lobes bristle-tipped. Leaves bronze to red in fall. Cup scarcely one-third the length of acorn. Tolerant of city conditions and wet soils, but often shows chlorosis of foliage, an unsightly yellowing, when soil is alkaline. Prefers a heavy, damp clay soil. E. North America. Zones 5–9.

robur 'Fastigiata' pp. 134, 135

Upright English Oak; Upright British Oak. The species is a broadly round-headed tree, not over 80 ft. (24 m) high. Leaves 3–5 in. (7.5–12.5 cm) long, broadest toward the tip, with 6–14 rounded lobes, without bristles. Cup one-third the length of acorn. The cultivar 'Fastigiata' is narrowly upright, only one-fifth as wide as tall when young, somewhat more with age. Except for powdery mildew on leaves in humid weather, this is a beautiful formal cultivar. Eurasia and n. Africa. Zones 5–8.

rubra pp. 144, 145

Red Oak. A tall, relatively quick-growing tree, to 100 ft. (30 m) high, broadly conical when young, generally rounded at maturity. Leaves oblongish, to 9 in. (22.5 cm) long, with 5–11 bristle-tipped lobes, shiny green in summer, deep to bright red in fall.

Acorn cup one-eighth to one-quarter the length of nut. Perhaps the fastest-growing oak and the easiest to transplant. An excellent shade tree, except in regions where oak wilt disease is prevalent. Prefers a light, sandy loam. New Brunswick to Wis. and south to Ala. Zones 4–8.

suber *pp. 226, 227*
Cork Oak. A round-headed tree, not over 60 ft. (18 m) high, with equal spread. Bark thick and corky, lending a picturesque, rugged appearance. Leaves evergreen, ovalish or oblong, to 3 in. (7.5 cm) long, without lobes but coarsely toothed; shiny green above, gray-felty beneath. Cup one-third to one-half the length of acorn. Its bark, harvested every 10–15 years, is the source of cork, mostly in Spain and Portugal. Drought resistant when established. Not hardy below 0° F (–18° C). S. Europe and n. Africa. Zones 7–9.

virginiana *pp. 230, 231*
Live Oak. An evergreen tree, usually round-headed and not over 70 ft. (21 m) high. Old trees may be twice as wide as high, often draped with Spanish Moss in the southern part of its range. Leaves elliptic or oblong, 3–5 in. (7.5–12.5 cm) long, without lobes, very rarely toothed, and with no bristles; green above, white-felty beneath. Acorn cup felty, one-quarter the length of nut. Temperatures below 0° F (–18° C) will kill leaves. Va. to Fla. and Mexico. Zones 7–10.

Salix
Willow family
Salicaceae

Say'licks. Willow. A huge group of quick-growing, often brittle-wooded deciduous shrubs and trees. About 300 species are known, chiefly from the cooler parts of the north temperate zone, a few in the southern hemisphere, none in Australia. Besides the great number of very similar species, there are innumerable natural and induced hybrids, so that the exact identification of willows is difficult even for experts. Willow branches break easily, roots invade drainage lines, and trees are messy and insect-prone. However, a Golden Weeping Willow at the edge of a large lot or in a

park is an inspiring sight, especially in early
spring when twigs brighten yellow and
leaves unfold.

Description

Leaves alternate, usually narrow, mostly
lance-shaped, and tapering both ends. Male
and female flowers on separate plants, both
in catkins that bloom before or when the
leaves expand. Petals and sepals none, the
flowers thus naked, but each flower borne in
the axil of a bract, the collection of which
forms the catkin—the female is the familiar
pussy willow. Fruit a 2–valved capsule.

How to Grow

Willows adapt to wet places, but also grow
vigorously in ordinary soil. They are easy to
transplant, and in fact may be started from
dormant branches of one or two years'
growth, 1–3 ft. (30–90 cm) long, simply
stuck into moist soil in early spring.
Pruning is seldom necessary, though
training to a central trunk early on may
prevent serious splitting later.

alba* var. *tristis *pp. 120, 121*
Golden Weeping Willow. A hardy and
popular weeping willow, reaching a
maximum of about 70 ft. (21 m) in height
with equal or greater spread. One-year-old
branches bright yellow. Leaves 3–4 in.
(7.5–10.0 cm) long, finely toothed, the
underside silky-hairy. Tolerates wet areas.
Confused in the trade; sometimes sold as
S. vitellina var. *pendula* and as Niobe
Weeping Willow. Eurasia and n. Africa,
often an escape in North America. Zones
3–9; semihardy 2.

Sapium
Spurge family
Euphorbiaceae

Say'pi-um. A genus of 100 species of
tropical trees with milky, poisonous sap, the
deciduous species below commonly grown as
a shade or screen tree with handsome fruit
and fall color. Chinese Tallow Tree casts
light shade, allowing grass and other plants
to grow beneath the canopy.

Description

Spreading, branching trunk, leaves
alternate, simple, poplarlike. Flowers lack

petals and are borne in spikes, the males
and females separated. Fruit a capsule.

How to Grow
Chinese Tallow Tree is not particular about
soil, and grows rapidly when young in dry,
wet, acid, and alkaline soils. It does require
full sun and cannot withstand 0° F (−18° C)
temperature. Insects and diseases are not
problems.

sebiferum pp. 164, 165
Chinese Tallow Tree; Popcorn Tree. A tree
to 50 ft. (15 m) high, less as cultivated
here, with alternate ovalish or angled leaves
1–3 in. (2.5–7.5 cm) long, slenderly long-
stalked, the stalks red-tipped. Fall color
variable from orange through red to purple
on different specimens. Flowers without
petals, not showy. Fruit a 3–lobed capsule,
½ in. (13 mm) wide, the seeds white,
hence Popcorn Tree. The plant is grown for
these decorative seeds in many regions, and
the waxy seed covering yields a tallowlike
substance used for soap and candles.
S. China and Japan; naturalized from S.C.
to Fla. and La. Fruit in fall. Zones 8–9.

Schinus
Poison ivy family
Anacardiaceae

Sky′nus. Chiefly South American resinous
trees comprising perhaps 28 species, those
commonly grown are broadleaf evergreen
trees planted for shade in semi-tropical
climates.

Description
Schinus have alternate, sometimes pinnately
compound leaves, the leaflets stalkless and
with an odd one at the end. Male and
female flowers on different trees, small,
white, in branched panicles. Petals 5,
stamens 10. Fruit a berrylike reddish drupe.

How to Grow
Schinus are easy to grow in almost any soil.
Young plants may need early staking and
pruning to encourage a tree shape. Some
people may be allergic to the pollen.

terebinthifolius pp. 232, 233
Brazilian Pepper Tree; Christmasberry Tree.
A small evergreen tree to 30 ft. (9 m),

umbrella-shaped. Leaflets 5–9, 2 in. (5 cm)
long, dark green above. Flowers yellowish,
not attractive. Fruit bright red, less than
¼ in. (6 mm) wide. Especially popular in
Fla., where its bright red berries persist
over the winter months. Brazil. Fruit in
winter. Zones 9–10.

Sequoia
Bald cypress family
Taxodiaceae

See-kwoy′ya. Redwood. A single surviving
species of massive evergreen trees, much
more widespread in earlier geologic times,
native to a narrow coastal area about 20
miles from sw. Oreg. to Monterey County,
Calif. In the proper climate and with the
necessary space, Redwood makes a noble
specimen tree. The genus is closely related
to *Sequoiadendron*. The burls of the Redwood
are often sold by florists and make
interesting growths when put in water.

Description
Small leaves of 2 kinds: on leading shoots
oblong, small, resembling a hemlock, with
a horny tip, arranged around the shoot in
several ranks; on lateral twigs larger,
oblongish, arranged in 2 ranks. Female
cones ovoid, persisting after the seeds are
shed.

How to Grow
Redwood needs full sun or very nearly so,
and a reasonably well-drained acid to neutral
soil. Water deeply and regularly for best
growth. Prune only if you wish to expose
the attractive bark of the lower trunk.

sempervirens pp. 252, 253
Redwood; Coast Redwood; California
Redwood. A narrow evergreen of extreme
height, up to 300 ft. (91 m) or more, and
exceeded only by some Australian trees of
the genus *Eucalyptus*. The trunk diameter is
less than the Giant Sequoia (*Sequoiadendron*),
not exceeding 28 ft. (8.5 m) and usually
10–20 ft. (3–6 m). Leaves ¼ in. (6 mm)
long, quite oblong, on leading branchlets;
¼–1 in. (0.6–2.5 cm) long, spreading, on
other branches. Cones 1 in. (2.5 cm) long,
not ornamental.
Scarcely adapted to the East but making
magnificent forests in its own region, far

more extensive than Giant Sequoia, and an important source of valuable timber. Cultivar 'Glauca' has bluish-green foliage. There is also a form with pendulous branches. On the West Coast it is a useful landscape tree, where conditions are favorable and space permits, growing 3–5 ft. (0.9–1.5 m) a year when young. N. Calif. and s. Oreg., in the fog belt. Zones 8–10; semihardy 7.

Sequoiadendron
Bald cypress family
Taxodiaceae

See-kwoy-a-den'dron. Giant Sequoia. A single species of massive evergreen trees, native on the western slopes of the Sierra Nevadas from Placer County to Tulare County, Calif., at altitudes between 4300 and 8000 ft. (1311 and 2438 m). Closely related to Redwood, Giant Sequoia are also fast-growing, magnificent specimen trees for very large properties.

Description
Leaves scale-like or needle-like, crowded and spirally arranged on the twigs. Female cones ripening the second year and persisting after the seeds are shed.

How to Grow
Giant Sequoia does best in a deep, well-drained soil in full sun, with occasional deep watering during dry seasons. Remove lower branches to expose the fluted trunk and red-brown bark.

giganteum pp. 250, 251
Giant Sequoia. The largest trunk girth of any coniferous tree in the world, up to 80 ft. (24 m). Height up to 250 ft. (76 m) in old age. Needle-like leaves ¼ in. (6 mm) long, crowded on twigs. Cones 2–3 in. (5.0–7.5 cm) long, inconspicuous, held throughout the year. Cultivar 'Glauca' has bluish-green foliage. Cultivar 'Pendula' has more drooping branches and in cultivation forms a narrow, columnar tree. A useful landscape tree on the West Coast, wherever conditions are favorable; growing 2–3 ft. (60–90 cm) a year. Cen. Calif. Zones 7–9; semihardy 6.

Sophora
Pea family
Leguminosae

So-for'ra. Handsome, profusely flowering shrubs or trees, most of the 50 known species Asiatic broadleaf evergreens, but a few in North America. The species below is a popular summer-flowering deciduous ornamental tree.

Description
Leaves arranged feather-fashion, with an odd leaflet at the tip. Flowers pealike, usually in showy panicles or racemes. Fruit a stalked pod constricted between the seeds, splitting very slowly if at all.

How to Grow
Pagoda Trees are best planted in a sandy, loam soil, acid or slightly alkaline, in full sun or nearly so. Young trees, especially in zone 5, are cold-tender. Prune away winter-killed branchlets and hope for mild winters until the trees mature. They have very few problems in warmer zones.

japonica pp. 96, 97
Pagoda Tree; Japanese Pagoda Tree; Chinese Scholar Tree. A spreading, round-headed tree, 40–70 ft. (12–21 m) high, sometimes more. Leaflets 7–17, stalked, ovalish or narrower, 1–2 in. (2.5–5.0 cm) long. Flowers ½ in. (13 mm) long, yellowish white, the panicles loose, 12–15 in. (30–38 cm) long, conical, vertical, very showy in late summer. Pods 2–4 in. (5–10 cm) long. Tolerates city conditions. The cultivar 'Regent' grows faster, has better foliage, and blooms at an earlier age. China and Korea. Blooms in summer. Fruit fall to winter. Zones 5–8.

Sorbus
Rose family
Rosaceae

Sor'bus. Mountain Ash. A genus of Eurasian and North American deciduous trees or shrubs, comprising perhaps 85 species, several species long-cultivated as ornamental trees with spring flowers and fall fruit.

Description

Leaves alternate, simple or compound, the leaflets arranged feather-fashion, sharply toothed. Flowers white, many and showy, in branching, flat-topped, leafy terminal corymbs. Petals 5, broad or narrow, clawed. Stamens 15–20. Fruit a small berrylike pome in clusters, usually orange or red, on some species white or yellow.

How to Grow

Mountain Ash trees suffer from summer heat, but need sunshine, and grow best in well-drained, acid soils. Mulching and watering deeply during drought increase vigor and reduce susceptibility to insect and disease attacks. Prune, if necessary, in winter or early spring.

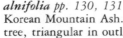

alnifolia pp. 130, 131

Korean Mountain Ash. A small to medium tree, triangular in outline when young, maturing to oval or round, reaching 50 ft. (15 m) in height. Bark gray, resembling American Beech, attractive in winter. Leaves alternate, simple, ovate, toothed, 2–4 in. (5–10 cm) long, lustrous-green, turning orange-brown in fall. Flowers white, ¾ in. (19 mm) in diameter, in flat corymbs 2–3 in. (5.0–7.5 cm) across. Fruit a rounded pome, pinkish orange to scarlet, about ½ in. (13 mm) wide, in clusters in fall. A tree of year-round beauty that deserves wider planting. E. Asia. Blooms in spring. Fruit in fall. Zones 4–7.

aucuparia pp. 130, 131

European Mountain Ash; Rowan Tree. A tree 50 ft. (15 m) or more high. Leaflets 9–15, 1–2 in. (2.5–5.0 cm) long, oblong or narrower, with a bloom beneath, hairy or smooth. Fall color ranges from none to yellow and red. Flowers ⅓ in. (8 mm) across, in compound terminal corymbs 4–6 in. (10–15 cm) across. Fruit round, orange to red, ¼ in. (6 mm) wide. Grows best in well-drained, acid soil. A popular cultivar developed at Michigan State University, 'Cardinal Royal', has larger clusters of redder fruits, coloring in summer. Europe to w. Asia and Russia. Blooms in spring. Fruit in fall. Zones 3–7.

Taxodium
Bald cypress family
Taxodiaceae

Tacks-o'di-um. Two magnificent coniferous
trees; one evergreen, from Mexico; the other
deciduous, from the se. U.S. Both are often
called cypress in the U.S., but are not the
traditional cypress, which is *Cupressus*. The
species below, the Bald Cypress, is a
valuable timber tree and also the most
decorative. Though its natural habitat is in
the cypress swamps, it will grow in ordinary
soils, and even on dry sites in the North.
The evergreen species is not hardy in the
North and is rarely grown even in s. Calif.
or Fla.

Description
Both species have light brown, scaly bark
and bear two sorts of branchlets, the upper
ones persistent, the lower ones on the shoot
deciduous. Leaves alternate, flat, needle-
like, and spreading. Male and female
flowers separate but on the same tree, the
male flowers consisting of only 6–8
stamens, mostly in drooping panicles.
Female flowers ultimately producing a scaly,
short-stalked cone, its seeds 3–angled and
3–winged. Neither flowers nor cones
are ornamental.

How to Grow
Bald Cypress transplants easily. Though
native to swamps and tolerant of wet soil, it
is quite at home in normal soils, even those
on the dry side, but the soil must be acid;
otherwise it may develop foliar chlorosis, an
unsightly yellowing of the foliage. It will
tolerate light shade.

distichum pp. 136, 137
Bald Cypress; Southern Cypress. A
deciduous tree, up to 100 ft. (30 m) high
but usually shorter northward in its range.
Its trunk is decidedly tapering, often
buttressed at the base, and in swamps and
moist soils producing "cypress knees,"
which are woody projections of the roots
4–6 ft. (1.2–1.8 m) high and up to 1 ft.
(30 cm) thick. Leaves light green, ¾ in.
(19 mm) long, very numerous, the foliage
graceful and feathery, russet-brown in the
fall, just before leaf drop. Cones 1 in.
(2.5 cm) long, not ornamental. A closely
related tree, var. *nutans,* Pond Cypress, with
less spreading leaves and rather upright

branches, is sometimes cultivated. Del. to
Fla., west to Ark. and La. Zones 5–10.

Thuja
Cypress family
Cupressaceae

Thew'ya. Arborvitae. Extremely valuable
evergreen trees found in North America and
e. Asia, comprising only 5 species but with
innumerable horticultural varieties, most of
which are low or at least not treelike. The
wild trees are magnificent forest evergreens
and widely cut for timber, especially in the
Pacific Northwest. Arborvitae grows
naturally in cool, moist areas, and the
cultivated species always do best in such
regions, but millions are cultivated in city
courtyards and suburban lots as accents and
as screen and background trees.

Description
Arborvitae usually form a narrow conical
head. Twigs densely covered with tiny,
scale-like leaves and standing in flat, fanlike
sprays or fronds, the leaves completely
covering the twigs. Flowers none, in the
usual garden sense, being represented by
6–12 stamens in the male flower, the female
flowers ultimately forming an egg-shaped or
oblongish cone with green scales, brown
when ripe, keeled, and not resembling the
familiar pine cone, and not ornamentally
important.

How to Grow
Arborvitae are easy to transplant almost any
time of year. They grow best in full sun or
light shade, and in good soils, moist and
well-drained. Soil pH is not usually
important. Mulching and deep watering
during drought prevent insects and diseases
that will almost certainly attack stressed
plants.

occidentalis pp. 246, 247

American Arborvitae; Eastern White Cedar.
A medium-sized, narrowly upright
evergreen tree, rarely over 60 ft. (18 m)
high, the trunk buttressed at the base, the
bark reddish brown and furrowed. Leaves
dark green or golden green, the frondlike,
fan-shaped, leaf-clothed twigs very
handsome. Foliage turns bronzy in winter.
Cones oblong, ½ in. (13 mm) long, green

at first, ultimately brownish, angled.
Hardy from zone 3 southward, but not in
the warm, dry parts of the coastal plain.
The common tree form, described above,
has been the origin of innumerable
horticultural varieties, all of them much
lower—shrubby or even dwarf. There are
also many forms with variously colored
foliage. Tolerates wet soil. Ne. North
America. Zones 3–7; semihardy 8.

orientalis pp. 274, 275

Oriental Arborvitae. Evergreen, narrowly
upright when young, more open with age.
Usually matures at about 25 ft. (7.5 m),
but may reach 40 ft. (12 m) under good
conditions. The bark is reddish brown and
scaly. Leaves all alike, the frondlike foliage
bright green. Cones egg-shaped, 1 in.
(2.5 cm) long, rather fleshy and bluish in
youth, only briefly ornamental in late
summer.
A better plant in the South than *Thuja
occidentalis.* The juvenile foliage is needle-
like and spreading. Some plants never lose
this condition and grow to a relatively large
size, but do not fruit. It is a variable plant,
and there are many named forms, most
slow-growing, available. Classified years ago
as *Biota orientalis;* recently as *Thuja orientalis,*
and more recently and controversially as
Platycladus orientalis. China and Korea.
Zones 6–8.

plicata pp. 248, 249

Giant Arborvitae; Western Red Cedar. A
magnificent forest evergreen and an
extremely valuable timber tree, reaching up
to 200 ft. (60 m) high—in cultivation
seldom reaching 100 ft. (30 m). Leaves
bright green, white-marked below,
remaining green in winter. Cones oblong,
¾ in. (19 mm) long. An extremely
ornamental tree, native mostly in regions of
copious rainfall and fog. Hardy in zone 4 in
cool-summer areas of New England.
Protracted summer droughts are not good
for this species. Often used as a specimen
and in groups, tall hedges, and screens.
Alaska to n. Calif. and to Mont. Zones 5–7;
semihardy 4 and 8.

Tilia
Linden family
Tiliaceae

Till'ee-a. Linden; Lime; Basswood. About
30 species of ornamental deciduous trees
native to the north temperate zone. Lindens
are handsome trees of good habit and
comparatively rapid growth; they make
excellent shade trees and are often planted
along streets and avenues. The abundant
nectar of the flowers attracts bees which
make a pleasant noise about the trees on
warm summer afternoons.

Description
Leaves are alternate, toothed, usually heart-
shaped at the base, with one side longer
than the other. Flowers are small, yellowish
white, fragrant, borne in long-stalked,
drooping clusters. Attached to the flower-
stalk for about half its length is a thin,
oblong bract that constitutes one of the
prominent characteristics of this group.
Fruit is the size of a small pea, dry and
hard.

How to Grow
Trees are easily transplanted when dormant.
Lindens grow best in full sun and in soils
neither wet nor dry, slightly acid to slightly
alkaline, and tolerate city air pollution.
Mulching is wise. Water deeply during
droughts.

cordata pp. *178, 179*
Little-leaf Linden. A shapely tree, to 90 ft.
(27 m) high. Leaves rounded, 1½–3 in.
(4.0–7.5 cm) long, heart-shaped at base,
with a short tapered tip, toothed, dark
green above; paler or whitish on the
undersurface, with tufts of brown hairs in
vein axils, a pleasant yellow-green in fall.
Flowers yellowish, fragrant, in 2–3 in.
(5.0–7.5 cm) cymes. Often used as a
specimen tree; also excellent for screens and
tall sheared hedges. Europe. Blooms late
spring to early summer. Zones 3–8.

tomentosa pp. *178, 179*
Silver Linden. A tree growing 90 ft. (27 m)
or more high, rather conical in habit, with
upright branches; young branchlets downy.
Leaves 2–5 in. (5.0–12.5 cm) long,
rounded, heart-shaped at base or straight
across, sharply toothed, occasionally slightly
lobed, dark green above, undersurface

covered with silvery white down, making a
pleasant silver-green tapestry on breezy
days. Flowers light yellow in pendulous
cymes, not conspicuous but highly fragrant.
Eurasia. Blooms in summer. Zones 5–8.

Trachycarpus
Palm family
Palmae

Tra-kee-kar′pus. Rather low-growing
Asiatic fan palms, among the hardiest
known, and generally not thriving in the
tropics. Two of the 6 species are cultivated,
and the species below is among the hardiest
cultivated palms, growing as far north as
zone 8 on the East Coast, on the West
Coast to Vancouver, B.C.

Description
Trunks solitary, covered with old leaf
sheaths. Leaves fibrous, palmate, ribbed.
Flowers in clusters at the crown, unisexual
or polygamous. Fruit drupelike, small, in
clusters.

How to Grow
Plant in ordinary soil, in sun or partial
shade, any time of the year. Water regularly
and thoroughly during drought. Remove
dead leafstalks to improve the plant's
appearance. Hose down the foliage regularly
to control sucking insects and dust.

fortunei pp. 190, 191
Windmill Palm; Hemp Palm. As
cultivated, a low, slow-growing palm with a
rounded crown, the trunk rarely over 30 ft.
(9 m) high—40 ft. (12 m) in the wild—and
densely clothed with the remains of the old
leaf sheaths, especially on the upper trunk,
giving a top-heavy effect. Leaves nearly
round, fanlike, stiff, 2–4 ft. (60–120 cm)
wide, divided nearly to the middle into
many narrow, pointed segments, in the
leafstalk rough. Flowers pale yellow, in
clusters 18 in. (45 cm) long, appearing
among the crown of leaves. Fruit drupelike,
3–lobed, ½ in. (13 mm) long, bluish, in
clusters. Tubbed specimens are suited for
patios, porches, and indoors. E. to cen.
China. Flowers spring to summer. Fruit
summer to fall. Zones 8–10; semihardy 7.

Tristania
Myrtle family
Myrtaceae

Tris-tay′ni-a. About 20 species of chiefly
Australasian broadleaf evergreen trees and
shrubs, related to *Eucalyptus,* but differing
in that the sepals and petals are persistent.
The species below is grown as a flowering
semi-tropical shade tree with decorative
bark.

Description
Leaves alternate or whorled on branchlets,
oval to lance-shaped, simple. Flowers small,
white to yellow, in cymes on the leaf axils,
5–petalled, with many stamens, usually
grouped in clusters. Calyx turban-shaped.
Fruit a 3–valved capsule.

How to Grow
Soil type is not critical with tristanias,
except that acid soil is necessary to preclude
foliar chlorosis. Trees grow best in fairly
good soil with deep weekly watering in dry
spells. Tristania endures drought after it is
well-established.

conferta *pp. 238, 239*
Brisbane Box. A tree, to 150 ft. (45 m)
high in nature. As cultivated in Calif., a
medium-sized tree, somewhat resembling a
eucalyptus, to 50 ft. (15 m), with reddish-
brown, exfoliating bark and alternate,
ovalish or narrower leaves, 3–6 in.
(7.5–15.0 cm) long, often grouped at the
ends of the twigs. Flowers ¾ in. (19 mm)
wide, white, fluffy, mostly in small cymes
4 in. (10 cm) across, in leaf axils. Scarcely
known outside of Calif., although it is very
attractive in flower. Australia. Blooms in
summer. Zones 9–10.

Tsuga
Pine family
Pinaceae

Soo′ga. Hemlock. In the U.S., beautiful
evergreen trees, as noted below, but in
Europe "hemlock" generally means the herb
Conium maculatum, the poison hemlock that
killed Socrates. The evergreen trees called
hemlock in America all belong to a genus of
10 species, chiefly from North America and
e. Asia. The 2 species below are excellent

screen and background evergreens
with delicate foliage, and *T. canadensis* is
among the most popular of hedge plants.

Description
Leaves 2–ranked, very numerous, their
arrangement resulting in fanlike sprays.
The leaves drop off quickly when dry and
are narrow, flattish, and minutely grooved
on the upper surface, with 2 white lines on
the underside. Cones usually small, the
scales somewhat woody, but not stiff. Seeds
2 under each scale.

How to Grow
Hemlocks fare poorly in windy spots with
dry summer air, and in dry or alkaline soils.
Give them the opposite conditions, as their
native habitats do, and they'll fare nicely.
To cheat a little in adverse climates, plant
them on eastern exposures, mulch
generously, and irrigate regularly. Prune
lightly for compact growth.

canadensis pp. 276, 277
Canada Hemlock; Eastern Hemlock. A
magnificent evergreen that may reach 90 ft.
(27 m), but is usually shorter in cultivation,
the branches gracefully drooping in age.
Needle-like leaves a lustrous dark green
above, bluish beneath, ¼–¾ in. (6–19 mm)
long, sometimes slightly notched at the tip,
about ¹/₁₂ in. (2.1 mm) wide, almost
microscopically saw-toothed on the margins.
Cones short-stalked, slightly egg-shaped,
about ¾ in. (19 mm) long. Tolerates moist,
shaded sites, but often fails in cultivation
because of unfavorable conditions. Useful
for hedges. Many cultivars exist, and among
the most notable is 'Pendula'. Also
called 'Sargentii', it is a compact, bushy
form, usually broader than high, with
pendulous branches, one of the most
graceful of all plants. E. North America.
Cones fall to winter. Zones 4–7; semihardy
3 and 8.

heterophylla pp. 276, 277
Western Hemlock. A majestic yet graceful
Pacific Coast evergreen tree of noble stature,
but not well suited to the East. May reach
200 ft. (60 m) high in nature, 100 ft.
(30 m) in cultivation. Leaves dark green and
glossy above, not notched, ¾ in. (19 mm)
long. Cones stalkless, 1 in. (2.5 cm) long.
Hardy in the East only from zone 7
southward and often failing because of

insufficient summer moisture and too much
heat. Alaska to Calif. Cones fall to winter.
Zones 6–8.

Ulmus
Elm family
Ulmaceae

Ul'mus. Elm. A genus of 18 mostly
deciduous species, all from the north
temperate zone of North America, Europe,
and Asia. The elms are excellent shade
trees, with broadly upright, high-branching
habits, creating a canopy of dappled shade.
The species below are all resistant but not
necessarily immune to Dutch elm disease,
which has decimated *U. americana,* the
beautiful American Elm. Good cultural
conditions improve the trees' resistance to
disease.

Description
Elms are mostly tall trees with alternate,
short-stalked leaves that are usually
somewhat oblique and double-toothed.
Flowers without petals, the calyx
bell-shaped and inconspicuous. Fruit a
compressed nut surrounded by a flat, often
hairy wing.

How to Grow
Elms are easily transplanted, and grow in a
wide variety of soils except wet and very
dry. They need more or less full sun. Prune
young trees to minimize narrow crotches
that are prone to split in later years. Some
species, notably the once overplanted
American Elm, which shaded the streets of
innumerable New England and Midwestern
towns, are highly susceptible to Dutch elm
disease, which is practically incurable.
Hybridization and selection of resistant elms
is ongoing, but replacement of the
spreading, vase-shaped American Elm is still
only a hope.

carpinifolia pp. 176, 177

Smoothleaf Elm. An upright tree, rarely
over 75 ft. (22.5 m) high. Leaves very
oblique, smooth both sides, glossy-green,
2–4 in. (5–10 cm) long. Flowers in dense
clusters, but seldom noticed. Fruit elliptic,
but wedge-shaped at the base, the seed close
to the closed notch, small and
inconspicuous. There are several cultivars,

the best known being 'Umbraculifera', with a globe-shaped crown; and 'Christine Buisman', resistant to Dutch elm disease. A new cultivar is 'Urban', a fast-growing, soil-tolerant selection from Ohio. Eurasia and n. Africa. Zones 5–8.

parvifolia pp. 176, 177
Chinese Elm; Lacebark Elm. A small tree, usually not over 60 ft. (18 m) high and inclined to forking. The bark attractively mottled and exfoliating in multi-colored patterns, some trees better than others. Leaves more or less elliptic, 1–2½ in. (2.5–6.0 cm) long, shining above, hairy beneath at first, at length smooth. Flowers in small clusters, in late summer, not ornamental. Flat circular fruit ¼–½ in. (6–13 mm) across, notched at tip, slightly ornamental.
A small, quick-growing tree whose foliage may turn yellowish or reddish purple in fall. Leaves are often evergreen in some cultivars used in southern Calif. A clean tree—bark particles, leaves, and fruits are all small. Often confused with *U. pumila.* E. Asia. Fruit in fall. Zones 5–10.

pumila pp. 180, 181
Siberian Elm. A medium to large tree, may reach 75 ft. (22.5 m) high. Somewhat resembles *U. parvifolia,* but usually much taller, the bark rough, the inconspicuous flowers appearing before the leaves unfold, and the branches still more inclined to fork than other elms. Leaves 1–3 in. (2.5–7.5 cm) long, smooth on both sides. Flat circular fruit nearly ½ in. (13 mm) across, in early summer, not ornamental.
Several cultivars exist; among the more notable is 'Coolshade', which is more resistant than the species to breakage in ice storms, though a slower-growing tree. Because of hardiness and drought tolerance, it is useful for planting on the Great Plains. Better trees are available elsewhere. Often incorrectly called Chinese Elm. Ne. Asia. Zones 3–9; semihardy 2.

Umbellularia
Laurel family
Lauraceae

Um-bel-you-lair′i-a. California Laurel. A single species, an aromatic broadleaf

evergreen tree native to Calif. and Oreg.
and grown as a shade or screen tree with
handsome flowers and foliage.

Description
Leaves alternate, oblongish. Flowers
clustered in several umbels, each with 6
sepals, no petals, and 9 stamens. Fruit a
drupe.

How to Grow
California Laurel will grow in poor, dry
soil, but slowly. A good deep soil and
regular watering speeds growth
considerably. Grows nicely in either sun or
shade—if not too dense. Train into a tree
with one or several stems.

californica pp. 238, 239
California Laurel; Spice Tree; Pepperwood;
Bay Tree. A handsome medium-sized tree,
slow-growing to 75 ft. (22.5 m), with
alternate, short-stalked, ovalish or oblongish
leaves, glossy-green, 1–5 in. (2.5–12.5 cm)
long and without marginal teeth. Leaves
strongly aromatic when bruised. Flowers
perfect, yellowish green, in dense umbels.
Calyx soon falling. Fruit a fleshy,
egg-shaped, purple drupe 1 in. (2.5 cm)
long. It prefers reasonably moist soils and
tolerates wind and shade. A beautiful shade
tree at maturity. Calif. to Oreg. Blooms
winter to spring. Fruit in spring. Zones
7–10.

Washingtonia
Palm family
Palmae

Wash-ing-tow'ni-a. Fan Palm. The genus,
named for General George Washington,
has only 2 species, both native in Calif.,
n. Mexico, and sw. Ariz. and widely planted
there, and also planted along the Gulf Coast
and in Fla. One species, *W. robusta,* the
Mexican Fan Palm, makes an extremely
handsome avenue tree.

Description
Trunks shaggy or densely clothed with a
petticoat of hanging withered leaves. Leaves
fanlike, but cut into numerous narrow
segments. Flowers perfect, nearly stalkless
on the flowering branches, which are long,
slender, and usually longer than the foliage.

Stamens 6. Fruit a 1–seeded, thin-fleshed drupe, scarcely ⅓ in. (8 mm) long. The individual flower clusters suggest a corn tassel.

How to Grow
Fan palms stand heat well, and tolerate some drought, but only grow well in a moist soil. For palms, they are relatively hardy, but are not safe from cold above zone 9.

filifera pp. 192, 193
California Fan Palm. A stout palm, 60 ft. (18 m) high, the upper part of the trunk clothed with persistent, withered, hanging leaves. Living leaves long-stalked, erect, the stalks prickly, the blade 3–5 ft. (0.9–1.5 m) wide, grayish green, cut to nearly the middle into many narrow, drooping, thready segments. Flowers and fruits inconspicuous. Less frequently planted than *W. robusta* and less satisfactory near the Calif. coast, but superior in dry soils in Fla. and Calif. Zones 9–10.

robusta pp. 190, 191
Mexican Fan Palm. To 90 ft. (27 m), the trunk more slender, usually clothed above with a dense, shaggy, fibrous network through which protrude the old, spiny leafstalks, but the trunk naked toward the base. Leaf blades cut only about one-third of the way to the middle, the stiffish or drooping segments not thready as in *W. filifera*. Flowers and fruits inconspicuous. Tolerates drought. Mexico. Zones 9–10.

Zelkova
Elm family
Ulmaceae

Zel-ko'va. Five species of elmlike Asiatic deciduous shrubs and trees. The species below is a neat, hardy shade tree free of the pests that plague many elms.

Description
Alternate, toothed leaves, slightly unequal at the base. Flowers small, polygamous, without petals, not showy; solitary, or the male flowers in small clusters on the leaf axils, all blooming early in the spring with the opening of the leaves. Fruit a 2–edged, oblique drupe, winged on the upper half.

How to Grow

Zelkova is not demanding, grows in acid to alkaline soils, quickly becomes wind and drought tolerant, and endures city air reasonably well. However, to produce a fine specimen, grow the tree only in deep moist soil, and give it mulch and supplemental irrigation.

serrata *pp. 174, 175*

Japanese Zelkova. Vase-shaped when young, rounded with age, often umbrella-like. Grows to about 70 ft. (21 m) in a century. Leaves sharply toothed, tapering at the tip, broader and about 2–3 in. (5.0–7.5 cm) long, turning purplish in fall. Touted as a good substitute for the American Elm, but it has not caught on for that purpose. Its relatively slow rate of growth is one drawback. However, it is a desirable tree, resistant to many elm troubles, including Dutch elm disease. Japan. Zones 5–8.

Appendices

Maintaining

You have selected a tree compatible with the soil and other conditions in its new environment, and you have planted it in the recommended fashion. To keep that tree healthy, you must now give it at least as much attention and care as you show to the other garden plants on your property.

Watering

The water needs of trees are often neglected. Some people water garden beds and allow trees to desiccate; others water lawns regularly and unknowingly overwater trees. Unfortunately, there is no easy formula for irrigating trees. But if you know the factors influencing soil and water relationships, you will be better able to judge when and how long to water your trees.

Judging Water Needs

Water retention varies according to soil type. Sandy soils hold the least water and dry out the fastest. Silt loams are intermediate, while clay loams hold the most water and dry out more slowly than other soil types. These basic soil conditions are influenced by a number of variables. Organic matter in soil improves its water-holding capacity. A porous or impervious subsoil obviously has great influence on the drainage of excess water. A tree's terrain is another important factor affecting its watering needs. Water applied equally to all parts of a rolling terrain, especially if applied rapidly, often runs off high spots and accumulates in low areas.

Soil coverings also influence water absorption and water loss. The same soil will have differing water needs if bare, grassed, planted with ground cover, or mulched. The type of cover within each category is also important. For example, ground with tall grass requires more water than grass mowed short, and ground with a wood chip mulch requires more waterings than if it were covered with black plastic.

Various tree species and cultivars have vastly differing water requirements and tolerances. Even the age of trees affects their water needs. Other factors to consider are the season, the amount of sun, the temperature, wind, pollution, and even, some say, the phase of the moon.

Watering Guidelines

Luckily, a few generalities do exist to guide you when watering a tree. Trees usually need water less often than flower beds because their roots penetrate more deeply. Also, trees need more water at one time than other plants because of these deeper roots. Apply water for trees slowly so that it will soak into the soil. A complete watering may take a long time: for example, to moisten dry clay soil to a depth of four feet may require a day and a half of irrigation.

Trees in normal soils usually need an inch of water per week in the

Trees

form of rain or applied water. In heavier soils, irrigation should be less frequent. During drought periods, water trees deeply each week. However, trees in lawns are often damaged by regular lawn irrigation, especially in zones 8 to 10.

Seek advice from local experts, and if necessary supplement your knowledge with a soil sampler probe to check soil moisture at 18 to 20 inches. Use a rain gauge; it is far more accurate than the local weather station.

Protective Staking
The Planting chapter discusses staking for support. However, two problems are so prevalent they are worth mentioning here—trees that do not need stakes are often given them, and stakes are usually left on newly planted trees too long. One growing season should suffice.

Protective staking is another matter, and in some cases it can save the life of a tree. Large stakes, painted white or plastic-ribboned, while not beautiful, will help protect young and even established trees from accidental damage in high-risk areas near streets and walks.

Trenching and soil movement 100 yards away from a mature tree can cause damage by changing soil and water relationships. If such activities are within twice the branch spread, they will surely cause damage. If earth changes are imminent, install stakes in the vicinity of prized trees and monitor the work to be sure earth-moving equipment does not encroach on the land near those trees.

Mulching
A mulch is an organic or inorganic material placed on the soil surface in relatively thin layers. Ideally for the gardener, a mulch should be inexpensive, readily obtainable, aesthetic, and resistant to blowing or washing away. Mulches benefit trees by increasing the moisture retention of soil, moderating soil temperatures, reducing water runoff and erosion, improving the soil's structure and fertility, and reducing the weed population.

Mulch Materials
The most common organic mulches are composted leaves, wood chips, shredded bark, bark nuggets, sawdust, peat moss, lawn clippings, peanut shells, buckwheat hulls, corn cobs, mushroom compost, manure, conifer needles, newspaper, sludge, and a wide assortment of locally available materials.

Inorganic mulches include limestone pebbles, granite pebbles, crushed brick, marble chips, polyethylene and other plastic films, synthetic fabrics, coal nuggets, and others. Stone and stonelike materials are formal and harsh to the eye, and are best reserved for large-scale urban landscaping or specialized gardens. Trees planted in the home landscape deserve organic mulches.

Potential Hazards
Unfortunately, not all mulches boast the ideal qualities, and the possible disadvantages of specific materials and their remedies are best mentioned at the outset.

Toxicity and Leaching
The rapid decay of a fresh organic material such as sawdust or grass clippings can deplete nitrogen in the soil. Compost the material before using it as a mulch, use shredded bark or another material that decomposes more slowly, or add nitrogen fertilizer to the soil to compensate for the loss.

Some plant products, especially when fresh, may be toxic to plants, especially young plants, mulched with them. Avoid the sawdust and leaves of eucalyptus; any parts of walnuts; the bark of spruces, Douglas-firs, and larches; and sawdust from cedars and redwoods. Limestone pebbles have a considerable alkalizing effect on soil, interfering with the ability of some species to obtain minerals, especially iron, resulting in foliar chlorosis. Use limestone only near alkaline-tolerant species, use other materials, or use a soil barrier such as black plastic sheeting, which will also inhibit weed growth, but may retain excess moisture.

Moisture Retention
Finely textured, compact organic materials such as peat moss or sawdust may retain excessive amounts of soil moisture for some tree species. If problems develop, use a material with a coarse texture and apply it no deeper than two inches.

Plastic sheet mulch, unbroken, can prevent water from entering the soil. Plastic with holes punched into it will allow water in but not out, often causing water-logged soil. The larger the surface area of the plastic, the more likely you are to encounter these problems. Don't use plastic on areas larger than 25 square feet.

Delayed Dormancy
Mulched trees, especially younger trees, may continue to grow in fall, delaying the onset of dormancy. This is most serious for those species at the limits of their hardiness, and could cause severe winter injury. If you plant a tree that you believe will be sensitive to cold, you should delay mulching until the second year; remove at least part of the mulch at the end of summer and replace it after a few winter freezes; and plant the tree in a protected site, usually an eastern exposure with a slight slope.

Other Dangers
Some materials, such as straw and dry peat moss, are fire hazards. Keep them moist, and use them only in nonpublic areas to reduce the possibility of fire caused by discarded matches or cigarettes. Inorganic mulches with sizable particles, such as marble chips and

Apply mulches 2–6 in. deep, under the dripline. A bare ring around the trunk prevents disease.

Fertilize every second year with nitrogen—broadcast by hand over the mulched area.

various pebbles, become dangerous projectiles when struck by rotary lawn mower blades. The particles, when they inexorably find their ways to walking surfaces, will turn an ankle or bruise a heel. Bark nuggets are only somewhat less hazardous. Use these materials only in areas with steel-strip edging or some other lawn barrier, or in areas edged regularly with a spade.

Applying Mulch

In cold climates, mulch should be applied to trees planted in fall only after several heavy frosts. In zones 1 to 5, trees planted in spring, especially those that are questionably hardy, may fare better if the mulch is withheld during the first summer and fall, and applied only after some freezing occurs.

Existing trees benefit from larger mulched areas as they grow, though mature trees often lack mulch altogether. The larger the mulched area, the better. A ten-foot circle under a tree spreading 40 feet will have much less benefit than mulch under the entire canopy.

Rather than strip sod with a spade, which may damage shallow roots or strain your back, use the herbicide glyphosate, sold as Roundup or Kleenup. Mark out the area to be treated. A can of spray paint is handy for this—mistakes can be crossed out and new lines drawn. Follow the application directions on the herbicide container. On a calm day, at the correct temperature, treat the expendable grass or other vegetation, working carefully within the lines.

A few days later, even though the grass is still more or less green, apply the mulch as uniformly as possible, about two inches thick for finely textured materials, four inches for coarse material. Large trees in light, sandy soil will tolerate as much as six inches of coarse mulch. Keep the mulch at least six inches away from trunks to deter mice and minimize fungal activity, and use a lawn barrier or edging to hold the mulch in place. Replenish organic mulches as they decompose, after the last frost of spring, or after the first freezes of early winter.

Animal Damage

Mulches may attract and harbor rodents. Materials such as corn cobs and peanut hulls usually contain stray edible seeds. Keep a six-inch bare ring around the tree trunk or use rodent poison in cans or jars with small openings so pets can't get in, buried under the mulch so children won't see them, and slanted slightly downward to keep water out.

Domestic animals sometimes cause problems. Sleeves made of hardware cloth will discourage cats from scratching small trees; be sure to adjust the size annually as trees grow. Urinating dogs can be a serious problem, especially in crowded suburbs. Experiment with commercial repellents.

Spraying and other pest control methods are discussed in the chapter on Pests and Diseases.

Lightning Protection
Trees are frequently hit by lightning, sometimes with extreme violence. Tall trees can be protected with properly installed lightning rods and cables, though an arborist with lightning protection expertise may be hard to find.

Some species of trees are more susceptible to lightning strikes than others. Lists vary, but the following trees are most vulnerable: oaks, maples, ashes, Tulip Trees, sycamores, pines, spruces, poplars, elms, and hemlocks. Those trees that are relatively safe are beeches, birches, and others with thin, smooth bark. Theoretical explanations differ, but thick bark seems pivotal to a tree's susceptibility to lightning.

Fertilizing
Trees, just as other plants, need essential elements, called fertilizer, for growth. Fertilizer can improve tree vigor, induce bigger, greener leaves, and improve resistance to various adversities, including attacks by certain insects and diseases. However, don't assume that normal lawn fertilization will help trees. Be aware that too much fertilizer is detrimental, and that fertilizer is not a panacea for the symptoms of trees affected by other agents than nutrient deficiencies.

The major elements, necessary in relatively large amounts, are nitrogen, phosphorus, and potassium. Commercial fertilizers specify the percentages they contain of these three elements. A package marked 25–5–10 contains 25 percent nitrogen, 5 percent phosphorus, and 10 percent potassium.

Minor elements, or trace elements, are necessary in minute quantities. Some commercial fertilizers indicate these in general, and label the product "including trace elements"; most make no mention of them but may contain some. Trace elements, particularly iron and manganese, may be lacking or simply unavailable to trees in alkaline soils. Acid, sandy soils may lack phosphorus, and certain local soils may be short of zinc or copper.

When to Fertilize
Visually assessing the fertilizer needs of trees is difficult. A tree with stunted, yellowed foliage may benefit from fertilizer, but may have other problems. A complete soil test, including tests for minor elements and toxic substances, is your best method of diagnosis. Some laboratories will also test leaves for element content. See your county Cooperative Extension office or other experts to obtain reliable, complete testing.

As a general rule, trees in good condition need little fertilizer, and then only nitrogen. If you employ soil testing, the test results will

To fertilize in lawn areas, drill evenly spaced 2 in. holes 2–3 ft. apart in the root zone.

Apportion a slow-release fertilizer, keeping it below grass roots, 4 in. or more from surface. Top holes with sand or mulch, or leave bare.

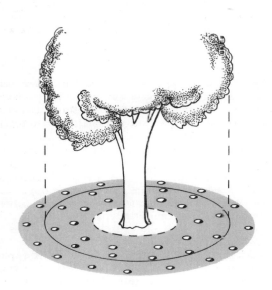

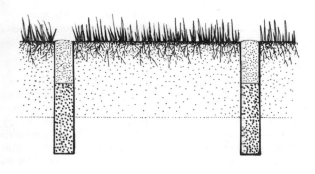

Maintaining Trees

include the proper application rates. If you haven't tested your soil, apply only nitrogen at a rate of three or four pounds of actual nitrogen for each 1,000 square feet every two years. For some trees in some soils, this rate may be light, or a bit heavy. If you have unusual conditions, don't trust the rule of thumb. Have your soil tested.

Timing
Many studies of fertilizer applications by qualified researchers have turned up a variety of results. Some have found little difference in effectiveness when changing the application seasons; others suggest avoiding summer and fall applications, especially of nitrogen, to minimize late growth that could be winterkilled. In sandy soils, some say nitrogen is best applied just before growth starts in spring to minimize loss by leaching before the tree can use it. Another recommendation is to apply nitrogen at the time of burgeoning spring growth, when tree needs are greatest and nitrogen uptake will be most efficient. Until more research gives solid answers, it seems we can fertilize trees, moderately, at any time.

Application Methods
Surface broadcasting of granular fertilizer is the easiest application method. It works well for nitrogen fertilizers, because nitrogen is soluble in water and will quickly enter the soil after rain or watering. Insolubles such as phosphorus, potassium, and most minor elements should be applied by other means.
If there is a sizable mulched area beneath a tree, scatter nitrogen atop the mulch by hand at any time. If grass is under the tree, apply nitrogen uniformly with a mechanical spreader in late winter or very early spring when grass is dormant. The grass should be dry at the time of application. Sprinkle with water slowly and thoroughly immediately, and again the following day, to soak the fertilizer down into the soil.

Drill Hole Fertilization
To apply insoluble or slow-release formulations of fertilizer, or nitrogen during the grass-growing seasons, the drill hole method is often chosen. Use a two-inch diameter bit in an electric or gasoline-powered drill. Never drill in wet soil or use a punch bar at any time—the sides of the hole will be compacted. Make holes a foot deep and two or three feet apart, beginning three feet from the trunk of a smaller tree, six feet for a large tree, and extending into a circle well beyond the dripline. Count the holes, estimate the surface area, and apportion the fertilizer to each hole.
In lawn areas, if the figured amount of fertilizer will fill the holes more than two-thirds full, drill more holes. The fertilizer must be at least four inches down, below the grass roots, or you will have rich green polka dots for several years. Use a funnel to prevent

spills and a measuring cup to ensure even distribution. The holes may be topped with coarse sand or mulch, or left alone—they are not a hazard and will gradually disappear.

Other Application Methods
The high-pressure injection of fertilizer solutions into the soil requires several applications over a growing season to be effective, but is often combined with waterings. The fertilizer can be applied by commercial operators with proper equipment. Foliage application of soluble fertilizer is expensive and is used as a short-term treatment of certain deficiencies. Sometimes a foliar-spray test is advisable—if the sprayed material corrects the tree's symptoms even briefly, it indicates the probable efficacy of soil application of the same element.
Trunk implants of fertilizer are available; more sophisticated trunk injection systems usually require licensed operators. Both are short-term methods that injure a tree and create the possibility of decay. But if a tree's roots are surrounded by paving or buildings, trunk treatment may be the only method available.

Vertical Mulching
Recent tests showed that if trees growing in poorly drained soil simply had holes drilled in the surrounding soil, they responded as well or better than similar trees with fertilizer placed in the holes. Drilling these holes is called vertical mulching by some arborists, and perhaps the term refers to the mulch material sometimes put into the holes. By whatever name, it is a great boon to trees that are sulking in heavy soil.

Pests & Diseases

Plant pests and diseases are a fact of life for shade and ornamental trees, and it is helpful to be familiar with the common plant pests and the methods used to control them.

Symptoms of Problems
Since yellowing leaves, loss of plant parts, stunting, weak growth, and wilting are general symptoms of plant problems, some experience is needed to determine their causes.

Diseases and Nematodes
Fungi and bacteria cause a variety of diseases, but plant tissues affected by bacterial diseases usually appear wetter than those attacked by fungi. Viruses and mycoplasma are often transmitted by aphids and leafhoppers. Affected trees display mottled yellow leaves, which also may be crinkled or deformed, and yellowed or stunted growth. Nematodes are microscopic roundworms that usually attack roots, causing stunting and poor plant growth.

Insect Pests
A variety of insects attack trees. The sap-sucking insects—including aphids, plant bugs, and scale insects—suck plant juices. The affected trees become yellow, stunted and misshapen. Aphids and scale insects also produce a sticky substance called honeydew which attracts ants and fosters sooty mold fungus. Pests with rasping-sucking mouthparts, such as spider mites, scrape plant tissue and then suck the juices which well up in the injured areas.
Leaf-chewers, the beetles and caterpillars, consume leaves whole or in part and can be very destructive. Borers tunnel into shoots and stems, and the young larvae consume plant tissue, weakening the tree.

Environmental Stresses
Other types of tree injuries are caused by environmental stresses, salt toxicity, rodents, nutritional deficiencies or excesses, pesticide injury, and damage from lawn mowers. Many of these injuries can be avoided if you are aware of potential dangers and take the proper precautions to protect trees.

Controlling Plant Problems
Cultural control measures should be included in the routine care of trees. They are far better than relying on haphazard pesticide applications which may be ineffective once the culprit is established. By observing your trees each week for signs of trouble, you can arrest or prevent a serious disease or infestation in its early stages, when it is most easily controlled. Prune and destroy infested and diseased branches and clean up fallen leaves and twigs in fall to help prevent insects and diseases from overwintering near susceptible trees. Regularly spray trees with water to dislodge some

insect pests and to keep the leaves free of suffocating dust.
Fertilize trees once every two to three years with a nitrogen
fertilizer, unless soil test results indicate otherwise. Provide
adequate air circulation by pruning and spacing trees properly.
Trees require approximately one inch of water per week in the form
of rain or applied water. During drought periods, water trees
deeply each week to avoid drought stress. Use a root-feeding
apparatus or lay a hose under the tree's dripline (the circular area
from the trunk to the branch tips). Mulch with several inches of
organic material around trees to conserve moisture, keep roots
cooler, and keep lawn mowers and weed-trimmers from trunks.
Do not apply herbicides, including "weed-and-feed" lawn
preparations, near a tree's dripline. Herbicide injury may cause
elongated, strap-like, or downward-cupping leaves. Spray weed-
killer only when the air is still, but not on very hot, dry days.

Insecticides and Fungicides

To protect plants from insect and disease injury, a number of
insecticides and fungicides are available. However, a few products
control diseases due to bacteria, viruses, and mycoplasma. Pesticides
are usually either "protectant" or "systemic" in nature. Protectants
shield uninfected foliage from insects or disease organisms, while
systemics move through the plant to provide some therapeutic or
eradicant action as well as protection. Botanical insecticides such as
pyrethrum and rotenone have a shorter residual effect on pests but
are considered less toxic and safer for the user and the environment
than inorganic chemical insecticides. Biological control, using
organisms like *Bacillus thuringiensis* (a bacterium toxic to moth and
butterfly larvae), is effective and safe.

Recommended pesticides may vary from region to region; consult
your local Cooperative Extension agent or plant professional. Always
check the pesticide label to be sure that it is registered for use on
the affected tree species and the pest you have identified. Follow the
label regarding safety precautions, dosage, and frequency of
application. Also, learn about the pest's life cycle so that you spray
when it will be effective. Employ professionals to spray or prune
trees over 20 feet high. They have the proper equipment and
training to handle the hazards involved.

Recognizing Pests and Diseases

Learn to recognize the most common insects and diseases that can
plague trees. The following chart describes the most common pests,
diseases, and environmental disorders that afflict trees, the damages
they cause, and the measures to take to control them.

Pest or Disease

Aphids

Borers

Cankers

Chlorosis

Decay

Description	Damage	Controls
Tiny green, brown, or reddish, pear-shaped, soft-bodied insects in clusters on buds, shoots, and undersides of leaves.	Suck plant juices, causing stunted or deformed blooms and leaves. Some transmit plant viruses. Secretions attract ants.	If control is necessary, spray with malathion or orthene.
Several kinds of wormlike, legless, cream-colored larvae tunneling in stems.	Holes, sawdust, or droppings on trunks or branches. Infestations may cause dieback of branches or entire tree.	Destroy infested branches, pruning several inches below swelling. Fertilize and water to increase vigor. Spray with dursban or lindane at proper time.
Fungal disease causing spots and dead areas on stems. Black dots of fungal spores in dead areas.	Discolored spots on stems. Spots enlarge, becoming light or dark and dry. Dieback and death of tree may occur.	Prune and destroy infected branches. Avoid wounding healthy stems in wet weather. Use proper pruning techniques.
Yellowed, unhealthy leaves usually caused by iron deficiency in alkaline soils. Also a symptom of viral and fungal diseases.	Unnaturally yellow or pale foliage and a general lack of vigor.	Apply iron chelate compound to root zone. Choose species tolerant of your soil conditions.
Internal weakening of tree by fungal growth.	Branches may die or drop from tree. Fungal conks may be visible on trunk or branches. Large cavities in trunk.	Prune affected limbs or remove tree. Cavity-filling does little to prolong the life of a tree.

Pests & Diseases

Pest or Disease

Fireblight

Fungal Blights

Fungal Leafspots and Needle Casts

Gall Formers

Girdling Root

Description	Damage	Controls
A bacterial disease that causes blackened foliage and oozing stem cankers on Rosaceous plants.	Blackens terminal shoots, causes stem cankers, often kills plant.	Cut out diseased shoots. Sterilize clippers in bleach solution between cuts. Streptomycin sprays or copper fungicides may help.
Leaves of deciduous trees turn brown and wilt. Branches of evergreen trees may be brown or gray.	Affects leaves and shoots of trees, killing portions of growth and stunting plant.	Prune badly affected plant parts. Avoid getting foliage wet. Provide adequate air circulation around trees.
Spots on leaves or needles, caused by fungi and encouraged by humid or wet weather.	Tan, brown, or black spots on leaves or needles. If serious, foliage may drop from plant.	Increase air circulation around plants. Remove badly diseased foliage. Spray with benomyl or Bordeaux mixture if serious.
Tiny insects or mites which produce unsightly growths called galls on plant parts.	Overgrowth of plant leaves, stems, or flowers. Leaf galls usually are not harmful; twig galls usually are.	For insects, spray malathion or orthene just before expected appearance of damage. For mites, use a miticide.
Root which encircles the base of the trunk or other roots. Trunk appears to go straight into ground.	Dieback of top branches, yellowing and decrease in size of leaves.	Cut or straighten encircling roots at planting time. Established girdling roots can be cut, but with difficulty.

Pest or Disease

Herbicide Injury

Leaf-feeding Beetles

Leaf-feeding Caterpillars

Leafminers

Leaf Scorch and Drought Injury

Description	Damage	Controls
Distortion of leaves and dieback of tree due to application of weed-killers.	Curling, puckering, or strap-like growth of leaves. May be dieback of twigs and branches.	Avoid applying weed-killers, including "weed-and-feed" products, near trees. Spray when air is calm, avoid very hot days.
Hard-shelled, oval to oblong insects on leaves and stems.	Chew plant parts, leaving holes. Larvae of some feed on roots.	If control is necessary, spray with malathion or carbaryl.
Soft-bodied, wormlike insects with several pairs of legs. May be smooth or spiny. Adults are moths or butterflies.	Consume part or all of leaves.	Spray with *Bacillus thuringiensis*, carbaryl, or orthene.
Small larvae of flies or beetles that feed between leaf surfaces.	Leaves show yellow, then brown, oval or meandering, papery blotches. Leaves may drop.	Remove badly infested leaves. Spray with malathion or orthene at first sight of small mines.
Drying of leaves or damage to roots by dry soil conditions.	Scorched and browned leaf margins. Wilted leaves, dieback of twigs and branches, or death of tree may occur.	Provide more water for trees, especially after transplanting and during hot, dry periods.

Pests & Diseases

Pest or Disease

Mechanical Injury

Nematodes

Plant Bugs

Salt Toxicity

Scale

Description	Damage	Controls
Injury to trees by lawn mowers, weed-trimmers, construction, vehicles, vandalism, or rodents.	Wounds on main trunk, often near ground line. Trees may die.	Avoid wounding trees. Mulch or fence trees to keep equipment away from trunks. Use ¼-inch mesh hardware cloth to deter rodents.
Microscopic roundworms, usually associated with roots, which cause various diseases.	Stunted, off-color plants that do not respond to water or fertilizer. Minute galls may be present on roots.	Nematocides are available for use around valuable plants.
Brownish, oval, sucking insects feed on leaves, leaving shiny, black droppings.	Leaves are curled, pale, and leaf margins may be brown. Trees may be defoliated.	Spray malathion or carbaryl when damage first appears and insects are present.
Death of leaves, branches, or roots due to application of salts to above-ground plant parts or root zone.	Yellowing or browning of leaves or needles. Early fall coloring, twig dieback, and branch death may occur.	Avoid use of de-icing salts near trees. Leach applied salts from soil with heavy watering.
Small, waxy, soft- or hard-bodied, stationary insects on shoots and leaves. May be red, white, brown, black, or gray.	Suck plant juices, causing stunted, off-color plants. Insects may cover large portion of stem.	Spray with malathion, or carbaryl when crawlers are present, or use a dormant oil spray in early spring before growth begins.

Pests & Diseases

Pest or Disease

Spider Mites

Tent-forming Caterpillars

Viruses

Wilts

Winter Injury

Description	Damage	Controls
Tiny golden, red, or brown arachnids on undersides of leaves. Profuse fine webs seen with heavy infestations.	Scrape leaves and suck plant juices. Leaves become pale and dry. Plant may be stunted.	Spray leaves with water. Use a miticide on undersides of leaves.
Wormlike larvae form weblike tents or bags in tree branches.	Larvae consume leaves on affected branches and may defoliate the tree.	Cut down and burn or dispose of webs.
Various diseases, including mosaics, that cause off-color, stunted plants. May be transmitted by aphids.	Crinkled, mottled, deformed leaves, stunted plants, and poor growth.	Control the insect vector (aphids), if present. Buy only healthy trees. Water and fertilize to improve vigor.
Fungal or bacterial diseases which cause wilting, stunting, and eventual death of plants.	Leaves turn yellow and entire tree may wilt and die.	If applicable, control insect vector. Remove severely diseased trees. If soil-borne, do not plant same type tree in that location.
Damage to plant leaves, stems, or roots by cold temperatures, drought, or sunscald during winter months.	Browning of evergreen foliage, dieback of branch tips, vertical cracks in trunk or branches. Death may occur.	Choose trees hardy for your region. Wrap stems of thin-barked species in fall with reflective tree wrap.

Propagation

The vast majority of ornamental trees are propagated by skilled horticulturists, and most gardeners purchase common and unusual trees in larger sizes. However, there is a special sense of satisfaction in raising trees from cuttings or by layering, and the processes are no more difficult than those used for other garden plants. The following is a short overview of the equipment and methods used to propagate trees. For detailed information, visit your library, your favorite garden center, or ask local professionals for advice.

Cold Frames and Mist Beds
Any box with a transparent lid—in ground or on top—is a cold frame, useful for starting seeds, rooting cuttings, and protecting small trees over winter. Cold frames should be made of treated lumber for durability, or may be purchased in many sizes from garden centers and mail-order dealers. Smaller propagating cases may be made or purchased for indoor use, and are usually supplemented by artificial light.
For cuttings that demand constant moisture, mist beds are ideal. Mist beds have one or more mist nozzles in an open-topped plastic enclosure of varying dimensions, and their sides are high to minimize wind disturbances. Mist systems can be constant, with a manually regulated water supply, or intermittent, with the water supply controlled by timers or other devices. Mist systems are often installed in greenhouses as well.

Seeds, Grafting, and Budding
Propagating trees by seed, though often not difficult, is a highly variable subject, and you should seek out detailed information on individual species at the outset. Be aware, as well, that seedlings are often of a mediocre type, inferior to asexually propagated cultivars. Grafting and budding are the ultimate triumphs of the propagator, but are difficult processes best left to professionals and devoted amateurs. The following methods will allow you to propagate many tree species.

Layering and Air Layering
An easy and nearly foolproof system of propagating trees with branches close to the soil is layering. A branch is scraped on its underside and pegged to the ground, with soil mounded over the wounded point. In mound layering, soil is mounded up over an entire many-branched shrub or tree, with each branch wounded at its base. The mounding is done in spring; the following spring the rooted shoots are removed and planted. If certain types of young trees—magnolias, especially—are cut off near soil level, many shoots arise; these can be mound layered the following year.
In air layering, damp sphagnum moss is placed around a wound on a small branch or trunk and covered with black polyethylene or aluminum foil and sealed with electrician's tape at either end,

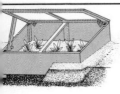

Cold frames are useful for starting seeds, rooting cuttings, and protecting small trees over winter.

Sink the frame into the soil or bank soil partially up the sides.

making a small pouch. After roots form in the moss, the branch is severed below the root mass and planted. This may be done at any time outdoors in frost-free climates. In colder areas, air layer trees as soon as possible after the last spring frost and remove rooted twigs just before the first winter frost.

Deciduous Cuttings

Hardwood cuttings are six- to eight-inch sections of firm new shoots taken during a tree's dormant season. Water sprouts make fine cuttings. In cold climates cuttings are often collected in early winter, stored in a cool, moist cold frame, and set out in spring with about an inch of cutting above the soil. Cuttings taken in early spring and planted immediately also root well. In warmer zones with little or no frost, cuttings may be taken whenever trees are dormant. Rooting may require two or three months, and not all species are successful. The easiest hardwood cuttings to root are taken from alder, mulberry, poplar, and willow species.

Softwood cuttings are taken during a tree's growing season. The cuttings are succulent and must not be allowed to dry out, and are best taken in the morning. They should be three to six inches long, with their terminal buds intact. Remove the lower leaves, then slightly wound the base of the stalk with a knife and dip it into a root-promoting hormone powder before planting. High humidity is paramount, so use a closed propagation unit or a mist system. After the cuttings root, which may take from two to ten weeks, harden them off by gradually exposing them to normal conditions before potting or planting. Young trees are often difficult to overwinter without a cold frame. Maples, Ginkgo, Silver-Bell, Crape Myrtle, Sweet Gum, magnolias, crabapples, Dawn Redwood, Empress Tree, cherries, willows, and elms all can be propagated from softwood cuttings.

Evergreen Cuttings

Cold frames or greenhouses are necessary for success with evergreen cuttings. The process is the same as for deciduous softwood cuttings. Broadleaf species and cultivars are best started in fall or early winter; needle-leaf evergreens in early or midwinter. Rooting takes from one to two months. The cuttings are then potted in spring and held in cold frames for a year, or are planted in lightly shaded beds for a year before being set out.

Record Keeping

Trees are valuable garden assets; to tend them properly, they deserve at least an inventory record, and ideally, maintenance and performance data as well. Such records are enjoyable to peruse on winter evenings, much like a photo album of family activities. Also, records can help you identify successful practices and discontinue deleterious ones.

Many gardeners keep a garden diary in which they note the changes that occur in their garden over the course of the seasons. The simplest diaries are dated jottings about tasks performed, the blooming times of plants, and personal impressions. This format is not really satisfactory if you want to follow closely the growth of your trees; it is usually better to devote a special file or diary to them, especially if you have many trees. If you already are keeping records of other garden plants, the system you are using will often adapt to include trees.

The following card file system presents the optimal method for the dedicated gardener, and it is easily adapted for use as a garden diary, if you find your own inclinations lean to that format. By whatever method, however, keep tree records. Chances are you'll be glad you did.

The Card File

Making a file with a card for each tree is a simple method of record keeping. Use scientific or common names to organize your entries, depending on your preference, but be consistent. The cards should be at least five by seven inches, preferably six by nine. A computer, if available and properly programmed, with back-up discs, of course, is ideal for compiling tree records.

Essential Data

The information you should record is not elaborate, but if not noted, it is often lost with time. First record the tree's scientific name, then the common name that makes you most comfortable—many trees have more than one. Second, record where you obtained the tree. For example: "Al's Nursery," "where new freeway is," or "grandma's yard." Then note the date of order or date of possession. Refinements here could be such as "arrived three weeks late." Next, note what stage of growth the tree was planted in: seed, cutting, seedling, grafted plant in three-inch pot, balled and burlapped six feet tall, and so on. The tree's size at the time of planting also should be entered here. Now, note the date planted and attendant data: "very dry day," "bad flood," "heavily pruned by nursery." Finally, record the tree's location. If your property is small, then "front," "west side," or other general notes are fine. Larger properties should be mapped and gridded. Use your landscape plan, or obtain a plat from county officials and mark it off in 100-foot by 100-foot squares. Code them, such as "Northwest" or "B–3," and enter the locations on your cards.

Maintenance and Performance Data

This data is also essential if you really care about your trees' performance. Use the backs of Essential Data cards, additional cards, or your computer to keep track of the information. Each tree's data can be arranged categorically, but it is more sensible to arrange it chronologically. By date, record what has been done to the tree, in what amounts, and by whom. Entries might read: "3/30/87: Zeke sprayed w/malathion at rec'd rate." "7/6/87: pruned by Expert Tree Co."

Don't forget activities in the area not directly related to trees. For example: "6/5/87: Zeke applied unidentified weed-killer to lawn around this tree at unknown rate." Make an occasional status note, and record any abnormalities, such as: "7/5/87: leaves twisted, distorted." Though you may have forgotten about the earlier weed-killer application, it becomes obvious to connect the events of June 5th and July 5th by using a record, and keeping and using such records may save a tree.

Every few years, measure each tree and add the data to the record system. Estimate its height, pace off its average spread, and measure the circumference of the trunk at four and a half feet high. If you have later casualty losses, such information will favorably impress insurance and tax examiners.

Photographs

Trees are fun to photograph, and the prints can be valuable. Next time cousin Mortimer visits, snap him dozing under the Green Ash tree. Get the entire tree in; Mort is just for scale. Or photograph your trees unencumbered, individually and in panoramic views, and date the prints. Do this at least every two or three years. If a tree is lost or damaged, photos will augment the golden written data you've collected.

Calendar

A healthy tree in a suitable environment requires little attention. But don't ignore your trees; examine them closely once a month. By the time a tree declines to the point of exhibiting severe symptoms, it may be impossible to save. This calendar offers seasonal planting and maintenance suggestions. Only you can decide whether to perform any or all of the tasks mentioned. Your own enthusiasm for gardening chores, an understanding of local conditions, and the needs of the trees you grow will determine your schedule.

The calendar is organized seasonally rather than monthly to offset geographic differences that cause variations in the onset and length of the seasons. For example, spring travels northward across the eastern U.S. at a rate of 16 miles per day. The last spring frost divides early spring and mid-spring. The first fall frost marks the end of fall and the beginning of early winter.

Late Winter
Order trees from mail-order sources.

In warmer climates, plant or transplant trees.

Remove dead or dying trees, especially deciduous ones. Lack of foliage reduces litter and eases clean-up.

This is a good time to prune trees. Minor pruning can be done by homeowners. Major pruning should be performed by qualified professionals.

Destroy insect egg masses on trunks, especially those of tent caterpillars and gypsy moths.

Spray with dormant oil or insecticide-oil combinations as recommended for mites, scale insects, and other pests, except on certain maple, beech, Douglas-fir, and other sensitive species.

Apply lime or sulfur to adjust soil pH, if necessary.

Fertilize.

Replenish mulches and vertical mulch.

Remove stakes, wires, trunk wraps, and identification labels from trees planted last season. Remove anti-snow wraps unless your area is subject to spring snows.

Early Spring
In colder climates, plant or transplant trees as soon as soil is workable.

Remember to apply dormant oil spray only before bud break. At bud break, spray as recommended for fungal leaf and twig diseases, especially if the weather is rainy or humid. Spray as recommended for specific insects on susceptible trees.

Head back low branches on young trees by a third to a half. Remove branches headed back previously on older trees.

Late Spring
Spray for leaf diseases a second or third time.

Control aphids and other early insects as recommended.
Employ branch-angle training.

Summer

Watch for mites, beetles, chewing larvae, and other summer insects
and control them as recommended.
Perform minor corrective pruning. Remove suckers and water
sprouts; treat wounds with a sprout-retardant compound.
Carefully enlarge mulch areas around trees that have outgrown their
installations.
Irrigate during drought—enough, but not too much or too often.
Know the needs and tolerances of your trees. Pay close attention to
trees planted in the last two years.
Inspect trees carefully. Is twig extension normal? Is leaf color
normal? If not, check for soil compaction and have your soil tested.
Call a consultant if you find problems.
Regularly spray trees with water to dislodge some insect pests and
to keep the leaves free of suffocating dust.
In late summer in most climates, plant new trees if
container-grown or balled and burlapped last spring. They are
nearly dormant now and their water needs will be modest.
Every other summer, photograph and measure all your trees.

Fall

In cold or windy areas, be sure trees, especially evergreens, have
reasonable soil moisture as winter approaches.
Rake up leaves. Healthy leaves make excellent compost. Destroy
diseased leaves.
Spray for certain insects according to instructions.
Transplant evergreens. Wait until leaf drop to transplant deciduous
trees, but avoid those sensitive to movement in fall.
Do not mulch newly planted trees until after heavy frosts.
In snow areas, in late fall, wrap narrow upright evergreens spirally
with soft cord to minimize snow damage.

Early Winter

Assess landscape needs and hire a designer if necessary.
Contract with qualified tree pruners for winter work, perhaps at
lower rates.
Consider lightning protection for large trees.
Select the desired species and cultivars from mail-order catalogues.
Consult local nursery people about trees you cannot find. Some may
be able to order trees from wholesale sources.
Keep snow from trunks of young trees to control rodents.
To repel deer, hang small bars of inexpensive scented soap four feet
above ground at the perimeters of trees.
Study this book. Make your own calendar to suit your needs.

Expert Help

Trained experts are available to design home landscapes, to plant trees, to care for them chemically by applying fertilizers and pesticides, and to attend to them physically by pruning and removing them. However, not all tree service personnel are qualified or competent. By knowing what to look for and what to avoid when choosing a tree service, you can easily select qualified, efficient personnel.

Landscape Designers

You may decide to have your landscape designed professionally. When choosing a designer, ask prospective candidates about their education, their previous experience, and any awards they may have won. Ask them for the locations of properties they have designed and go to view them. Beware of the haughty who won't listen, and also of the oversolicitous who agree with everything you say. Give special consideration to those who try to find out what effects you want and what functions you need, and who can clearly explain why some of your ideas may be unsound.

After choosing a designer, obtain a written contract stating what specific services the designer will do, when they will be completed, and for what payment. The simplest contract would be for a planting plan only, a drawing indicating the sites of plants and landscape features—earth mounds, retaining walls, steps, terraces, and the like. More complete services could include a site analysis, planting specifications, suggested sources for plants, acceptable substitutes, detailed blueprints, and the supervision of construction and planting.

Chemical Specialists

Specialists—those applying pesticides and fertilizers—should have the pertinent training and education. Be sure to inquire about the time, manpower, and equipment a specialist estimates would be necessary for the job you propose, and use those estimates to compare services. Specialists should also have decent, even impressive, equipment. Neighbors often can refer you to a qualified company. Check with your county Cooperative Extension office about required licensing, and be sure that the personnel you hire have obtained the necessary local, state, and federal sanctions. Ask about relevant degrees and certificates, and be sure the company has proper and adequate insurance.

Tree Removers and Pruners

To prune a tree, an operator must be both an artist and a technician. You may have to take the pruner's artistry on faith, but his technical knowledge is fairly easy to determine. The operator, or at least the company, should hold membership in the American Association of Arborists or the International Society of Arboriculture, preferably both.

Before signing the essential contract, ask about insurance. Read the chapter Pruning, then ask whether your prospective pruner advocates tree wound dressing. Also ask what he or she knows about branch collars, branch bark ridges, and compartmentalization. Before you sign a contract, decide who will dispose of the wood and debris, especially if you do not want firewood.

In rural areas, it may be impossible to find a qualified tree pruner nearby, and mileage costs for distant experts run high. You will be tempted to do the work yourself. Caution! If the job requires more than a stepladder, if you would be sawing from above your waist with or without a ladder, or if the cut portion could possibly—even remotely—cause damage or injury, pay the mileage costs for a good tree surgeon, or have the tree pruned by an unschooled sawyer with insurance and experience. Above all, resist the temptation to hire local tree hackers. Even if the job is done without mishap, you may be left with a truncated caricature of a tree.

Tree Appraisers

Lightning, an ice storm, sudden high winds, vandals, fire, an errant vehicle, or some other phenomenon may someday damage or kill a tree of yours. The loss is physically irreparable, but you may be entitled to compensation. You can file a claim with your insurance company, if you have coverage, or you can claim compensation from the perpetrator's insurance company, if any exists. And you also may be able to obtain an income tax deduction in the amount of the reduction in the value of your property.

In the first two cases, the expertise of a qualified tree appraiser, preferably a member of the American Society of Consulting Arborists, will be valuable, perhaps valuable enough to cover the professional fee. Ask about the fee at the outset. The value of the damage is based on either the tree's replacement cost, or a damage value calculated by the tree species, its location and condition before damage, and the extent of the damage. If your prospective tree appraiser doesn't know about those factors, find one who does. If the case goes to court, you will need a credible witness.

The IRS deduction is the province of real estate appraisers and your tax consultant. The dollar amount is based on the value of your property before and after the damage or loss.

Tree Chart

	Page Numbers	Zones, Hardy; Semihar...
Deciduous Ornamentals		
Acer campestre	126, 127	5–8
Acer griseum	126, 127	5–8
Aesculus × carnea 'Briottii'	76, 77	5–9
Albizia julibrissin 'Rosea'	80, 81	6–9
Amelanchier × grandiflora	128, 129	4–8; 3
Amelanchier laevis	128, 129	4–8; 3
Bauhinia blakeana	78, 79	10
Betula pendula 'Purpurea'	122, 123	3–9
Carpinus betulus 'Fastigiata'	134, 135	5–9
Catalpa bignonioides	90, 91	5–9
Catalpa speciosa	90, 91	4–8
Cercis canadensis	86, 87	5–8; 4
Chorisia speciosa	78, 79	9–10
Cladrastis lutea	94, 95	4–8
Cornus florida	114–117	5–9
Cornus kousa	112, 113	5–8
Cornus mas	118, 119	5–7
Cornus nuttallii	110, 111	7–9
Crataegus crus-galli	98, 99	5–9
Crataegus × lavallei	98, 99	5–9
Crataegus phaenopyrum	100, 101	5–9
Crataegus viridis 'Winter King'	100, 101	5–7
Delonix regia	80, 81	10
Fagus sylvatica 'Pendula'	120, 121	5–8
Fagus sylvatica 'Riversii'	122	5–8
Fagus sylvatica 'Tricolor'	123	5–8
Halesia carolina	88, 89	5–8
Jacaranda mimosifolia	84, 85	10; 9
Koelreuteria bipinnata	96, 97	8–10; 7
Koelreuteria paniculata	94, 95	5–8
Lagerstroemia indica	76, 77	7–9

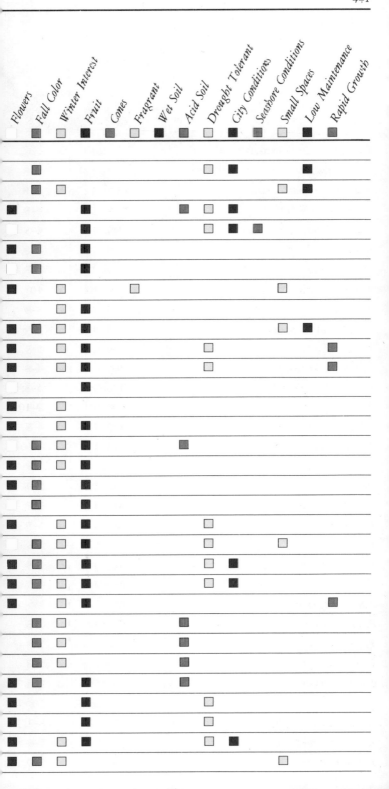

	Page Numbers	Zones, Hardy; Semihar...
Deciduous Ornamentals continued		
Larix kaempferi	138, 139	4–6
Magnolia × soulangiana	82, 83	5–10
Malus 'Bob White'	107	4–8
Malus 'Candied Apple'	102, 103	4–8
Malus 'Coralburst'	104, 105	4–8
Malus 'Dolgo'	102	4–8
Malus 'Donald Wyman'	106, 107	4–8
Malus floribunda	106	4–8
Malus 'Indian Magic'	105	4–8
Malus 'Liset'	104	4–8
Malus 'Makamik'	103	4–8
Malus 'Mary Potter'	108, 109	4–8
Malus sargentii	108, 109	4–8
Malus 'White Angel'	110, 111	4–8
Melia azedarach	118, 119	7–10
Metasequoia glyptostroboides	138, 139	5–8
Oxydendrum arboreum	132, 133	5–9
Paulownia tomentosa	84, 85	6–9
Prunus padus	92, 93	4–7
Prunus sargentii	124, 125	5–8
Prunus serrulata 'Kwanzan'	82, 83	5–8
Prunus subhirtella 'Pendula'	86, 87	6–8; 5
Prunus virginiana 'Schubert'	124, 125	3–5
Prunus yedoensis	88, 89	6–8
Pyrus calleryana 'Bradford'	132, 133	5–9
Pyrus calleryana 'Chanticleer'	92, 93	5–9
Quercus palustris	136, 137	5–9
Quercus robur 'Fastigiata'	134, 135	5–8
Salix alba var. *tristis*	120, 121	3–9; 2
Sophora japonica	96, 97	5–8
Sorbus alnifolia	130, 131	4–7

Flowers	Fall Color	Winter Interest	Fruit	Cones	Fragrant	Wet Soil	Acid Soil	Drought Tolerant	City Conditions	Seashore Conditions	Small Spaces	Low Maintenance	Rapid Growth

	Page Numbers	*Zones, Hardy; Semihar...*
Deciduous Ornamentals continued		
Sorbus aucuparia	130, 131	3–7
Taxodium distichum	136, 137	5–10
Deciduous Shade Trees		
Acer platanoides	152, 153	4–7
Acer rubrum	154, 155	4–9
Acer saccharinum	154, 155	3–9
Acer saccharum	152, 153	4–8
Aesculus glabra	150, 151	4–8
Alnus cordata	166, 167	5–10
Alnus glutinosa	164, 165	3–9
Betula lenta	170, 171	4–8
Betula maximowicziana	168, 169	5–7
Betula nigra	170, 171	5–10
Betula papyrifera	168, 169	3–7
Betula platyphylla	166, 167	5–7
Celtis occidentalis	172, 173	4–8
Cercidiphyllum japonicum	182, 183	5–8
Eucommia ulmoides	156, 157	5–7
Fagus grandifolia	148, 149	4–9
Fagus sylvatica	148, 149	5–8
Fraxinus americana	158, 159	4–9
Fraxinus excelsior 'Aurea'	160, 161	4–9
Fraxinus pennsylvanica	158, 159	3–8
Ginkgo biloba	184, 185	5–9; 4
Gleditsia triacanthos var. *inermis*	162, 163	5–9; 4
Gymnocladus dioica	156, 157	5–8; 4
Liquidambar styraciflua	150, 151	5–9
Liriodendron tulipifera	184, 185	5–9
Morus alba	174, 175	5–9
Nyssa sylvatica	182, 183	4–9
Phellodendron amurense	180, 181	4–7

Flowers	Fall Color	Winter Interest	Fruit	Cones	Fragrant	Wet Soil	Acid Soil	Drought Tolerant	City Conditions	Seashore Conditions	Small Spaces	Low Maintenance	Rapid Growth

	Page Numbers	Zones, Hardy: Semih
Deciduous Shade Trees continued		
Pistacia chinensis	160, 161	7–9
Prosopis glandulosa	162, 163	7–9
Pyrus ussuriensis	172, 173	4–6
Quercus alba	144, 145	4–9
Quercus coccinea	146, 147	5–9
Quercus imbricaria	146, 147	5–8
Quercus kelloggii	142, 143	8–10
Quercus lobata	142, 143	7–10
Quercus rubra	144, 145	4–8
Sapium sebiferum	164, 165	8–9
Tilia cordata	178, 179	3–8
Tilia tomentosa	178, 179	5–8
Ulmus carpinifolia	176, 177	5–8
Ulmus parvifolia	176, 177	5–10
Ulmus pumila	180, 181	3–9; 2
Zelkova serrata	174, 175	5–8
Broadleaf Ornamentals		
Acacia baileyana	216, 217	9–10
Araucaria bidwillii	216, 217	9–10; 8
Arbutus menziesii	208, 209	6–9
Arbutus unedo	202, 203	6–9
Archontophoenix cunninghamiana	196, 197	8–10
Arecastrum romanzoffianum	196, 197	10; 9
Brahea armata	192, 193	9–10
Butia capitata	194, 195	8–10
Eriobotrya japonica	206, 207	8–10
Eucalyptus ficifolia	212, 213	9–10
Eucalyptus sideroxylon	210, 211	9–10
Ficus elastica	198, 199	10
Ficus microcarpa	198, 199	10; 9
Ilex opaca	204, 205	5–9

Flowers	Fall Color	Winter Interest	Fruit	Cones	Fragrant	Wet Soil	Arid Soil	Drought Tolerant	City Conditions	Seashore Conditions	Small Spaces	Low Maintenance	Rapid Growth
■	■	□	■	▦	□	■	▦	□	■	■	□	■	▦
	▦		■					□			■		
■			■					□					
■			■										
	▦												
	▦												
		□											
	▦												
		□											▦
	▦												▦
	▦		■								■		▦
■	▦				□			■	■				
■					□			■					
	▦	□	■							▦			
							□	■	▦				■
	▦						□	■					
■		□		■				□					▦
				▦									
■		□	■			▦							
■		□	■					□					
■			■						▦				
■			■										
■		□	■					□					
■		□	■										
■			■	□				□					
■			■					□					
■		□	■	□				□					
								□					
		□	■			■	▦			▦			

Tree Chart

	Page Numbers	Zones, Hardy; Semiha...
Broadleaf Ornamentals continued		
Laurus nobilis	204, 205	8–10
Magnolia grandiflora	200, 201	7–9; 6
Magnolia virginiana	200, 201	5–9
Melaleuca linariifolia	212, 213	10; 9
Olea europaea	210, 211	9–10; 8
Phoenix canariensis	194, 195	9–10
Pittosporum undulatum	208, 209	9–10
Podocarpus gracilior	214, 215	9–10
Podocarpus macrophyllus	214, 215	8–10
Prunus lusitanica	206, 207	7–10
Pyrus kawakamii	202, 203	8–10
Trachycarpus fortunei	190, 191	8–10; 7
Washingtonia filifera	192, 193	9–10
Washingtonia robusta	190, 191	9–10
Broadleaf Shade Trees		
Acacia dealbata	220, 221	9–10
Acacia melanoxylon	220, 221	8–10
Brachychiton populneus	234, 235	8–10
Ceratonia siliqua	230, 231	9–10
Cinnamomum camphora	224, 225	8–10
Cupaniopsis anacardioides	232, 233	10; 9
Erythrina caffra	234, 235	9–10
Eucalyptus camaldulensis	236	9–10; 8
Eucalyptus citriodora	237	9–10
Eucalyptus gunnii	237	8–10; 7
Eucalyptus polyanthemos	236	8–10
Ficus benjamina	224, 225	10
Ficus macrophylla	226, 227	9–10
Fraxinus uhdei	222, 223	9–10
Grevillea robusta	222, 223	10; 9
Quercus agrifolia	228, 229	9–10

Flowers	Fall Color	Winter Interest	Fruit	Cones	Fragrant	Wet Soil	Acid Soil	Drought Tolerant	City Conditions	Seashore Conditions	Small Spaces	Low Maintenance	Rapid Growth
								■					
■			■		■					■			
■			■		■	■							
■								■					
			■		■			■					
			■										
■			■		■				■	■			
											■		
			■							■			
■			■										
■		■			■								
■			■										
								■					
								■		■			
■		■			■			■					■
■					■			■					■
■			■					■					
■			■					■					
										■		■	
■		■								■			
								■					■
					■			■					■
■					■								
								■					■
										■			
			■										
													■
■								■					
										■			

	Page Numbers	Zones, Hardy; Semih
Broadleaf Shade Trees continued		
Quercus chrysolepis	228, 229	8–10;
Quercus suber	226, 227	7–9
Quercus virginiana	230, 231	7–10
Schinus terebinthifolius	232, 233	9–10
Tristania conferta	238, 239	9–10
Umbellularia californica	238, 239	7–10
Needle-leaf Ornamentals		
Araucaria heterophylla	254, 255	10
Chamaecyparis nootkatensis 'Pendula'	250, 251	5–9
Cryptomeria japonica	252, 253	6–8
× *Cupressocyparis leylandii*	248, 249	6–10
Cupressus sempervirens 'Stricta'	244, 245	8–10
Juniperus scopulorum	244, 245	4–10
Juniperus virginiana	246, 247	3–9
Picea abies	256, 257	3–7
Picea omorika	256, 257	4–7
Pinus canariensis	254, 255	9–10; 8
Sequoia sempervirens	252, 253	8–10; 7
Sequoiadendron giganteum	250, 251	7–9; 6
Thuja occidentalis	246, 247	3–7; 8
Thuja plicata	248, 249	5–7; 4,
Needle-leaf Screens		
Abies concolor	284, 285	4–7
Abies homolepis	286, 287	5–6
Abies koreana	286, 287	5–6
Abies procera	282, 283	5–8
Abies veitchii	284, 285	4–6
Cedrus atlantica 'Glauca'	270, 271	6–9
Cedrus deodara	272, 273	7–8
Cedrus libani	272, 273	6–7
Cupressus macrocarpa	274, 275	8–10

Tree Chart

	Page Numbers	Zones, Hardy; Semih
Needle-leaf Screens continued		
Picea glauca	280, 281	3–6
Picea orientalis	278, 279	5–8
Picea pungens	280, 281	3–7
Pinus bungeana	270, 271	5–8
Pinus contorta	268, 269	7–10
Pinus densiflora	262, 263	5–8; 4
Pinus flexilis	260, 161	4–7
Pinus halepensis	262	8–10
Pinus lambertiana	263	6–8
Pinus nigra	266, 267	4–8
Pinus parviflora	282, 283	5–7
Pinus resinosa	264, 265	3–7
Pinus strobus	268, 269	4–7
Pinus sylvestris	266, 267	3–8
Pinus taeda	264, 265	7–9
Pinus thunbergiana	260, 261	5–9
Pseudotsuga menziesii	278, 279	6–8; 5
Thuja orientalis	274, 275	6–9
Tsuga canadensis	276, 277	4–7; 3,
Tsuga heterophylla	276, 277	6–8

Flowers | Fall Color | Winter Interest | Fruit | Cones | Fragrant | Wet Soil | Acid Soil | Drought Tolerant | City Conditions | Seashore Conditions | Small Spaces | Low Maintenance | Rapid Growth

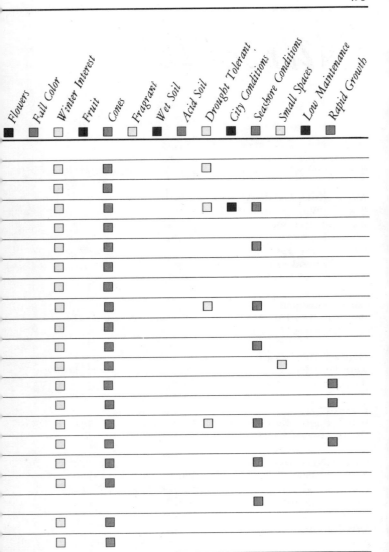

Nurseries

Mail-Order Association of Nurseries
404 Hawthorne Drive, Crawfordsville, IA 47933
(Helpful with queries and complaints about members)

Appalachian Gardens
Box 82, Waynesboro, PA 17268
(Unusual trees and shrubs in small sizes)

Brooks Tree Farm
9785 Portland Road N.E., Salem, OR 97305
(Conifers and deciduous trees in small sizes)

Carroll Gardens
Box 310, 444 East Main Street, Westminster, MD 21157
(Unusual trees)

Dauber's Nurseries
Rear 1705 North George Street, Box 1746, York, PA 17405
(Uncommon trees and shrubs)

Forestfarm
990 Tetherow Road, Williams, OR 97544
(Western natives and unusual Eastern species)

Girard Nurseries
Route 20 East, P.O. Box 428, Geneva, OH 44041
(Ornamental deciduous and evergreen trees in small sizes,
some rare grafted cultivars, tree seeds)

Gossler Farm Nursery
1200 Weaver Road, Springfield, OR 97477
(Magnolias and other trees)

Gurney Seed & Nursery Co.
Yankton, SD 57079
(Trees and shrubs for the Plains)

Kelly Nurseries
Dansville, NY 14437
(Shade, ornamental, fruit, and nut trees)

Krider Nurseries, Inc.
Box 29, Middlebury, IN 46540
(General nursery stock)

Louisiana Nursery
Route 7, Box 43, Opelousas, LA 70570
(Magnolias and uncommon ornamental trees)

This list includes some of the best sources of trees in the country. Some offer large and varied selections of popular forms, others carry rare variations, and a few specialize in certain groups of plants. Catalogues may be free, or the fee may be refunded with your first order.

Try to order trees from nurseries in climates similar to your own.

Maxalea Nurseries
900 Oak Hill Road, Baltimore, MD 21239
(Unusual woody plants)

Earl May Seed & Nursery Co.
208 North Elm Street, Shenandoah, IA 51603
(General nursery stock)

Mellinger's, Inc.
2310 West South Range, North Lima, OH 44452
(Numerous tree species in small sizes)

Musser Forests
Box 340, Indiana, PA 15701
(Conifers and other trees, many in seedling sizes)

The National Arbor Day Foundation
Arbor Lodge 100, Nebraska City, NE 68410
(Flowering, shade, and evergreen trees in small sizes)

Salter Tree Farm
Route 2, Box 1332, Madison, FL 32340
(Southern trees and shrubs)

Spring Hill Nurseries
6523 North Galena Road, Peoria, IL 61632
(General nursery stock, some unusual trees)

Stark Brothers Nurseries
Louisiana, MO 63353
(Fruit tree specialists; limited selection of flowering, shade, and evergreen trees)

Wayside Gardens
Hodges, SC 29695
(Some trees. Beautiful catalogue)

Weston Nurseries
East Main Street, Hopkinton, MA 01748
(Landscape-sized trees. Will deliver in Boston area)

Woodlanders
1128 Colleton Avenue, Aiken, SC 29801
(Plants for Southern and coastal areas)

Leaf Shapes

Simple Leaves	The majority of broadleaf trees have simple or lobed leaves. Simple leaves have a central midrib and secondary veins. On pinnate leaves, the secondary veins are fewer and more pronounced, creating distinct lobes.	On palmate leaves, the central midrib is only one of several major ribs radiating out from the tip of the leafstalk.
Compound Leaves	Compound leaves are composed of several simple leaflets arranged on a shared leafstalk. Pinnate compound leaves have a long central stalk with leaflets appearing in pairs or staggered along it.	Bipinnate—or double—compound leaves are made up of pairs of pinnate compound leaves attached to a central stalk. The leaflets of palmate compound leaves radiate from a single point at the end of a leafstalk.
Leaf Margins	Leaf margins may be smooth or toothed. Serrate margins are finely toothed; dentate margins are more deeply toothed.	
Conifers	Conifers have three leaf types. Scale-like leaves are small and keeled, and lie flat against the twig. Awl-like leaves are small and tightly pointed, and usually occur as a juvenile stage of growth.	Needle-like leaves are often bunched along a twig, as with the pines and larches, or arranged in double rows, as with the hemlocks, firs, and spruces.

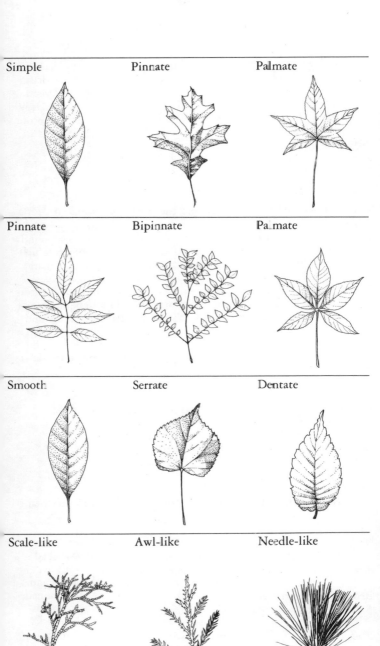

Simple	Pinnate	Palmate
Pinnate	Bipinnate	Palmate
Smooth	Serrate	Dentate
Scale-like	Awl-like	Needle-like

Glossary

Acid soil
Soil with a pH value of less than 7.

Alkaline soil
Soil with a pH value of more than 7.

Alternate
Arranged singly along a twig or shoot, and not in whorls or opposite pairs.

Axil
The angle formed by a leafstalk and the stem from which it grows.

Balled and burlapped
Dug out of the ground with a ball of soil around the roots, which is tied with burlap and string for support.

Bare-rooted
Dug out of a loose growing medium with no soil around the roots. Some trees are sold by nurseries in this condition.

Berry
A fleshy fruit, with one to many seeds, developed from a single ovary.

Bipinnate
Doubly pinnate; the primary leaflets being again divided into secondary leaflets.

Bisexual
A flower with functional stamens and pistils.

Bloom
A whitish powdery or waxy covering on some fruits or other plant parts.

Bract
A modified and often scale-like leaf, usually located at the base of a flower, a fruit, or a cluster of flowers or fruits.

Broadleaf evergreen
An evergreen plant that is not a conifer.

Bud
A young and undeveloped leaf, flower, or shoot, usually covered tightly with scales.

Calyx
Collectively, the sepals of a flower.

Candle
The tender spring growth of the pine and a few other needle-leaf evergreen species.

Capsule
A dry fruit containing more than one cell, splitting along more than one groove.

Carpel
One of the units composing a pistil or ovary.

Catkin
A compact and often drooping cluster of reduced, stalkless, and usually unisexual flowers.

Clone
A group of plants all originating by vegetative propagation from a single plant, and therefore genetically identical to it and to one another.

Compound leaf
A leaf made up of two or more leaflets.

Conifer
A cone-bearing tree or shrub, often evergreen, usually with needle-like leaves.

Container-grown
Raised in a pot that is removed before planting. Many trees are sold by nurseries in this form.

Corolla
Collectively, the petals of a flower.

Corymb
A flower cluster with a flat top, in which the individual pedicels emerge from the axis at different points, rather than at the same point as in an umbel, and blooming from the edges toward the center.

Cultivar
An unvarying plant variety, produced and maintained by vegetative propagation or by inbred seed.

Cutting
A piece of plant without roots; set in a rooting medium, it develops roots, and is then grown as a new plant.

Cyme
A flat or rounded branching flower cluster that blooms from the center toward the edges, and in which the tip of the axis always bears a flower.

Deciduous
Dropping its leaves; not evergreen.

Dentate
With sharp, spreading teeth that are perpendicular to the leaf margin; more pronouncedly toothed than serrate.

Dieback
The death of tops of plants—naturally, due to climatic conditions, or unnaturally, due to disease.

Dioeceous
Bearing male and female flowers on different plants.

Dissected leaf
A deeply cut leaf, the clefts not reaching the midrib; same as a divided leaf. See also Lobed leaf.

Double-flowered
Having more than the usual number of petals, usually arranged in extra rows.

Drupe
A fleshy fruit with a single seed enclosed in a hard covering.

Dwarf
A plant that, due to an inherited characteristic, is shorter or slower-growing than normal forms.

Epiphyte
A plant growing on another plant but not deriving nourishment from it.

Escape
An exotic plant that has spread from cultivation and grows successfully in the wild.

Espalier
A plant trained to grow flat against a wall or framework.

Evergreen
Retaining green leaves for more than one annual growth cycle.

Excurrent
A growth habit with a single vertical trunk, the branches obviously secondary.

Exfoliate
To peel off in shreds, thin layers, or plates.

Family
A group of plants in related genera, all of which share characteristics not found in other families.

Fertile
Able to produce seed.

Follicle
A usually dry, one-chambered fruit which splits only along one seam.

Form
A small but constant variation within a population of plants, such as a white-flowered plant in a normally purple-flowered population.

Fruit
The fully developed ovary of a flower, containing one or more seeds.

Genus
A group of closely related species; plural, genera.

Habit
The characteristic growth form or general shape of a plant.

Hardiness
The ability of a plant to withstand winter cold and summer heat; often expressed as a numerical range.

Hardpan
A layer of compact clay or silt below the topsoil which often prevents the penetration of water and shrub or tree roots.

Hardwood cutting
A cutting taken from a dormant plant after it has finished its yearly growth.

Glossary

Hilum
The scar or mark on a seed indicating the point of attachment.

Horticulture
The cultivation of plants for ornament or food.

Humus
Partly or wholly decomposed vegetable matter; an important constituent of garden soil.

Hybrid
The offspring of two parent plants belonging to different species, subspecies, genera, or clones.

Inflorescence
A flower cluster.

Invasive
Spreading aggressively from the original site of planting.

Involucre
One or more close spirals of small leaves or bracts surrounding the base of a flower or an inflorescence.

Keel
A sharp ridge or rib on the underside of a petal, leaf, or other plant part.

Key
A dry, one-seeded fruit with a wing; a samara.

Layering
A method of propagating plants in which a stem is induced to send out roots by surrounding a section of it with soil.

Leaflet
One of the subdivisions of a compound leaf.

Leaf mold
A type of humus consisting of partially decayed leaves.

Legume
A simple, one-chambered fruit of the pea family.

Lime
A substance containing calcium added to soil for increased alkalinity and nutrient content.

Loam
A humus-rich soil containing up to 25 percent clay, up to 50 percent silt, and less than 50 percent sand.

Lobe
A segment of a cleft leaf or petal.

Lobed leaf
A leaf whose margin is shallowly divided.

Margin
The edge of a leaf.

Midrib
The primary rib or mid-vein of a leaf or leaflet.

Mulch
A protective covering spread over the soil around the base of plants to retard evaporation, control temperature, or suppress weeds.

Naturalized
Established as a part of the flora in an area other than the place of origin. Also, of a planting, tended so as to give the appearance of spontaneous or "wild" growth.

Neutral soil
Soil that is neither acid nor alkaline, having a pH value of 7.

Node
The place on a stem where leaves or branches are attached.

Nut
A hard, bony, one-celled fruit that does not split.

Nutlet
One of several small, nutlike parts of a compound fruit; or the hard inner core of some fruits, containing a seed and surrounded by softer flesh.

Opposite
Arranged along a twig or shoot in pairs, with one on each side.

Ovate
Oval, with the broader end at the base.

Palmately compound
Having veins or leaflets arranged like the fingers on a hand, arising from a single point. See also Pinnately compound.

Panicle
A compound, branching flower cluster, blooming from bottom to top, and never terminating in a flower.

Peat moss
Partly decomposed moss, rich in nutrients and with a high water retention, used as a component of garden soil.

Pedicel
The stalk of an individual flower.

Persistent
Remaining attached, even though withered.

Petal
One of a series of flower parts lying within the sepals and outside the stamens and pistils, often large and brightly colored.

Petiole
The stalk of a leaf.

pH
A symbol for the hydrogen ion content of the soil, and thus a means of expressing the acidity or alkalinity of the soil.

Pinna
A primary division or leaflet of a pinnate leaf.

Pinnately compound
With leaflets arranged in two rows along an axis.

Pistil
The female reproductive organ of a flower, consisting of an ovary, style, and stigma.

Pod
A dry, one-celled fruit, with thicker walls than a capsule.

Pollen
Minute grains containing the male germ cells and produced by the stamens.

Polygamous
Bearing male and female flowers on the same plant.

Pome
A fruit with fleshy outer tissue and a papery-walled inner chamber containing the seeds.

Propagate
To produce new plants, either by vegetative means involving the rooting of pieces of a plant, or by sowing seeds.

Prune
To cut the branches of a woody plant to spur growth, maintain vigor, or shape the plant.

Raceme
A long flower cluster on which individual flowers are borne on small stalks from a common, larger, central stalk.

Rachis
The main stalk of a flower cluster or the main leafstalk of a compound leaf.

Root
The underground portion of a plant that serves to anchor it and absorb water and minerals from the soil.

Samara
A dry, one-seeded fruit with a wing; a key.

Screen
A single plant or grouping of plants used to bar certain parts of the landscape from view.

Scurfy
Covered with tiny, broad scales.

Seed
A fertilized, ripened ovule, almost always covered with a protective coating and contained in a fruit.

Semi-evergreen
Retaining at least some green foliage well into winter, or shedding leaves only in cold climates.

Semihardy
Questionably hardy in a given temperature zone; susceptible to damage by extreme cold or heat.

Sepal
One of the outermost series of flower parts, arranged in a ring outside the petals, and usually green and leaflike.

Serrate
Having teeth like those of a saw. See also Toothed.

Shrub
A woody, perennial plant, smaller than a tree, usually with several stems or trunks.

Simple leaf
A leaf with an undivided blade; not compound or composed of leaflets.

Softwood
The immature stems of woody plants.

Solitary
Borne singly or alone; not in clusters.

Spathe
A bract or leaf surrounding or enclosing a flower cluster.

Species
A population of plants or animals whose members reproduce by breeding with each other, but which is reproductively isolated from other populations.

Specimen
A plant placed conspicuously alone, usually in a prominent place, so as to show off its ornamental qualities.

Spike
An elongated flower cluster, each flower of which is without a stalk.

Spine
A strong, sharp, usually woody projection from the stem or branches of a plant; not usually from a bud.

Spreading plant
A plant whose branches grow in a more or less horizontal direction.

Spur
A tubular elongation of the petals or sepals of certain flowers, usually containing nectar.

Stamen
The male reproductive organ of a flower, consisting of a filament and a pollen-containing anther.

Sterile
Incapable of producing seeds, either because of a lack of stamens and pistils or because of internal genetic incompatabilities.

Stipule
A small, leaflike appendage at the base of some petioles.

Stone
A single seed surrounded by a large, hard shell and covered by pulp.

Style
The elongated part of a pistil between the stigma and the ovary.

Sucker
A secondary shoot arising from underground buds on the roots of a plant. See also Water sprout.

Terminal
Borne at the tip of a stem or shoot, rather than in the axil.

Thorn
A short, sharp, woody outgrowth of a stem or branch.

Tier
A radial, layered branching habit of excurrent trees. See also Whorl.

Toothed
Having the margin shallowly divided into small, toothlike segments.

Topiary
The art of shearing trees and shrubs into unusual shapes.

Tree
A woody, self-supporting perennial plant reaching at least 20 feet at maturity, usually with a single trunk.

Umbel
A flower cluster in which the individual flower stalks grow from the same point, like the ribs of an umbrella.

Unisexual flower
A flower bearing only stamens or pistils and not both.

Valve
One of the separable parts of the wall of a pod or capsule.

Variegated
Marked, striped, or blotched with some color other than green.

Glossary

Variety
A population of plants differing slightly but consistently from the typical form of the species, and occurring naturally. More loosely applied to forms produced in cultivation. See also Cultivar.

Water sprout
A sucker produced on the trunk, stem, or large branch of a plant.

Weeping
Having drooping branches.

Whorl
Three or more leaves, flowers, or twigs, attached radially. See also Tier.

Wing
A thin, dry, leaf-like membrane found on many fruits, seeds, and leafstalks.

Winterkill
To be killed by harsh winter weather.

Woody
Producing hard rather than fleshy stems and having buds that survive above ground in winter.

Photo Credits

Jean Baxter, PHOTO/NATS
A member of the board of the New England Wildflower Society.
91B, 175B, 279B

Gillian Beckett
A well-known English horticultural photographer.
82B, 83B, 90B, 93B, 125B, 128B 129B, 137B, 139B, 148B, 153A,
178B, 179A, 198E, 207A, 209B, 226A, 236A, 239A, 246B, 247B,
249B, 250A, 255E, 256A, 257B, 262B, 266B, 267A, 263A, 268B,
269A, 278A, 279A, 283A, 287A

John E. Bryan
A garden writer and president of a horticultural consulting firm.
81A, 82A, 84B, 208B, 222B

Gay Bumgarner, PHOTO/NATS
A professional landscape designer and photographer.
132A

Al Bussewitz, PHOTO/NATS
A conservationist and a photographer for the Arnold Arboretum.
95B, 135A, 139A, 161A, 167B, 169B, 181A, 201B, 285B, 287B

David Cavagnaro
A freelance nature photographer and author.
81B, 89A, 118A, 143A, 143B, 155B, 166A, 177A, 193A, 204A,
211A, 211B, 217B, 220B, 222A, 226B, 229A, 229B, 234B, 235B,
245B, 253A, 269B, 273B, 275A, 277A

Alan D. Cook
The author of this guide and a director of the Dawes Arboretum.
286B

Gordon Courtright
A retired nurseryman and landscape architect.
78B, 83A, 96B, 97B, 98B, 99B, 110B, 119A, 162A, 164A, 176A,
183B, 192B, 196B 206B, 210A, 213B, 214A, 214B, 220A, 221A,
221B, 223B, 224A, 230B, 236B, 237B, 238A, 238B, 244A, 252B,
254B, 263B, 266A, 274A

Jack Dermid
A freelance biological photographer and retired professor.
155A, 163B, 230A, 233A

Michael Dirr
A professor of horticulture at the University of Georgia.
92A, 92B, 122A, 123A, 134A, 134B, 150B, 164B, 166B, 169A,
173B, 180A, 200B, 206A, 248B, 270A, 271A, 276A

Thomas E. Eltzroth
A dedicated gardener, writer, and professor of horticulture.
203A

Derek Fell
A widely published garden writer and photographer.
76A, 77A, 79A, 80B, 85A, 88A, 90A, 94B, 101A, 102B, 112A,
120A, 120B, 121B, 122B, 123B, 131B, 133B, 136B, 138A, 144A,
146A, 148A, 150A, 152A, 154B, 154B, 158A, 160A, 165A, 184B,
190A, 195A, 198A, 212A, 213A, 216B, 217A, 227A, 227B, 228A,
228B, 232A, 242, 250B, 252A, 257A, 284A, 284B

Charles Marden Fitch
A media specialist and horticulturist.
74, 80A, 88B, 191A, 193B, 225B, 263A, 271B, cover

Bruce Hamilton
A professor of horticulture and landscape architecture at Rutgers
University.
280B, 282B, 286A

Walter H. Hodge
The author of *The Audubon Society Book of Wildflowers*.
79B, 87A, 87B, 89B, 91A, 133A, 135B, 142A, 191B, 194A, 195B,
197B, 205B, 207B, 215A, 223A, 225A, 231A, 233B, 245A, 251A,
253B, 254A, 255A, 260B, 273A, 281B

Philip E. Keenan
A freelance photographer specializing in horticulture.
86A, 98A, 99A, 100A, 106A, 106B, 107A, 107B, 132B, 152B, 153B,
180B, 184A, 256B, 277B

Helen Kittinger
A nature photographer, conservationist, and lecturer.
185B, 201A

Ken Lewis, Jr.
A contributor to the Audubon Society Field Guides.
137A, 264A, 265A, 267B, 285A

John A. Lynch
A photographer specializing in gardening and wildflowers.
117A, 144B, 171B, 247A, 265B, 278B

Robert E. Lyons, PHOTO/NATS
A professor of horticulture at Virginia Polytechnic Institute.
115A, 116B, 185A, 276B

Elvin McDonald
Director of Special Projects at the Brooklyn Botanic Garden.
168A

Monrovia Nursery Co.
A wholesale grower of trees and shrubs in Azusa, California.
162B, 232B

Muriel Orans/Arthur Norman Orans, HORTICULTURAL PHOTOGRAPHY
A landscape designer and an architect, respectively.
76B, 78A, 160B, 174B, 188, 190B, 192A, 194B, 196A, 199A, 199B, 202A, 202B, 210B, 212B, 216A, 218, 224B, 231B, 234A, 235A

Joy Spurr
A writer, photographer, and owner of a photographic agency.
93A, 109B, 111B, 119B, 142B, 171A, 177B, 186, 203B, 205A, 208A, 209A, 237A, 239B, 251B, 260A, 261A, 274B, 275B

Alvin E. Staffan
A widely published freelance photographer.
147A, 147B, 149A, 159A, 159B, 163A

Steven M. Still
A photographer, professor, and widely published garden writer.
72, 77B, 84A, 86B, 94A, 95A, 97A, 100B, 101B, 102A, 103A, 103B, 104A, 104B, 105A, 105B, 108B, 109A, 110A, 111A, 112B, 113B, 114A, 114B, 115B, 116A, 117B, 121A, 124A, 125A, 126A, 126B, 127B, 128A, 129A, 130A, 131A, 136A, 138B, 145B, 146B, 149B, 151A, 151B, 156A, 156B, 157A, 157B, 158B, 161B, 165B, 167A, 168B, 170A, 170B, 172A, 173A, 174A, 175A, 176B, 178A, 179B, 181B, 182A, 182B, 183A, 200A, 204B, 215B, 240, 244B, 246A, 248A, 249A, 262A, 270B, 272A, 280A, 281A, 282A, 283B

David M. Stone, PHOTO/NATS
A freelance nature and life-science photographer.
118B, 140, 145A

George Taloumis
Garden columnist for the *Boston Globe* and *Flower and Garden*.
85B, 108A, 96A, 113A, 124B, 127A, 130B, 172B, 258, 261B, 264B

Sondra Williamson
A freelance nature photographer with decades of experience.
197A

Marilyn Wood, PHOTO/NATS
Owner of Photo/Nats, an agency of nature photographers.
272B

Index

Chanticleer Staff

Publisher: Paul Steiner
Editor-in-Chief: Gudrun Buettner
Executive Editor: Susan Costello
Managing Editor: Jane Opper
Project Editor: Andrew Zega
Assistant Editor: Amy Hughes
Production Manager: Helga Lose
Production Assistants: Gina Stead-Thomas,
Helen L.A. Brown
Art Director: Carol Nehring
Art Associate: Ayn Svoboda
Art Assistant: Cheryl Miller
Picture Library: Edward Douglas
Drawings: Robin A. Jess, Margaret
Kurzius, Edward Lam, Dolores R.
Santoliquido, Alan D. Singer, Mary Jane
Spring, Stephen Thurston, Robert Villani
Zone Map: Paul Singer

Design: Massimo Vignelli